Contemporary Research in Business & Management

Editor

Manoj Sharma

Copyright © 2018 Manoj Sharma

All rights reserved.

Disclaimer: The view expressed in the articles/papers/chapters are those of the Authors/contributors and not necessarily of the editor and publisher. Author/Contributors are themselves responsible for any kind of plagiarism found in their articles/papers/chapters.

Email: manoj.nith@gmail.com

ISBN: 1979434336
ISBN-13: 978-1979434331

DEDICATION

To Academicians, Scholars and Researchers

CONTENT

	Contributors	vii
	Preface	ix
1	Determinants of Corporate Performance: A Review of The Literature *A.K. Sharan and Rajneesh Prakash Verma*	1
2	A Review Study on Prevalence of Stress and its Management among Banking Professionals in India *Manpreet Kaur and Rajesh Kumar*	20
3	Lending Practices and Customers' Satisfaction of District Central Cooperative Bank: with Special Reference to Kangra Central Cooperative Bank *Pradeep Kumar*	35
4	A Study of The Human Resource Development Practices in The Kangra Central Cooperative Bank *Ravi Kumar and Shagun Sood*	47
5	A Review Analysis on Antecedents of Organizational Citizenship Behaviour *Jitendra Singh and Pawan Kumar Chand*	59
6	Mapping Organizational Culture of Indian Banks: An Octapace Approach *Mitu Mandal*	74
7	Micro and Macroeconomic Determinants of Corporate Financial Performance: Empirical Evidence from Indian Textile Firms *Rajneesh Prakash Verma and A.K. Sharan*	87
8	Factors Responsible for Share Price Fluctuations with Special Reference to Infrastructure Sector in India *Amit Kumar and Deepika Jhamb*	106
9	Motive for Mergers and Acquisitions in the Indian Banking Industry *Tirth Raj; Shrekant Sharma and Pinky*	121
10	Awareness Regarding Life Insurance: A Case Study of Shimla Town *Leena Devi and Ranjana*	131

11	Knowledge and Concerns among Millennials of North India Regarding Online Advertising *Sahil Dupta and Rajesh Kumar*	140
12	Financial Inclusion through Pradhan Mantri Jan Dhan Yojana – An Empirical Analysis *Rajneesh Kumar Sharma*	149
13	Critical Appraisal of Disaster Prevention Preparedness and Mitigation Management in Himachal Pradesh *Kewal Ram and S.S. Chauhan*	159
14	A Comparative Study on Financial Inclusion of Public and Private Sector Banks – A Case Study of North Eastern Region *Nitin Gupta*	174
15	Effectiveness of Public Distribution System in Ensuring Food Security in Himachal Pradesh *Tilak Raj and Anuradha Negi*	187
16	Problems & Prosperity of Public Distribution System in Himachal Pradesh - A Case Study with Special References to Kangra District *Ranju*	200
17	Globalization and Indian Identity *Jitender K. Bhanwal*	217
18	Textile Export Performance in Post Reform Regime: A Study at Disaggregate Level *Manoj Sharma and Rahul Dhiman*	226
19	Women Entrepreneurship and Financial Performance: Moderating Role of Spouse Support *Stanzin Mantok*	237
20	A Fuzzy Logic Approach to Optimize Low Cost Carriers Performance *Pratima Mishra and Somesh Kumar Sharma*	251

CONTRIBUTORS

A.K. Sharan, Professor, National Institute of Financial Management, Faridabad, Haryana, India.

Amit Kumar, MBA Student, Chitkara Business School, Chitkara University Punjab, India.

Deepika Jhamb, Associate Professor, Doctoral Research Centre - Chitkara Business School, Chitkara University Punjab, India.

Anuradha Negi, Research Scholar, Department of Economics, Panjab University, Chandigarh, India.

Jitender K. Bhanwal, Associate Professor (Commerce) Govt. Degree College, Thural, Kangra, Himachal Pradesh, India.

Jitendra Singh, Research Scholar, Chitkara Business School, Chitkara University, Punjab, India.

Kewal Ram, Research Scholar, Department of Public Administration Himachal Pradesh University, Shimla, India.

Leena Devi, Research Scholars, Department of Commerce, Himachal Pradesh University, Shimla, India.

Manoj Sharma, Assistant Professor, Department of Management & Humanities, NIT Hamirpur, Himachal Pradesh, India.

Manpreet Kaur, Research Scholar, Chitkara Business School, Chitkara University, Punjab, India.

Mitu Mandal, National Institute of Technology, Hamirpur, Himachal Pradesh, India.

Nitin Gupta, Assistant Professor, Faculty of Management Sciences and Liberal Arts, Shoolini University, Solan, Himachal Pradesh, India.

Pawan Kumar Chand, Associate Professor, Chitkara Business School, Chitkara University, Punjab, India.

Pinky, Assistant Professor, L.R. Institute of Management, Solan, Himachal Pradesh, India

Pradeep Kumar, Research Scholar, Department of Accounting & Finance, SBMS, Central University of Himachal Pradesh Dharamshala, India.

Pratima Mishra, Project Associate, National Institute of Technology, Hamirpur, Himachal Pradesh, India.

Rahul Dhiman, Assistant Professor, Chitkara Business School, Chitkara University, Punjab, India.

Rajesh Kumar, Associate Professor, Chitkara Business School, Chitkara University, Punjab, India.

Rajneesh Kumar Sharma, Assistant Professor Government Degree College Dhaneta, Hamirpur, Himachal Pradesh, India.

Rajneesh Prakash Verma, Department of Management & Humanities, National Institute of Technology, Hamirpur, Himachal Pradesh, India.

Ranjana, Research Scholars, Department of Commerce, Himachal Pradesh University, Shimla, India.

Ranju, Research Scholar, Department of Commerce & Management, Himachal Pradesh University, Shimla, India.

Ravi Kumar, Research Scholar, Department of HRM and OB, SBMS, Central University of Himachal Pradesh, Dharamshala, India.

S.S. Chauhan, Professor, Department of Public Administration Himachal Pradesh University, Shimla, India.

Sahil Gupta, Research Scholar, Chitkara Business School, Chitkara University, Punjab, India.

Shagun Sood, Research Scholar, Department of HRM and OB, SBMS, Central University of Himachal Pradesh, Dharamshala, India.

Shreekant Sharma, Assistant Professor, L.R. Institute of Management, Solan, Himachal Pradesh, India.

Somesh Kumar Sharma, Associate Professor, Mechanical Engineering Department, National Institute of Technology, Hamirpur, Himachal Pradesh, India.

Stanzin Mantok, Assistant Professor, Government Degree College Basohli, Jammu, India.

Tilak Raj, Assistant Professor, University Business School, Panjab University, Chandigarh, India.

Tirth Raj, Assistant Professor, L.R. Institute of Management, Solan, Himachal Pradesh, India.

PREFACE

Research in business and management generate understanding and disseminate knowledge about the different issues and aspects pertaining to business and management amongst its stakeholders. It requires placing the results and outcome of these research exercises. The placing of results and outcome can be done through seminars and conferences. Hence, it is in this background the Department of management & Humanities, NIT Hamirpur organized a National Conference on Management, Economics and Social Sciences (NCMESS 2017) on July 14-15, 2017. The conference covered a whole range of issues of concern to General Management, Advances in Finance, Marketing, Human Resource Management, Banking and Insurance and other vital issues related to Business and Management.

The present book is a collection of select research papers/articles presented in NCMESS 2017. It is expected that this book will provide sensible and useful guidance to the budding researchers, practitioners and analyst in these fields. Due care has been taken by the editorial board to shortlist papers/articles having innovation, depth of thoughtful and workability in application, nevertheless, the Authors have the ultimate responsibility with respect to the novelty.

The editor duly acknowledges the support and help provided by the advisory committee, experts and authorities of National Institute of Technology, Hamirpur, Himachal Pradesh, India.

Editor

CHAPTER 1
DETERMINANTS OF CORPORATE PERFORMANCE: A REVIEW OF THE LITERATURE

A.K. Sharan and Rajneesh Prakash Verma

Abstract

Substantial attention has been waged to the determinants of firm's financial performance. However, despite the research efforts in ascertaining and determining the impact of such determinants, the existing literature is portrayed by assortment and disintegration, deterring the theory development and as well as the practical progress in the field. The paper intends to review and synthesise the research knowledge on the nexus among firm performance, capital structure, and other control variables. As an aftermath, this study reviews and examines 36 research articles published during 1997 and 2016 to assess the evolution of arguments on the determinants of firm performance in the Asian context. This study also presents a comprehensive literature review specifically in the Indian context. The assessment of these studies reveals that both classical and modern indicators are engaged in gauging firm's financial performance. The empirical debates over the determinants of the financial performance show the disjunction of the variables employed and this has eventually unbolted new dimension for further exhaustive research. The conclusion drawn is that dedicated literature has been amplified with extensive empirical debates that led to the expansion of the field of investigation in the performance context. This paper may be an expedient source of information to the researchers and managers who are willing to explore the concept of financial performance and its determinants.

1.1. Introduction

The effective financial performance of organizations is important to achieve and sustain market capitalization expected to end up or stay prolific native and international development organizations. An examination of the relative effectiveness of firms and factors impacting effectiveness is thus indispensable in an inexorably worldwide economy. International markets are ending up noticeably more coordinated and this has brought about escalated worldwide competitiveness. Measures of corporate financial performance are pointers of performance originated from data on financial statements of companies. Ratios that emphasis on the profit-elevating performance of companies are "profitability ratios"; and these ratios reflect risk and operating performance of the organisations. The most generally utilized profitability ratios are "return on asset" and "return on equity".

The assessment of financial performance is a relevant issue to researchers, managers, and industry examiners. Data about the financial performance of companies is utilized for different purposes. Creation of value is imperative to investors and when company's value escalates, shareholder wealth also escalates. Going further to the limits of the theory of irrelevance, literature showed that there is a connection between the organization's value and its capital structure; consequently, the studies in the field turned out to be less intrigued by the way in which capital structure applies impact over the company's value. This study aims to explore the expansion of arguments encompassing the issues of capital structure and various imperative financial performance determinants that have affected the performance of firms, which eventually ad to highlight advance accomplished in the range of scientific research, specifically in the Asian context.

Subsequent sections of this study discuss in detail about the prevailing debates over the issues of financial performance and its determinants in the Asian context; specifically in the Indian Context.

1.2. Studies in Indian context

Majumdar (1997) investigated the impacts of age and size of

companies on firm-level profitability and productivity by using a data of 1020 Indian corporations. Larger organizations in India were found to be less profitable and more productive, whereas older firms were less productive and more profitable. They argued that the performance differences are described as ascending from the "market-restricting industrial policies" that have been trailed in India during the last three decades.

Majumdar & Chhibber (1999) determined the linkage between performance and the capital structure for a dataset of 1,000 Indian companies over the period 1988 and 1994. They argued that existing theory suggests a positive association; however, data analysis outcomes revealed that the relationship to be significantly negative for Indian companies. This negative influence was due to the framework of capital market in India, where government-own both long and as well as short-term lending institutions.

Khanna & Palepu (2000) argued that emerging nations like India have ineffective operational institutions, leading to severe information and agency problems. They also believed that business associations in emerging markets have the caliber both to offer paybacks to member companies and to eradicate value. The sample of their study comprised of 1309 firms, of which 654 firms were affiliated with any other business group and 655 companies were affiliated to diversified business associations. They examined the performance of affiliates of diversified Indian business associations compared with unaffiliated companies by using Tobin's Q ratio. They found that stock market and accounting gauges of firm performance at first waning with associations diversification and afterward rise once associations diversification goes beyond a certain level.

Kakani et al. (2001) offer an empirical validation of the extensively held prevailing theories on the determinants of organisation financial performance. Their study mined data from capital market and financial statement of 566 Indian corporations over a span of eight years (viz., 1992-2000) to study financial performance of Indian firms across numerous dimensions viz., "accounting profitability" and its components, shareholder value, risk and growth of the sample companies. Their results reveal that difference exists between the determinants of accounting-based performance estimates and market-based estimates. The study finds that firm's operating parameters such as marketing expenses, size, and worldwide diversification had a positive association with a company's market valuation. Further, they found that ownership composition of the company (i.e. equity held by Domestic Institutional Investor and Public Shareholders) and the leverage were important determinants of corporate performance.

Bhaduri (2002) studied the capital structure choice of Indian Corporate sector by using data from 363 firms by using two-stage model. The study aimed to achieve an output model that explains for the likelihood of restructuring expenses in attaining an optimal capital structure and discourses the measurement issue that ascends owing to the unobservable nature of the characteristics influencing the optimal capital structure. Three proxies were used to measure leverage, namely, "short-term borrowing to asset ratio (STB/TA)", "long-term borrowing to asset ratio (LTB/TA)" and "total borrowing to asset ratio (TB/TA)". Nine independent variables were used, namely, "Size", "Age", "Asset structure", "Profitability", "Financial Distress", "Non-Debt Tax Shield", "Growth", "Signalling" and "Uniqueness" as a determinant of capital structure. They found that the selection of optimal capital structure can be impacted by factors like "size", "cash flow", "growth", and "product as well as industry characteristics".

Chander & Aggarwal (2008) empirical ascertained the determinants of profitability of fifty Indian firms from 1995-1996 to 2004-2005. The profitability of organizations was measured by "average return on capital employed" and for studying the determinants of profitability they considered 10 predictor variables, i.e., "age", "size (total assets)", "advertising intensity", "liquidity", "efficiency ratios (inventory turnover ratio, debtor turnover ratio, asset turnover ratio)", "past profitability (OPR, NPR)", "market share", "retention ratio", "long term finance", and "research and development intensity". They used multiple regression analysis for developing a model to ascertain the contributing factor of company's profitability. The outcomes showed that "age", "past profitability", "efficiency ratio", and "research and development intensity" were statistically significant determinants of profitability of companies.

Ghosh (2008) in his study investigated the relationship between profitability and corporate leverage by utilizing the firm-level data on Indian manufacturing sector (i.e. 1390 firms) over the period 1995–2004. The outcomes of the study were robust as it has taken control of various firm-specific factors and economic environment. The study shows that cash flows and corporate profitability lessens as leverage increases. Further, it shows that the marginal influence of a rise in leverage on company's earnings is greater for those who engage in global debt markets in comparison to other organisations. Mahakud & Misra (2009) studied the impact of leverage, adjustment costs (i.e. lagged value of corporate performance, investors' perception, etc.) and other control variables on the performance of the organisations by using a dataset of 5258 Indian manufacturing organisations for the period 2000-01 to 2006-07. Five predictor variables were used, namely "leverage", "size", "tangibility", "inventory" and "short-term liability". Four explained variables used in the model were "return on equity", "earnings per share", "return on capital employed" and "economic value added". The study estimated panel data model by "Generalized Method of Moments (GMM) method" and found that leverage has significant influence on the performance of the organisations. Further, control variables such as "tangibility", "firm's size", "short-term liabilities", "inventory ratio" and "time dummy" have also significantly impacted on numerous corporate performance measures.

Bhayani (2010) studied the influence of internal as well as external variables, i.e., "growth of organisations", "size of organisations", "operating profit ratio", "age of the firm", "liquidity ratio", "fixed asset turnover ratio", "receivable turnover ratio", "debt-equity ratio", "inflation rate" and "interest rate" on the profitability of the firms. The sample comprised of all listed cement companies operating in India during the period 2001 to 2008 and evaluated the relationship by using backward regression analysis. The outcomes of the study depict that "age of the firm", "liquidity", "operating profit ratio", "inflation rate" and "interest rate are the vital determinants of the company's profitability.

Gupta et al. (2010) studied the effect of financial leverage on the performance of the 100 Indian companies over the 5-year time horizon (i.e. 2006-2010). Financial performance of the firms was measured with numerous proxies, namely, "Return on investment (ROI)", "Return on equity (ROE)", "Return on stock (RET)", "earnings before tax to sale ratio (EBT / S)", and "operational profit to sale ratio (OPR/S)". They adopted both "book value and market value of equity and debt" as proxies of leverage. The outcomes of the study demonstrated that the significance of the effect of capital structure on organisation's performance is correspondingly appertained to measures of "book value", "market value", and "adjusted value". It was further concluded that firm that has good performance and high profitability have less debt.

Azhagaiah & Gavoury (2011) analysed the influence of capital structure on profitability of Indian corporations. They categorized the selected companies into three groups based on two characteristics, viz. "asset size" and "business revenue". The sample dataset of the study was comprised of 102 IT firm for a duration of 8 years, i.e. for the period 1999–2000 to 2006–2007 and they employed regression analysis for the purpose of analyses. "Return on Capital Employed (ROCE)" and "Return on Assets (ROA)" were used as a proxy for performance. Four proxies' variables were used to quantify capital structure namely, "current ratio", "total debt to total asset", "debt-equity ratio" and "expense to income ratio". The outcomes showed a strong association between Profitability and capital structure variables.

Mistry (2012) aimed to ascertain the determinants of firm profitability of Indian Automobiles Industry for the duration of 5years ranging from 2004-05 to 2008-09 by using multiple regression models. "Return on capital employed" was used as a measure of firm profitability and they used four independent variables in the study, namely, Total Asset (SIZE), Inventory Turnover Ratio (ITR), Liquidity (LIQ), and Debt-Equity Ratio (DE). They found that SIZE, ITR and DE were the most significant determinants of the firm profitability. All variables have positively affected the profitability of the firm except LIQ which showed negative influence on it.

Banerjee & De (2014) studied the influence of numerous firm-specific variables on the financial performance of 319 Indian iron and steel firms for the duration from 1999–2000 to 2010–2011 using multiple regression analysis. They undertaken one independent variable, i.e. return on asset (ROA) and eight independent variables, namely, "firm's age", "debt service capacity", "business risk", "firm size", "dividend payout", "growth rate", "degree of operating leverage" and "financial leverage". They found that "debt service capacity (interest)", "firm size" and "leverage" are significant factors affecting that profitability of the organizations and further, they also explored the relationship during the pre- and post-recession periods.

Narang & Kaur (2014) examined the effect of company-specific characteristics on the value of the shareholders by taking a sample of 100 Indian organisations. They explored whether the significant characteristics are identical to both the measures of shareholder value, i.e., "market-based (Tobin's Q and market value added (MVA))" and as well as "accounting-based measurements (economic value added (EVA))" over the period from the financial year 1997–1998 to 2008–2009. They employed regression method for analysis and the outcomes revealed that investors have a tendency to reward the firms which have "high leverage", "lower market risk", "higher profitability", "efficient resource management", "higher marketing expenditures", "more liquidity", and "robust market capitalization". They found that certain organisations attributes describe about 34% of the variation in the EVA, whereas these attributes account for greater than 55% variation in the company's shareholder value when determined by Tobin's Q and MVA.

Chadha & Sharma (2015) studied the effect of the capital structure or financial leverage on the performance of the firm using a data of 422 listed Indian manufacturing firms on BSE over a duration of 10 years from 2003–2004 to 2012–2013. Three proxies were used to estimate the performance of the firm, namely, "Return on equity", "Return on asset" and "Tobin's Q". Panel data approach and Ratio analysis were employed and the outcomes showed that financial leverage has no effect on Tobin's Q and return on asset. However, it was significantly negatively correlated with return on equity. They also found that other independent variables like age, size, asset turnover, sales growth, tangibility, and ownership structure were significant determinants of performance. Their study covers the phase of both pre- and post-recession of 2008–2009 and they demonstrated the adverse impact of the recession on the performance of the Indian manufacturing organisations.

Chaudhuri et al. (2016) employed MIMIC model to measure the firm performance and "true" firm performance in his study was viewed as a latent variable but argued that there are several observable indicators of it. The latent firm performance measures in the MIMIC model was linked with some observed independent variables like size, age, R&D intensity, advertising intensity, debt-equity ratio and the shareholder pattern of the foreign promoter. "Return on Asset (ROA)" and "Tobin's Q" were used as measures of latent firm performance and they used firm specific data from India over the duration 2001-2008. Lastly, they estimated two stochastic frontier models and evaluated Pearson's correlation between a couple of performance measures. They also found a high rank correlation between the pairs of firm efficiency/performance, which validates the implementation of the MIMIC model as a complementary technique of performance measures.

Batra & Kalia (2016) addressed the value and effect of firm-specific factors on the corporate profitability, i.e. they analysed the pervasive association between the firm-specific factors of liquidity, firm size, and capital structure (financial leverage) with a sample of 50 Indian listed firms by using correlation as well as multiple regression techniques. The outcomes revealed a significant positive association between corporate profitability and firm size. With an upsurge in the scale of investment, the firm's profits showed an increase. The capital structure shows a significant negative connexion with corporate profitability, thus with an increase in debt-equity ratio, the firm's profits exhibited a downstream. Conversely, liquidity had an insignificant negative relationship with profitability. The value of this research lies in highlighting those specific firm factors that need to be revamped to augment corporate profits.

1.3. Studies in the Asian context

Krishnan & Moyer (1997) empirically studied the capital structure and corporate performance of large organisations from four emerging market and newly industrialised economies of Asia, namely, Malaysia, Hong Kong, Korea and Singapore. They studied 81 corporations from these four emerging nations and found that both capital structure and financial performance were affected by the source nation. Specifically, they found that Hong Kong organisations have significantly greater invested capital and "Returns on Equity" than organisations from the other nations, probably revealing the concentrated conglomerate business structure. The performance differences among companies from other countries were not found statistically significant. Korean firms exhibited significantly higher leverage in comparison to firms from the other nations.

Muslumov (2005) examined the post-privatization performance of all privatized cement industry firms in Turkey. The results show that privatization lead to significant performance decline in cement industry. Return on investment and total value added decreases significantly after privatization. This decline was due to deterioration in productivity of asset. The decrease in productivity of asset, however, did not originate by a rise in capital investment. While, a significant rise in financial leverage and reduction in total employment after privatizations; were the main research outcomes. Privatization through domestic ownership, gradual privatization, and public offering was found to stimulate the operating as well as financial performance of companies following privatization.

Zeitun et al. (2007) examined the influence of total economic risk on an organization's performance by using dataset of 167 firms during 1989-2003 period in Jordan. The crucial macroeconomic gauges used were the "production manufacturing index", "inflation", "nominal interest rate", "exports", "changes in money supply", "the availability of credit", and including "Islamic credit". They also considered key microeconomic measures, namely, capital structure variables, firm size, firm growth, tax rate, cash flow, risk factors and ownership structure. "Return on assets (ROA)" and "market value of equity to the book value of equity (MBVR)" were used as a measure to evaluate a company's performance. The study employed "Population Average (PA)", "Random-Effects Autoregressive" and the "Feasible Generalized Least Square (FGLS)" estimations; and they found that interest rate increase negatively affects a performance while "production manufacturing index" along with "Islamic credit facilities" positively influence performance. They also found that the firm's age and capital structure have negative influenced firm's performance; while firm's size and growth have positively influenced firm's performance.

Zeitun & Tian (2007) also studied the influence of capital structure on the performance using an unbalanced panel of 167 firms over the duration 1989-2003 in Jordan. "Tobin's Q", "market value of equity divided by book value of equity (MBVR)", "earning per share (P/E)", "book value of liabilities and market value of equity divided by book value of equity (MBVE)" were the four measures used, which represents market performance of the Companies. While, the "ROE", "ROA", and "earnings before interest and tax plus depreciation divided by total assets (PROF)" were engaged as measures demonstrating accounting performance measures. Numerous explanatory variables were considered in the study, namely, leverage (five different measures were used), growth, firm size, tax rate, risk and tangibility. The outcomes of the study showed that a organization's capital structure has negatively impacted performance estimates, in the market as well as in accounting measures. They found that the "short-term debt to total assets (STDTA)" level had a significant positive influence on "Tobin's Q".

Pratheepkanth (2011) constituted an attempt to ascertain the association between performance and capital structure by using data of companies operating in Sri Lanka over the five year duration from 2005 to 2009. Four proxies were used to measure financial performance of the organisation, namely, "gross profit margin", "net profit margin", "return on asset", and "return on capital employed" and on the other hand, ratio of debt to equity and total funds represents the firm's capital structure. The study employed correlation and regression techniques for empirical assessment, and the outcomes revealed that the association between the financial performance and capital structure is negative relationship at -0.114. While the outcomes of regression model were insignificant and they concluded that Business firms mostly depend on the debt capital.

Muzir (2011) examined the associations among "firm size", "capital structure", and "financial performance" by using a data set of 114 Turkish companies over the period 1994 – 2003. They argued on the validity of 3 key capital structure theories – "Static Trade-Off Theory", "Irrelevance Theorem", and "Pecking Order Theory" - on a comparative rationale. They modelled insolvency by using financial ratios and employing logistic regression technique. The outcomes presented some robust evidence signifying that the impact of size on sustainability and financial performance may vary in relation to the way how firm size growth is financed. Any asset growth financed with debt has evidenced to upsurge risk exposure specifically during economic depressions, that recommends the "Static Trade-off Theory" in comparison to the others.

Salim & Yadav (2012) studied the association between organisation performance and capital structure by using panel data of 237 Malaysian listed firms during 1995-2011. They used 4 performance measures (i.e. predictand variables), namely, "return on asset (ROA)", "return on equity (ROE)", "Tobin s Q" and "earning per share (EPS)". Five measures were used for capital structure (predictor variable), namely, "short term debt (STD)", "long term debt (LTD)", "total debt ratios (TD)" and "growth". Size was used as a control variable. The outcomes indicated that "firm performance (ROA, ROE & EPS)" measures have negative association with STD, LTD and TD. Furthermore, they found positive linkage between the performance and growth. Tobin s Q showed significant positive association between STD and LTD. They also reported that TD has significant negative association with the corporate performance.

Salameh et al. (2012) examined the effect of the capital structure determinant on financial performance by using a dataset of 27 companies in Saudi-Arabia over the period 2004-2009. The study employed OLS technique to examine the influence of capital structure factors (i.e. "liquidity", "business risk (BR)", "growth rate", "tangibility", and "firm size") and leverage on two gauges of financial performance, namely, "Return on Asset (ROA)" and "Return on Equity (ROE)". The outcomes showed that no significant association among between "leverage ratio", "capital structure determinants", and "ROE". They also found insignificant relationship between a few of the capital structure determinants (Risk & Tangibility) and ROA.

Ahmad et al. (2012) investigated the influence of capital structure on the corporate performance by examining the association between operating performance of corporations in Malaysia, measured by "return on equity (ROE)" and "return on asset (ROA)" with "long-term debt (LTD)", "short-term debt (STD)" and "total debt (TD)". Four control variables were considered to have an effect on company operating performance, namely, "size", "asset growth", "sales growth" and "efficiency". Two main sectors, specifically, industrials and consumers sectors of Malaysian equity market were considered. Sampling frame of the study comprised of 58 firms over the year 2005-2010. The study found that TD and STD have significant association with ROA, while degree of debt does not impact the firm's ROE.

Pouraghajan et al. (2012) examined the influence of capital structure on the financial performance of companies which represents 12 industrial groups in Tehran over the period 2006 to 2010 by using regression methods. "Return on equity ratio (ROE)" and "return on assets ratio (ROA)" were used as a gauge of firms' financial performance. Outcomes suggested that there was a significant negative association between "firms' financial performance" and "debt ratio", and a significant positive association between "firm size", "asset tangibility ratio", "growth opportunities", and "asset turnover" with firms' financial performance determinants. But they found insignificant relationship between financial performance (i.e. both ROA & ROE) measures with the firm age. Moreover, research outcomes showed that by reducing "debt ratio", management can augment the firm's profitability and thus the volume of the its performance determinants and can enhance shareholder wealth.

Sheikh & Wang (2013) investigated the effect of capital structure on the performance of 240 companies in Pakistan during 2004-2009 by using "Pooled Ordinary Least Squares (OLS)", "panel fixed effects estimation", and "random effects estimation". Three proxies were used to measures of capital structure, i.e. "short-term debt ratio", "long-term debt ratio" and "total debt ratio"; and two proxies were used to gauge firm performance, i.e. "market-to-book ratio (market-based)" and "return on assets (accounting-based)". The outcomes of their study indicated that all gauges of capital structure were negatively associated to ROA in all regressions. Pooled OLS model outcomes indicated that "long-term debt ratio" and "total debt ratio" were negatively associated to "market-to-book ratio", whereas these gauges are positively associated to "market-to-book ratio" when "fixed effects model" was considered. They argue that negative association between capital structure and organisation performance shows that agency issues may lead the organisations to exploit greater than suitable degrees of debt in their capital structure.

Pratheepan (2014) studied the determinants of profitability of firms in Sri Lankan by using a sample of 55 manufacturing firms over the span of 2003-2012. The study considered "Return on Assets (ROA)" as a profitability measure whereas "size", "tangibility", "liquidity" and "leverage" were considered as predictor variables. The study employed "panel Ordinary Least Square (OLS)", "random effects and fixed affects" estimations for the analysis; and found significant relationship of both size and tangibility on profitability, specifically size was positively associated whereas tangibility associated with profitability. The other two variables i.e. leverage and liquidity exhibited insignificant effect on profitability.

Hunjra et al. (2014) examined the impact of firm-specific variables such as "size", "age", "firm's growth" (i.e. sales growth) and leverage on the firm performance of twenty six Pakistani cement manufacturing firms. The study extracted data from the annual reports of all the firms from 2002 to 2012 and applied panel OLS approach for the analysis purpose. Findings of the study indicate that all predictor variables have significant effect on the organisation performance. Specifically, the study found that "leverage" has a positive effect on "firm performance", when "Return on Asset (ROA)" was considered as a measure of firm performance. However, in case of "Return on Equity (ROE)" as a firm performance measure, outcomes of the study show that "age", "size" and "growth" have a positive influence on "ROE" while "leverage" has a negative influence.

Rehman et al. (2014) explored the relationship between "firm size", "macro-economic variables", and "firm performance" by considering the seven non-financial sectors of economy in Pakistan over a period 1999-2010. Six variables were used for measuring firm performance, namely: "current ratio", "inventory", "gearing ratio" and "total asset turnover"; and two macro-economic variables, namely: "interest rate" and "gross domestic production". The dependent variables used in the study were "return on asset" and "earning per share". Ordinary Least Square regression and Fixed Effect Model were used for analysis. The outcome of the study shows that the performance and size of companies both depend upon macroeconomic variables and financial ratios. They also found significant difference in terms of performance and size among all considered sectors.

Javed et al. (2014) analysed the effect of capital structure on the firm performance of 63 Pakistani firms over the 5 years duration from 2007 to 2011 by using the panel fixed effects model. Three proxies were used to determine firm performance, namely, "return on asset (ROA)", "return on equity (ROE)" and "return on sales (ROS)". In contrast, three proxies, namely, "equity over assets ratio (EQA), "debt over assets ratio (DTA), and "long term debts over assets ratio (LDA), measured Capital structure. They also used control variables like assets utilization, size of the firm, dividend payout ratio, earnings per share, share performance and firm growth. Capital structure exhibited positive influence on firm performance when ROA was employed as predictand variable. When ROE was employed as predictand variable then DTA depicted positive effect but EQA and LDA showed negative influence on predictand variable and when ROS was employed as predictand variable then DTA and EQA indicated negative relationship but LDA showed positive influence over ROS.

Xin (2014) studied the effect of capital structure and ownership structure on financial performance of the firm in the backdrop of an emerging transitional economy by using a sample of 134 Vietnamese companies for the duration from 2009-2012. They found that capital structure has a negative influence on firms' financial performance (measured by ROE & ROA). They argued that greater extent of state ownership in ownership structure leads to improved financial performance. While they remained unsuccessful to find significance of the influence of managerial ownership on firms' financial performance.

Twairesh (2014) empirically investigated the effect of capital structure on the firm performance of companies operational in Saudi Arabia. Sample of the study consist of 74 firms for the period 2004 to 2012 and they employed "panel fixed effect regression model" for analysing the association between capital structure and operating performance. Three proxies were used to estimate capital structure, namely, "long-term debt (LTD)", "short-term debt (STD)" and "total debt (TD)"; and two proxies were used to estimate the operating performance, namely, "return on equity (ROE)" and "return on assets (ROA)". He used firm's size as a control variable. They found that LTD, STD, and TD have significant influence on ROA. While only LTD has significant influence on ROE. They also found that firm size has significant influence on firm performance, when ROA was considered as a firm performance measure but does not impacted when ROE was a dependent variable.

Al-Jafari & Al Samman (2015) examined the determinants of profitability for 17 companies in Oman over the period 2006-2013 using panel ordinary least squares model. For measuring profitability, "net profit margin" and "return on assets" were used. The outcomes of the estimation revealed that significant positive relationship exist between "profitability", "growth", "firm size", "working capital" and "fixed assets". On the other hand, the financial leverage and the average tax rate variables showed a negative association with profitability. Though, this relationship is insignificant only for average tax rate variable.

Demirgunes & Ucler (2015) analysed the inter-relationship between firm profitability, size and growth for Turkey by using quarterly data of manufacturing industry comprising of Borsa Istanbul (BIST) listed manufacturing companies over the period 1991.Q2-2014.Q4. The study checked whether the data series are stationarity or not by using unit root test and further ascertained co-integration relationship by employing co-integration test. The co-integration coefficients were estimated by means of "dynamic ordinary least squares (DOLS)" method. Causal relationships between the series were also tested. Co-integration test outcomes show that the series were having long-run co-integration relationship. Long-run parameters evaluated by DOLS method posited a significantly negative association between size and profitability. Causality test outcomes show the presence of one-way causality run from size to profitability.

Conclusion:

The contemporary literature on the nexus among corporate financial performance, capital structure, and other control variables have been criticised for offering only fragmented outcomes and for not having the capacity to build up a broadly acknowledged model of firm's financial performance, consequently restricting theoretical advancement in this field. There is a need, along these lines, to move towards conceptualizations and framework that clarify the firm financial performance in a more persuading way. This study means to display a survey of the literature on the nexus among these variables in the Asian Context which includes Malaysia, Hong Kong, Korea, Singapore, Turkey, Jordan, Sri Lanka, Turkey, Saudi-Arabia, Tehran, Pakistan, Vietnam, and Oman. Furthermore, it shows an extensive review particularly in the Indian Context. A few vital discoveries were featured in the examination. Literature demonstrate that numerous proxy variables were used to gauge firm's financial performance, namely, "return on assets", "return on equity", "return on capital employed", "earnings per share", "Tobin's q ratio", "economic value added", "return on investment", "market value added", "market value of equity to the book value of equity", "book value of liabilities and market value of equity divided by book value of equity", "gross profit margin, and "net profit margin". Correspondingly, to quantify leverage a number of variables were used, in particular, "short-term borrowing to asset ratio", "long-term borrowing to asset ratio" and "total borrowing to asset ratio", "book value and market value of equity and debt", "debt equity ratio", and "expense to income ratio".

Apart from capital structure variable, different controlled variables, namely, "size", "age", "asset structure", "profitability", "financial distress", "non-debt tax shield", "growth", "shareholder value", "risk", "growth", "advertising intensity", "liquidity", "efficiency ratios (i.e. inventory turnover ratio, debtor turnover ratio, and asset turnover ratio)", "market share", "retention ratio", "research and development intensity", "dividend payout", and "past profitability" were additionally considered as a significant determinant of firm's financial performance. A few studies have also considered macroeconomic variables, in particular, "gross domestic production", "inflation", "interest rate", "production manufacturing index", "exports", "changes in money supply", "availability of credit", "Islamic credit", and "tax rate" as the significant determinants of firm's performance. All in all, it can be concluded that most of the studies have shown that the relationship between capital structure and firm's financial performance is either negative or non-existent. However, the nexus between other control variables and firm's performance on the above survey of the literature is still ambiguous. As the relationship depends upon the sample dataset pertaining to a particular manufacturing sector or nation.

References

Ahmad, Z., Abdullah, N. M. H., & Roslan, S. (2012). Capital structure effect on firms performance: Focusing on consumers and industrials sectors on Malaysian firms. *International review of business research papers*, *8*(5), 137-155.

Al-Jafari, M. K., & Al Samman, H. (2015). Determinants of Profitability: Evidence from Industrial Companies Listed on Muscat Securities Market. *Review of European Studies*, *7*(11), 303.

Azhagaiah, R., & Gavoury, C. (2011). The Impact of Capital Structure on Profitability with Special Reference to IT Industry in India vs. Domestic Products. *Managing Global Transitions*, *9*(4), 371.

Banerjee, A., & De, A. (2014). Determinants of Corporate Financial Performance Relating to Capital Structure Decisions in Indian Iron and Steel Industry An Empirical Study. *Paradigm*, *18*(1), 35-50.

Batra, R., & Kalia, A. (2016). Rethinking and Redefining the Determinants of Corporate Profitability. *Global Business Review*, *17*(4), 921-933.

Bhaduri, S. N. (2002). Determinants of capital structure choice: a study of the Indian corporate sector. *Applied Financial Economics*, *12*(9), 655-665.

Bhayani, S. J. (2010). Determinant of profitability in Indian cement industry: an economic analysis. *South Asian Journal of Management*,

17(4), 6.

Chadha, S., & Sharma, A. K. (2015). Determinants of capital structure: an empirical evaluation from India. *Journal of Advances in Management Research*, *12*(1), 3-14.

Chander, S., & Aggarwal, P. (2008). Determinants of corporate profitability: an empirical study of Indian drugs and pharmaceutical industry. *Paradigm*, *12*(2), 51-61.

Chaudhuri, K., Kumbhakar, S. C., & Sundaram, L. (2016). Estimation of firm performance from a MIMIC model. *European Journal of Operational Research*.

Demirgunes, K., & Ucler, G. (2015). Inter-Relationship between Profitability, Growth and Size: Case of Turkey. *Journal of Business Economics and Finance*, *4*(4).

Ghosh, S. (2008). Leverage, foreign borrowing and corporate performance: firm-level evidence for India. *Applied Economics Letters*, *15*(8), 607-616.

Gupta, P., Srivastava, A., & Sharma, D. (2010). Capital structure and financial performance: Evidence from India. *Gautam Buddha University, Greater Noida, India, Staff Working Paper*.

Hunjra, A. I., Chani, M. I., Javed, S., Naeem, S., & Ijaz, M. S. (2014). Impact of Micro Economic Variables on Firms Performance.

Javed, T., Younas, W., & Imran, M. (2014). Impact of Capital Structure on Firm Performance: Evidence from Pakistani Firms. *International Journal of Academic Research in Economics and Management Sciences*, *3*(5), 28.

Kakani, R. K., Saha, B., & Reddy, V. N. (2001). Determinants of financial performance of Indian corporate sector in the post-liberalization era: an exploratory study. *National Stock Exchange of India Limited, NSE Research Initiative Paper*, (5).

Khanna, T., & Palepu, K. (2000). Is group affiliation profitable in emerging markets? An analysis of diversified Indian business groups. *The Journal of Finance*, *55*(2), 867-891.

Krishnan, V. S., & Moyer, R. C. (1997). Performance, capital structure and home country: an analysis of Asian corporations. *Global Finance Journal*, *8*(1), 129-143.

Mahakud, J., & Misra, A. K. (2009). Effect of Leverage and Adjustment Costs on Corporate Performance: Evidence from Indian Companies. *Journal of Management Research*, *9*(1), 35.

Majumdar, S. K. (1997). The impact of size and age on firm-level performance: some evidence from India. *Review of industrial organization*, *12*(2), 231-241.

Majumdar, S. K., & Chhibber, P. (1999). Capital structure and performance: Evidence from a transition economy on an aspect of corporate governance. *Public Choice*, *98*(3-4), 287-305.

Mistry, D. S. (2012). Determinants of profitability in Indian automotive industry. *Tecnia Journal of Management Studies*, *7*(1), 20-23.

Muslumov, A. (2005). The financial and operating performance of privatized companies in Turkish Cement Industry. *METU Studies in Development*, *32*(1), 59-100.

Muzir, E. (2011). Triangle Relationship among Firm size, Capital Structure Choice and Financial Performance: some evidence from Turkey. *Journal of Management Research*, *11*(2), 87.

Narang, S., & Kaur, M. (2014). Impact of Firm-specific Attributes on Shareholder Value Creation of Indian Companies: An Empirical Analysis. *Global Business Review*, *15*(4), 847-866.

Pouraghajan, A., Malekian, E., Emamgholipour, M., Lotfollahpour, V., & Bagheri, M. M. (2012). The relationship between capital structure and firm performance evaluation measures: Evidence from the Tehran Stock Exchange. *International journal of Business and Commerce*, *1*(9), 166-181.

Pratheepan, T. (2014). A Panel Data Analysis of Profitability Determinants: Empirical Results from Sri Lankan Manufacturing Companies. *International Journal of Economics, Commerce and Management*, *2*(12).

Pratheepkanth, P. (2011). Capital structure and financial performance: Evidence from selected business companies in Colombo stock exchange Sri Lanka. *Researchers World*, *2*(2), 171.

Rehman, R. U., Zhang, J., & Ali, R. (2014). Firm Performance And Emerging Economies. *Journal of Applied Business Research*, *30*(3), 701.

Salameh, H. M., Al-Zubi, K. A., & Al-Zu'Bi, B. (2012). Capital structure determinants and financial performance analytical study in Saudi Arabia market 2004-2009. *International Journal of Economic Perspectives*, *6*(4), 18.

Salim, M., & Yadav, R. (2012). Capital structure and firm performance: Evidence from Malaysian listed companies. *Procedia-Social and Behavioral Sciences*, *65*, 156-166.

Sheikh, N. A., & Wang, Z. (2013). The impact of capital structure on performance: An empirical study of non-financial listed firms in

Pakistan. *International Journal of Commerce and Management*, *23*(4), 354-368.

Twairesh, A. E. M. (2014). The Impact of Capital Structure on Firm's Performance Evidence from Saudi Arabia. *Journal of Applied Finance and Banking*, *4*(2), 183.

Xin, W. Z. (2014). The impact of ownership structure and capital structure on financial performance of Vietnamese firms. *International Business Research*, *7*(2), 64.

Zeitun, R., & Tian, G. G. (2007). Capital structure and corporate performance: evidence from Jordan. *Australasian Accounting, Business and Finance Journal*, *1*(4), 3.

Zeitun, R., Tian, G. G., & Keen, S. (2007). Macroeconomic determinants of corporate performance and failure: evidence from an emerging market the case of Jordan. *Corporate Ownership and Control*, *5*(1), 179.

CHAPTER 2
A REVIEW STUDY ON PREVALENCE OF STRESS AND ITS MANAGEMENT AMONG BANKING PROFESSIONALS IN INDIA

Manpreet Kaur and Rajesh Kumar

Abstract

One of the fast developing and important sector in the financial system in India is banking sector. Employees working in public and private sector banks are constant subjects of facing challenges throughout their working career originating from their workplace. Work stress causes psychological, physiological and financial costs on both the individual employees and to their organization. Study of explosive growth especially in the last decade of the study clearly indicate that work-related stress has a negative impact on productivity, absenteeism, turnover of workers and their health. Numbers of attempts have been made to understand & quantify the job stress. The present study is based on secondary source of data and various papers have been studied and reviewed for this study. An attempt has been made through this paper to study the reasons of stress among the bank employees and different ways used by employees to cope with stress generated at workplace. Findings of the paper indicates that maximum number of employees in banks are stressed where work overload with time management, working environment, long working hours, unhelpful colleagues, incompetent subordinates, technological incompetency etc are some of the major reasons for work stress. According to the study, the level of job stress for permanent employees in public sector has affected more because of the unsupportive behavior of team leaders, strict organizational structure etc. Despite of the modern technology and banking sectors innovations, the employees are facing more job load and are stressed out.

Some measures are also suggested in the paper to overcome work stress that affects the physical and mental health of the employees. The study also illustrates different ways of stress management and managerial implications which should be considered to help employees overcome and cope with work stress that affects their mental and physical behavior.

2.1. Introduction

The word "Stress" (Goel & Kamboj, 2014) is taken from Latin word "Stringers" which means "to draw tight". Stress is a component of modern life; with growing difficulties of life, stress is likely to increase. Variety of actions and elements in life cause stress, beginning from the birth of a child and ending in the death of a near or beloved one. Stress is those vibrant situations in which an individual faces opportunity demand related to its requirements for which the results are considered valuable. Work stress in an organization is turning up as a rising concern for an organization and scholarly research both. According to Selye (1956), any external or internal drive which threatens to upset the organism equilibrium is stress. He has defined stress as the non-specific response of the body to any demand made upon it.

The stress at work (Anamika, 2016) is planned worldwide considering as a main task for the workers' health and the organization healthiness. It can be measured by a situation of anxiety practiced by individuals that faces constraints/opportunities and extraordinary demands. The Indian economy even has shown a tremendous growth in all sectors but the stress has taken its place in this growth as well. People are facing number of psychological and psychosomatic disorders, feeling of dissatisfaction and frustration in life are common now. The workplace stress is considered as a hurtful biological response for those who have a poor matching with the profile of the job with their resources, capabilities and worker needs. The mentioned condition not only affects the performance but the health as well of the individual.

Stress is taken as negative as well as positive. Less amount of stress can be considered healthy for the organization. Level dependence is the major factor that can help the individual to increase or decrease the performance (Awan & Asghar, 2014). Number of studies has shown that stress is maximizing its level in the banking sector (Azad & Tilottama, 2014). According to Sonnentag and Frese (2001), the organizations need highly working employees to deliver the products or services they are dealing in and finally to accomplish the competitive edge in the market. Different reasons for stress in banking organizations are changes in the Environment, changes in the economy, technological changes, challenges by management in the dynamic scenario, gender discrimination, job conditions, job demands, cultural differences etc. Therefore, work stress is defined as the working roles when work demands go beyond the working capability of the employees.

Varied numbers of challenges are being faced by the banking sector because of the recession in the worldwide market with the cut-throat rivalry. So, banks (Chaterjee & Chattopadhyay, 2015) are making efforts for growing the efficiency and constructing themselves again. As stress is rising as a problem for everyone, so stress management is needed for controlling and preventing level of stress for individual. Effectual stress management can be considered at organizational level and the individual level (Chahal et al., 2013). It can be managed at the different phases, firstly, stress copying and secondly, at experiencing the stress by relaxation techniques like meditation, yoga etc.

2.2. Need of the study

In the present scenario, the intensity and nature of stress (Samartha et al., 2014) is so unstable that the era is named as "Age of anxiety, stress and depression". Most of the time of an individual is being spend at the work place and is considered as the effective supplier and stress influencer. Various roles are performed by the individuals at the workplace that are coordinated with the role of home/other places. The stress is being induced as the performance of roles by individuals because employees are one of the influential organizational stressors. The researchers have applied the role-theory for understanding the problems of the stress at the workplace and assessing the role pressure contribution to professional stress. Though, the earlier study in this research area (Gopika,2014) specify that the role stress is like a fact which is hardly to understand entirely and expansively in commercial banks case mainly in the Indian context . Private and public banks are also being witnessed as the effort less for analyzing the stress role phenomenon thoroughly.

Banks (Joshi et al., 2012) are playing a role of significant economic consequence as mediators in mobilizing public economy and channelizing the funds flow for the purpose of productivity for economic expansion of country. Reserve Bank of India's branch expansion plan aimed at the development of the country, especially in rural areas and semi-urban areas and providing the necessary banking facilities. Due to structural changes, rationalization, indeed, is essential that the banks are public or private sector and should apply appropriate incentive tool to improve performance. Roots of motivation to achieve the desired goals can vary with the individual. For example, an employee may be excited in his work in order to earn higher commissions, while another employee can satisfactorily provided by it or by surrounding environment alone (Rizzo et al.,1970).

The organizations that are unhealthy in nature never get best from the employees and affect their survival rate with the performance. The employee may face the following while having the work stress:

i. May become irritable and distressed.
ii. Unable to concentrate or relax.
iii. May face problems in decision making and logic thinking.
iv. Less committed to work.

v. May feel anxious, depressed and tired.
vi. Cannot have good sleep.
vii. Can have problems like headaches, heart disease and blood pressure.

The organization got affected by work stress by:
i. Decrease work commitment.
ii. Absenteeism may increase.
iii. Staff turn-over may increase.
iv. Complaints from clients/customers may increase.
v. Can affect the recruitment of staff.
vi. The image of organization may be damaged

2.3. Objectives of the Study

- To study the reasons of stress among banking professionals.
- To identify the different ways used by employees to cope with stress generated at workplace.

2.4. Review of Literature

Researches from past has shown that nearly one-third of the working population in developed countries has reported a very high level of stress. Similarly, the evidence also shows that the newly industrialized countries prevails stress. Time pressure, role conflict, excessive demand, ergonomic defects, relations with customers and job security in the financial services sector employee's particularly common pressures.

2.4.i. Stress Among Banking Professionals

Stress is not always negative by nature and the full satisfaction doesn't mean positive attitude for fulfilling organizational goals. Duo of job satisfaction at high level and stress at lower level could build innovation required for social demand (Dahiya & Hooda, 2016). Stress at workplace stems from variety of stressors like organizational Culture, communication lack, role conflict, performance pressure, and lack of support with inadequate resources (Jadeja & Verma, 2016). It is difficult to predict the accurate impact; the basic impact is on the mind, impact on body, employee's emotions and behavior. Numbers of variables in the working environment have direct impact on the performance of the employee in a positive and negative way. Positive impact can lead to better results and achievements on the contrary negative impact can cause harm to the employees and to the organization both. Variables such as long working hours, improper incentive system, lack of job autonomy, organizational culture, role conflict, change in government policies and lack of management support banking sector stress. It has been shown that the stress among respondents is more because of more work load than time management efficiency (Azad & Tilottama, 2014) and job satisfaction (Samartha et al, 2014).

(Ayyappan & Sakthi, 2013) found that there is a important relationship between type of the banks, gender, age, education, marital status, length of service, job role, family type of the respondents and impact of occupational stress. But Organizational factors have major relation with the level of work stress and there is no such difference in the work stress level by means of demographic factors like gender, age, education qualification, and status and job pessimism (Das & Srivastav, 2013).

According to (Vishal et al, 2013), both public and private sector bank employees face same level of stress. Factors like lack of efficient manpower, performance pressure, family demands and unexpected emergencies with job stiffness are some of the major stressors among public sector bank employees. Similar stressors are experienced by private sector bank employees with some new characteristics like adaptability to change and performance pressure. Education qualification level as compare to work experience of an employee working in a banking organization have significant contribution to job stress (Bano & Jha, 2012). Organization structure has negative relation with the efficiency of the employees whereas the monetary rewards given to the employees at work have positive relation with their work efficiency. Further, administrative support have no significant relationship with employee efficiency (Shah et al., 2012). Research by Diefendor et.al (2002) reveals that job participation is an influence of stress as employees get more focused towards unfavourable situations, where lack of social experience is the main cause of stress over which job involvement is forerunner of stress.

2.4.ii. Coping with Stress by Banking Professionals

The causes of stress cannot be banned but we can defeat and rise above from its results by adopting right strategies for coping with stress. Coping with stress can be performed with different coping strategies under different situations. Studies have found that the organizations which follow stress management programs have accomplished an edge of competitiveness from the organizations that works successfully (Kaur & Sharma, 2016). Different strategies used for managing stress such as audit, appraisals, social support, programs for occupational growth, role clarifications etc (Jadeja & Verma, 2016).

Some studies also came up with contradictory results for gender differences for coping tactics (Gonzalez, Rodriguez, & Peiro, 2010; Haarr & Morash, 1999; He, Zhao, & Archbold, 2002; Kieffer & MacDonald, 2011; Piko, 2001). It was found that women suffer more from stress than men and hence have higher score for emotional and avoidant coping than men Matud (2004). The study by Hart et al. (1995) found that there are mainly two type of coping namely problem-focused coping and emotional focused coping. According to the author there is positive work experience with problem focused coping while negative work experience with emotional focused coping. The process of coping with stress in a particular situation is through cognitive appraisal in which a person appraises chain of communications between the individual and the surroundings is stressful or not (Lazarus & Folkman, 1984).

2.5. Findings of the Study

The workplace stress is measured as an unkind biological response for the employees with a poor matching with the job profile by their resources, capabilities and worker needs.

Varieties of challenges are faced by the banking sector since the recession with the cut-throat rivalry.

One should be self-confident, self-aware with self-control at the workplace.

Stress is considered as the individual's role for their performance as employees are the one for influential organizational stressors.

Private and public banks are witnessed as the effort less for analyzing the stress role phenomenon carefully.

Overall banking sector in India is considered being mature for supply, product range.

Stress can be lessen by regular training, by conducting stress management programs and with suitable communication

Stress among private sector employees is more as compare to public sector banks.

For achieving the required output, the banks need to focus on the employee's satisfaction.

Conclusion

Work efficiency growth in any industry is the most decisive factor. More emphasis on employment, health and the importance of the family is the main reason for reducing the stress of a job behind. Stress, in the present case has become a deep-rooted evil that need to eradicate. Stress is itself a problem, which in turn creates some problems. This paper aims to study the need of stress management program, because of the increasing stress due to which employees cannot work. The research study is certainly conducive to the organization that they need to share understanding of stress management plan to spend, so, they can maximize their profits, which also help to produce employee satisfaction and creating a stress-free environment. The research has led us to conclude that the public and private sector employees are facing moderate pressure; they are most vulnerable to erosion and the role of inadequate resources. India is one of the fastest growing countries in the world. India's economy is greatly influenced by the national banking system, relating to control and help in the process of development in all fields. As the stress of banking sector is mainly because of the excessive pressure of work, so the organizations must support and encourage the employees for taking up the decisions properly to manage the family and work. Since stress in banking sector is mostly due to excess of work pressure and work life imbalance the organization should support and encourage taking up roles that help them to balance work and Family. The stress factors related to organizations, work, individuals, environmental health, stress management, psychological, avoidance of stress-related pressures factors are important steps to reduce the stress factor.

Recommendations

Recommendations to employees

- To survive in the competitive world always be prepared to face the changes or challenges to avoid stress.
- Face the stressful situations in personal life and at work life with positive attitude.
- Try artistic imagination for different situations.
- Re-appraise and prioritize your goals.
- Give time by refreshing, re-motivating yourself.
- While under constant stress avoid smoking, taking alcohol or any other substance abuse.
- Always seek social support to discuss problems and stress related issues from your friends and family at home and peers at work.
- Consult a health professional in case of chronic stress.

Recommendations to the organizations

- Identification of the job roles for eliminating the role ambiguity.
- The grievances of the employees need to be handled so that they can cop up with organization environment.
- The objectives of the organization should be clear for the employees because it is known that the satisfied employee can satisfy the customer which is the priority of all organizations.
- Employment of the psychiatrist should be conducted in the organizations at all levels; this can improve the job conditions and can alleviate the job stress.
- The management of the people at organization level should be done differently; the treatment should be given in respectful manner and should value the contribution.
- The training should be given as per the profile of the employee and the implementation of policy should be the priority when the activities of the bank turn into complexity. The employee should have the knowledge about his work for less stress and more efficiency of work.
- Jobs that are inhibiting employees' abilities with capacities that must be redesigned or eliminated as per the employee's potential.
- The training programs and job orientation should be conducted for improving the skills of employees and can effectively boost up their confidence.

Continuous training to the employees for updating and refining about the new technical competencies is needed. Incorporated programs for creating self awareness, motivational development, role and value clarification for positive reinterpretation of own and others actions has to be initiated. To give more exposure and opportunity to the employees, job rotation, job enrichment and enlargement must regularly be done by the superiors. It is seen from previous researches that proper interpersonal feedback from the employees supports and strengthens the working of the organization. These all aspects brings stress free working environment and brings positive attitude to face upcoming challenges in future.

References

Anuj Goel, Akshita Kamboj. (2014). A Study on Stress Management Among the Employees of Nationalised Bank. *Journal of Commerce and Trade*.

Anamika. (2016). Stress and Job Satisfaction level among Government and Private Sector Bank Employees: A Study on Urban Area in Patna India. *The International Journal of Indian Psychology*.

Awan G.A, Asghar I. (2014).Impact of Employee Job Satisfaction on their Performance- A Case Study of Banking Sector in Muzaffargarh District, *Global Journal of Human Resource Management*.

Ayyappan, Valdivel M. Sakthi(2013) " The Impact of Occupational Stress of Selected Banking Sector Employees in Tamil Nadu", *International journal of Finance and Banking Studies*. Vol. 2

Azad, Tilottama. (2014). Managing Stress among Banking Sector Employees in Bhopal. *Irc's International Journal of Multidisciplinary Research in Social & Management Sciences*, 1(7), 132-137.

B. Bano and R. Kumar Jha, "Organizational role stress among public and private sector employees: a comparative study," *TheLahore Journal of Business*, vol. 1, no. 1, pp. 23–36, 2012.

Chatterjee I, Chattopadhyay M. (2015).The Impact of Motivational Factors on Job Satisfaction of Public and Private Sector Bank Employees. *International Journal of Science Technology and Management*.

Chahal A.,Chahal. S, Chowdhary. B & Chahal. J. (2013). Job Satisfaction among Bank Employees: An Analysis of the Contributing Variables towards Job Satisfaction.

International Journal of Scientific & Technology Research, 2 (8), 11-20.

Dr. Beulah Viji Christiana. M, Dr. V. Mahalakshmi. (2013). Role Stress and its Impact on Public and Private Sector Managers in Chennai: An Empirical Study. *International Journal of Management & Business Studies*, 3(1), 22-27.

Dr. N. Balraj.(2016) .Role Stress Among Employees In Public And Private Sector Banks. *Asia Pacific Journal of Research*.

Dr. Vishal Samartha, Dr. Mushtiary Begum, & Lokesh. (2014). A comparative analysis of occupational stress among the employees in public and private sector banks in dakshina kannad district. *International Journal of Conceptions on Management and Social Sciences*, 2(2), 32-36.

Ms. Rishampreet Kaur,Mrs.Poonam Gautam Sharma (2016). Stress Management in the Banking Sector. *Imperial Journal of Interdisciplinary Research*, 2(3), 113-117.

D. Duffie. (2011). A 10-by-10-by-10 approach. NBER Working Paper, 17281.

G., Gopika. (2014).A Quantitative Analysis on The Correlation between Industrial Experience and Stress Level Changes in Banking Industry. *International Journal of Advance Research in Science and Engineering*.

Gonzalez, M. G., Rodriguez, I, & Peiro, J. M. (2010). A longitudinal study of coping and gender in a female dominated occupation: predicting teachers' burnout. *J Occup Health Psychol, 15*, 29-44.

H. C. Triandis, M. Gelfand. (1998). Converging measurement of horizontal and vertical individualism and collectivism. Journal *of Personality & Social Psychology*, 74, 118-128.

Haarr, R. N., & Morash, M. (1999). Gender, race, and strategies of coping with occupational stress in policing. *Justice Quarterly, 16*(2), 303-336.

Hart, P. M., & Wearing, A. J. (1995). Police stress and well-being: Integrating personality, coping and daily work experiences. *Journal of Occupational & Organizational Psychology, 68*(2), 133-156.

He, N., Zhao, J., & Archbold, C. A. (2002). Gender and police stress: The convergent and divergent impact of work environment, work-family conflict, and stress coping mechanisms of female and male police officers. *Policing: An international journal of police strategies & management, 25*(4), 687-708.

Hiteshwari Jadeja, Dr. Monica Verma (2016). Investigating Sources of Occupational Stress: A Conceptual Framework. *International Journal of Advance Research in Computer Science and Management Studies*,4(1), 239-247.

J. M. Diefendorff, D. J.Brown, A. M. Kamin, & R. G. Lord. 2002. Examining the roles of job involvement and work centrality in predicting organizational citizenship behaviors and job performance. *Journal of Organizational Behavior*, 93-108.

J. R. Rizzo, R. J. House, & S. I. Lirtzman.(1970).Role conflict and ambiguity in complex organizations. Administrative Science Quarterly.

Jayashree, Rajendran. (2010).Stress Management with Special Reference to Public Sector Bank Employees in Chennai. *International Journal of Enterprise and Innovation Management Studies.* 1(3), 34-39.

Joshi, Vijay, Goyal & K.A. (2012).Stress Management among Bank Employees: With Reference to Mergers and Acquisitions. *International Journal of Business and Commerce,* 1(5), 22-31.

Kavita Dahiya, Dr. Shweta Hooda (2016). A Study of influence of job satisfaction on stress in banking sector employees in India. *International Journal of Institutional and Industrial Research*, 1(1),50-55.

Kieffer, K. M., & MacDonald, G. (2011). Exploring factors that affect score reliability and variability: In the Ways of Coping Questionnaire reliability coefficients: A meta-analytic reliability generalization study. *Journal of Individual Differences, 32*(1), 26-38.

Khurram Zafar Awan, & Faisal Jamil.(2012).A comparative analysis: Differences in overall job stress level of permanent employees in Private and Public sector banks. *International Journal of Economics and Management.*

Lazarus, R. S., & Folkman, S. (1984). *Stress, appraisal, and coping*: Springer Publishing Company.

Matud, M. P. (2004). Gender differences in stress and coping styles. *Personality and Individual Differences, 37*(7), 1401-1415.

Nadeem Malik. (2011).A study on occupational stress experienced by private and public banks employees in Quetta City. *African Journal of Business Management.*

Piko, B. (2001). Gender Differences and Similarities in Adolescents' Ways of Coping. *Psychological Record, 51*(2), 223.

Priyanka Das, Alok Kumar Srivastav (2013). A study of stress among employees of public sector banks on Asansol, West Bengal. *International Journal of Science and Research*, 4(7), 108-113.

R. Cardarelli, S. Elekdag, & S. Lall.(2011).Financial stress and economic contractions. *Journal of Financial Stability.*

S. Vishal, Vidyavathi, and B. Mustiary, "Regression analysis of stress, a comparative study of employees in public and private sector banks," *Excel International Journal of MultidisciplinaryManagement Studies*, vol. 3, no. 7, pp. 68–76, 2013.

Selye, H. (1974). "Stress without Distress." *Harper and Row Publications*, U.S.A.

Shah Syed Saad Hussin,Aziz jabran, Jaffari Ahsan, Waris Sidra, Ejaz Wasiq, Fatima Maira and Shirazi Syed Kamran(2012) "Impact of Stress on Employees's Performance: A Study on Teachers of Private Colleges of Rawalpindi", *Asian Journal of Business Management*, 4(2)

Shavita Dhankar.(2015).Occupational stress in banking sector,1(8),132-135.

Shukla, Harish and Garg, Rachita. (2013).A Study on Stress Management among the Employees of Nationalised Banks, 2(3), 72-75.

Shri N. Ramanathan, Dr S. Chnadra Mohan.(2014).Occupational stress- A comparative study of employees in Public and Private sector banks in Tamil Naidu. *International journal of Innovation and scientific Research.*

T. P. Ference, A. F. Stoner & -E. K. Warren. (1977). Managing the career plateau. Academy of Management Review, 2, 602-612.

T. Gautama, D. P. Mandic & M. M. Van Hulle. (2000). A differential entropy based method for determining the optimal embedding parameters of a signal. In Proc. Acous. Speech Sig. Proc.

CHAPTER 3
LENDING PRACTICES AND CUSTOMERS' SATISFACTION OF DISTRICT CENTRAL COOPERATIVE BANK: WITH SPECIAL REFERENCE TO KANGRA CENTRAL COOPERATIVE BANK

Pradeep Kumar

Abstract

Cooperative banks play vital role in financial inclusion, especially in rural areas. These banks help in the development and growth of local communities, access of banking services to farmers and low and middle income households, increases their purchasing powers, encourages for small saving habits, and mobilize savings into investment. These banks provide financial assistance to small business/enterprises which helps in employment generation and economic growth. Cooperative banks are based on the principle of mutual cooperation and interest of their members belonging to same local communities. These banks are controlled and managed by their own members or elected board of directors by the members.. There are three tier short term cooperative structures in our financial system, i.e. State Cooperative Banks (SCBs) at apex level, District Central Cooperative Banks (DCCBS) at district level and Primary Agricultural Cooperative Societies (PACS) at the local level. This paper is an attempt to study the lending practices and level of customers' satisfaction towards the lending practices of the Kangra Central Cooperative Bank (KCCB) which came into existence on March 17, 1920 (Himachal Pradesh). A Descriptive research has approached. Structured questionnaire, interview tools and observation method are used in primary sources. A sample size of 70 respondents is taken and convenience sampling technique is used in the present study. Annual reports and various research articles are used as secondary sources of data. As far as results are concerned KCCB has comprehensive lending policies in various sectors. Documentation and Terms & Condition are to be the major factor for the customer satisfaction. The majority of the customers is satisfied with all the factors considered for the purpose of this study.

> "There should be one cooperative for every village and every village should be covered by one cooperative".
>
> *Maclagan committee-1915*

3.1. Introduction

Cooperative banks help in the development and growth of local communities, access of banking services to farmers and low and middle income households, increases their purchasing power, encourages for small saving habits and mobilize savings into investment. The present study is conducted to answer the questions like what are the lending practices and what is the level of customers' satisfaction of District Central Cooperative Banks (DCCBs).

Cooperative banks play vital role in financial inclusion, especially in rural areas. The Government of Madras was the first to identify the possibilities of cooperative movement in India. And, in 1892, appointed F. H. Nicholson as the special officer to study the theory and practices of cooperative banks in Europe. The Cooperative Society Act-1904 was the first in India related to the legal aspects of cooperative banks. Another more comprehensive Act was enacted for the encouragement and promotion of cooperatives named as The Cooperative Society act- 1912. Maclagan Committee (1915) advocated that "there should be one cooperative for every village and every village should be covered by one cooperative". Provisions were made in RBI Act-1934 for the establishment of an agricultural Credit Development Bank and extending refinance facility to cooperative system. The Royal commission's maid observation that "if cooperative fails, there will be full of the best of the rural India".

The international cooperative Alliance has defined as cooperative:-
"An autonomous association of persons united voluntarily to meet their common economic, social and cultural needs and aspiration through a jointly owned and democratically controlled enterprise. And cooperative are based on the values of self-help, self-responsibility, democracy, equality, equity and solidarity"

Barou N has defined cooperative credit (Bank) association as:-
"A voluntary association of individual with unrestricted membership and collectively owned resources, formed by small procedure, conducted on a democratic basis under joint management and by mutual services by accumulating the savings of members and granting them credit on easy terms of interest and repayment, the surplus being placed for reserves or distribution between depositors, borrowers and shareholders".

Cooperative banks works on the Rochdale principal firstly Set out in 1844 by the Rochdale Society of Equitable formed in Rochdale in United Kingdom. Updated version of these principles were adopted by the International Cooperative Alliance (ICA) in 1966 and further in 1995.

3.2. Structure of Cooperatives in India

There are three tier cooperative structures in India
- State Cooperative Bank (SCB) at state (apex) level.
- District Central Cooperative Bank (DCCB) at district (intermediate) level.
- Primary Agricultural Credit Society (PACS) at local or village level

3.3. District Central Cooperative Banks (DCCBs)

The District Central Cooperative Bank is the federation of Primary Agricultural Credit Societies (PACS). These banks fulfill their financial needs from share capital, deposits, loans and overdraft from NABARD and State Cooperative Bank (SCB). DCCBs provide finance to member societies and other members within specified limits of borrowing. DCCBs generally located in district headquarter and works in the territory of that particular district. DCCBs act as intermediate between Primary Agricultural Credit Societies at (local level) and State Cooperative Banks (apex level). There are 371 DCCBs working in 20 states in India with 14060 branches. As on March 31, 2015 loan advances of DCCBs in India was 23242126 (in lakhs) and loan outstanding was 20720549 (in lakhs) (National federation of State Cooperative Banks, 2015-2016).

3.4. Kangra Central Cooperative Bank (KCCB)

The Kangra Central Cooperative Bank came into existence on March 17, 1920, headquarter at Dharmshala, District Kangra (Himachal Pradesh). KCCB is currently operating with 214 branches in five districts of Himachal Pradesh. The total deposits and loans of KCCB are 8427.57 crore and 3820.57 crore respectively (Annual Report 2015-16, KCCB). The net worth of KCCB is 67951.57 (in lakhs) as per balance sheet of March 31, 2016.

3.5. Literature Review

Bawa Committee (1971) recommended setting up large multipurpose cooperative banks in the tribal area. National Commission on Agriculture (1976) recommended setting up farmers services cooperative societies with collaboration with the national banks. Maxima Committee (1991) laid the foundation for the reformation of India banking sector in the form of reduction of the statutory liquidity ratio, progressive reduction in cash reserve ratio, redefinition of priority sector, stipulation of minimum capital adequacy ratio. Gupta and Jain (2012) in their paper 'A study on Cooperative Banks in India with special reference to Lending Practices' suggested that cooperative bank should introduce new plans to attract more customer and satisfy existing customer, technological up gradation (related to internet banking, credit card, ATM etc.), expansion of branches and improvement of customer satisfaction of the bank.

Cooperative bank should improve their recovery practices, computerized system of monitoring loans and organization of regular workshop for survival in a competitive banking environment (Dutta and Basak, 2008). Singh and Kaur (2011) concluded that satisfaction of customer is affected by six major factors- responsiveness, tangible, social responsibility, service innovation, positive word of mouth, competency and reliability. Sabir et al., (2014) in their paper 'the factor affecting customer satisfaction in banking sector of Pakistan' concluded that service quality attribute and customers' satisfaction has positive relation.

In 2014, a study analyzed the productivity in term of per employee and per branch of the district central cooperative bank in India

(Hooda). There are six major factors of customers' perception related to performance and services of UCBs (tangible customer service, basic banking services, customer grievances and Redressal system, soft skill of employees and technology provision of convenient banking and customer empowerment) amongst which tangible customer service factor is the most important factor for customer satisfaction (Singh and Soni, 2015). In 2013, a study on cooperative bank in India found that most of the customers (borrowers) taken house loan and for more than three years. The simple procedure and less formalities are the main factors determining customers' selection of loan (Soyeliya). In 2016, an another study found that a majority of borrowers reasoned for borrowing from DCCB is less rate of interest and suggested that the bank should modify its loan sanctioning policy (Varalakshmi and Deepika).

3.6. Objectives of the Study
- To know the lending practices of the Kangra Central Cooperative Bank (KCCB).
- To know the level of customers' satisfaction from the lending policies of the bank.
- To identify the problems faced by KCCB and give appropriate suggestion.

3.7. Research Methodology

This study is based on lending practices and customers' satisfaction of KCCB and descriptive research is used for the purpose. Both, Primary and secondary source of data collection is used. Structured questionnaire and interview tools and observation method is used in primary sources. Annual reports of KCCB, and various research articles uses as secondary sources of data. A sample of 70 customers is used for the purpose of this study. Only those customers are considered as respondents who has taken loan form the Bank. All the customers of the KCCB, who have taken loan are the population of the study and individual customer is the sampling unit for the purpose. A convenience sampling technique, a non-probability sampling method is used for selection of respondents.

3.8. Data Analyses and Interpretation

This study has been conducted with four major factors (i.e. Basic

Banking Services, Documentation and Terms & Conditions, Employees' Attitude and Behavior and Grievances and Redressal) to analyze the level of customers' satisfaction. The responses of 70 respondents have drawn with Five Point Likert Scale rating from Strongly Agree to Strongly Disagree. Simple statistical tools (tables, charts, diagrams, and percentage) have been used for the analyses of data.

3.8.i. Lending Practices of KCCB

As per the Balance Sheet (31-3-2016), KCCB has granted 3820.57 crores of loans and advances of various categories in which 896.08 crores in agricultural sector only.

Table 1: Loan products of KCCB

Sr. No.	For societies	For individuals
1	Agriculture	Agriculture
2	Non-farm sector	Non-farm sector
3	Personal vehicles	Housing
4	Weavers/industrial/housing	Personal vehicles
5	Cash, credit	Cash, credit

Sources: http://www.kccb.in

As on March 31, 2016 Gross NPA to total advances has 11.43 percentage and net NPA to Net Advances has a 8.66 percentage (Balance Sheet, 2015-16, KCCB)

Table 2: Loan and Advances of KCCB

Sr. No.	Years	Amounts (crores)
1	2007	1095.58
2	2008	1150.40
3	2009	1328.23
4	2010	1497.30
5	2011	1825.00
6	2012	2421.58
7	2013	2855.34
8	2014	3141.78
9	2015	3527.42
10	2016	3820.57

Source: Annual reports, KCCB

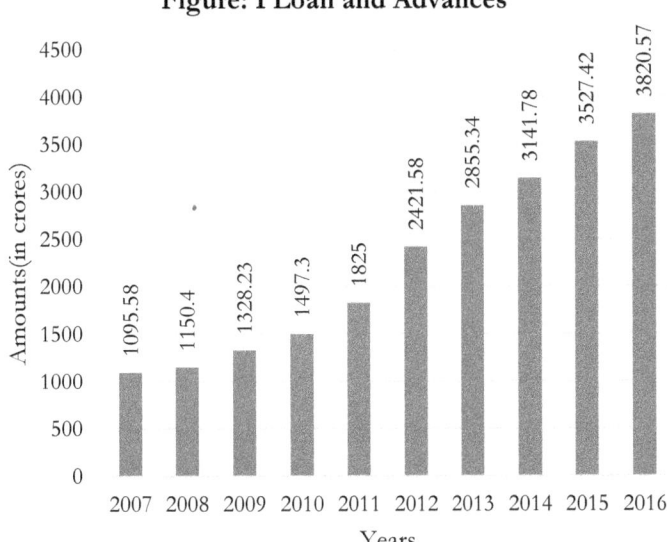

Figure: 1 Loan and Advances

Sources: Annual Reports, KCCB

For the objective, to know the perception and customers' satisfaction of KCCB, the responses of 70 customers have been drawn on four major factors. Responses and analyses of each factor are as:

Table. 3: Loan Preferences of the Respondents

Sr. No.	Loan type	No. of Respondents	Percentage
1	House loan	24	34.28
2	Agriculture loan	19	27.14
3	Personal vehicle loan	13	18.58
4	Personal loan	9	12.86
5	Others	5	7.14
	Total	70	100

Sources: Primary Data

3.8.ii. Basic Banking Services

Deposits and Borrowings, location of the branch, service charges and seating, water, parking facility are the first major factor which has an impact on customers' satisfaction.

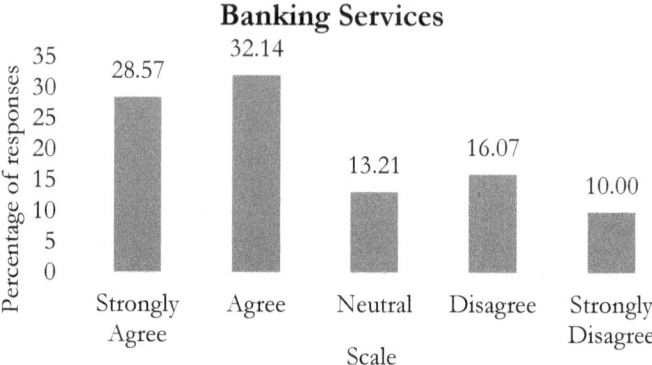

Figure 2: Percentage of responses to Basic Banking Services

The above graph shows that 28.57 percent respondents are highly satisfied and 32.14 percent respondents are satisfied with the basic banking services of KCCB. 13.21 percent respondents are neutral with their responses on this factor. It reports that respondents disagree and strongly disagree with 16.07 percent and 10 percent respectively.

3.8.iii. Documentation and Terms & Conditions

It is the second major factor which is considered in this study, which impact customers' satisfaction. Statement for the purpose includes documents formalities, the rate of interest on loan, terms and conditions of loan, amounts and numbers of EMIs and time taken to provide a loan.

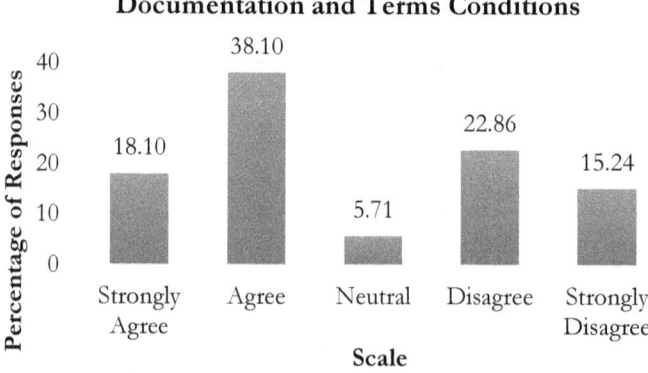

Figure 3: Percentage of responses on Documentation and Terms Conditions

From the above graph, it is revealed that Majority of respondents is satisfied with the Documentation and Terms & Conditions of KCCB. A very less number of respondents disagree and strongly disagree with the 22.86 percent and 15.24 percent respectively.

3.8.iv. Employees' Attitude and Behavior

Two statements, behavior of employees with the customers and employees having up-to-date knowledge related to the rules and policies of the bank are used in this factor to draw responses of customers.

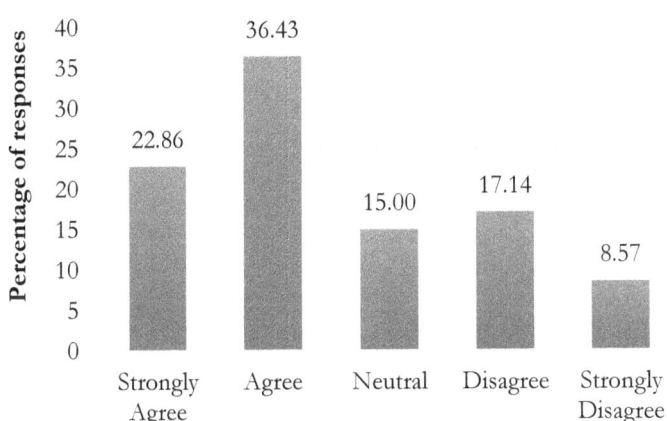

Figure 4: percentage of responses on employees' attitude and behavior

Above graph reveals that more than 50 percent respondents are satisfied with the employees' behavior of KCCB.

3.8.v. Grievances and Redressal of customers

In this factor responses are drawn on three statement- handling of telephonic enquiries, feedback system in the bank and speed of handling problems

Figure 5: Percentage of response on Grievances and Redressal factor

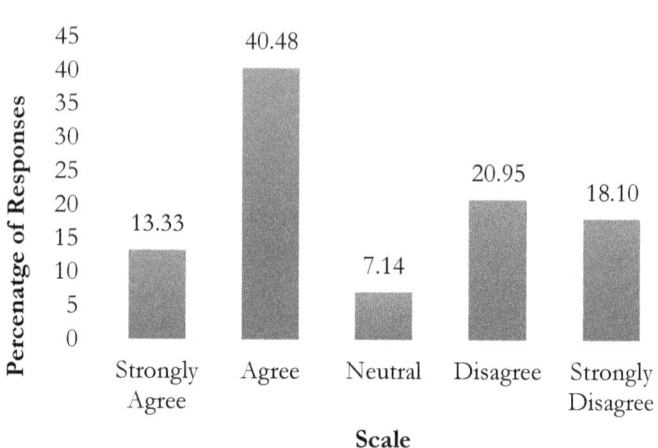

This graphs reveals that 40 (apprx.) respondents are not satisfied with the grievances and redressal procedures of the KCCB. Although more than 50 percent are satisfied with the statements on this factor.

Suggestions

As per the results of this study maximum respondent are satisfied with overall services of the KCCB, however, some major issues have been pointed out from the study as:
- The bank should focus on lending to the Agriculture sector and education.
- The bank should improve their NPAs and profitability.
- The bank should expand their Branches and ATMs network in other districts of Himachal Pradesh.
- The bank should also focus on transparency as they are not getting any funding from RBI.

Conclusion

As per the analyses and results of the study KCCB has comprehensive lending practices and policies in various sectors like agriculture, housing, vehicles, SHGs, SSIs etc. and member societies. As far as satisfaction of the customer is concerned, four factors, basic banking services, documentation and terms & conditions, employees' attitude and behavior and grievance and Redressal have discussed in the study. As per the responses from customers', documentation and terms & condition is the major factor for their satisfaction. The majority of the respondents' have satisfied with the lending practices of KCCB in all the four segments considered in the study.

References

Annual Reports of KCCB, 2014, 2015, 2016.

Devi, R. U. (2013). The Role of District Central Co-operative Banks in the Agricultural Development of EG District of Andhra Pradesh. *International Journal of Innovative Research and Development, 2* (2), 101-124.

Dutta, U. K., & Basak, A. (2008). Appraisal of financial performance of urban cooperative banks-a case study. *MANAGEMENT ACCOUNTANT-CALCUTTA-, 43* (3), 170.

Garg, Y., & Gupta, J. (2017). A Study on Lending Practices of Cooperative Banks in India. *International Journal of Technology in Engineering and Science,* 5 (1), 532-544.

Gupta, J., & Jain, S. (2012). A study on Cooperative Banks in India with special reference to Lending Practices. *International Journal of Scientific and Research Publications, 2* (10), 1-6.

Hooda, V. S. Progress of District Central Co-operative Banks in India: A Snapshot on Productivity. *Pacific Business Review International,* 7 (2), 77-84.

Kavitha, N. A. (2016). A Study of Customer Satisfaction and Perception Towards the Services of Co-operative Banks. *International Journal of Engineering Technology, Management, and Applied Sciences,* 4 (10), 127-130.

Sabir, R. I., Ghafoor, O., Akhtar, N., Hafeez, I., & Rehman, A. U. (2014). Factors affecting customer satisfaction in banking sector of Pakistan. *International Review of Management and Business Research, 3* (2), 1014

Singh, B., & Soni, R. (2015). Customer satisfaction in Urban Cooperative Banks. *International Journal of Research in Finance and Marketing, 5* (8), 26-32.

Singh, J., & Kaur, G. (2011). Customer satisfaction and universal banks: An empirical study. *International Journal of Commerce and Management,* 21 (4), 327-348.

Soyeliya, U. L. (2013). A study on Co-operative Banks in

India. *International Journal of Research in Humanities and Social Sciences*, *1* (7), 26-30.
www.kccb.in
www.nafscob.org

CHAPTER 4
A STUDY OF THE HUMAN RESOURCE DEVELOPMENT PRACTICES IN THE KANGRA CENTRAL COOPERATIVE BANK

Ravi Kumar and Shagun Sood

Abstract

In a skill based economy and competitive era of globalization, human resource development practices are the backbone for the development of any organization. Human resource development plays a vital role in attracting, developing, retaining and satisfying employees to achieve organizational goal. Human Resource Development is a continuous process of overall development of employees in the form of competency, efficiencies and effectiveness, morale, motivation, dynamism etc. Human resource development is a system in which includes subsystems like training, performance appraisal, career counseling, mentoring, job rotation, rewards, and feedback. Human resource development subsystem helps in developing a mutual trust and collaboration, spirit of team work, better superior-subordinate relationship (Rao, 1985). Human resource development practices help to sharpen capabilities and explore the inner potential of employees for their own career enhancement and organizational development (Rao, 1991). This paper is an attempt to study the Human Resource Development practices in Kangara Central Cooperative Bank (KCCB) was founded on March 17, 1920 headquarter at Dharamshala, district Kangara (Himachal Pradesh). This study is to know human resource development practices in KCCB. It also aims to examine the relationship between Human Resource Development Subsystem and their effectiveness. A Descriptive research design has used. For primary source of data collection, Interviews and Questionnaire tools are used, whereas publications and research articles are used for secondary data collection. Sample size of 75 respondents has taken to using Convenience sampling technique for the purpose of this study. The study revealed that employees are satisfied with HRD subsystem, especially development initiatives and working environment. The organization needs for improvement in Performance management and Compensation policy subsystem.

"All the activities of any enterprise are initiated and determined by the people who make up the institutions. Plants, offices, computers and automated equipments, those are unproductive in the absence of human efforts and directions".

Rensis Likert

4.1. Introduction

Human resource development is a management philosophy which directly associated with growth, development, career, welfare, dignity and respect of employees (Ramu, 2008). The present study is an attempt to answer the question that does HRD practices followed by the Knagra Central Cooperative Bank has an impact on the effectiveness of employees' performance.

Human resource development plays a vital role in attracting, developing, retaining and satisfying employees to achieve organizational goal. To make pace with the changing environment of industries, competencies and the efficiencies of employees are very essential (Kumari, (2012). In a skill based economy and competitive era of globalization, human resource development practices are the backbone for the development of any organization. Human Resource Development is a continuous process to acquire, to enhance, to change, to improve of employee's skills, abilities, attitudes, beliefs, values, personalities, etc. in relating to perform their current or future jobs/roles in respect of objective's achievement of organization (Rodrigues and Chincholkar, 2005).

Human resource development subsystem helps in developing a mutual trust and collaboration, spirit of team work, better superior-subordinate relationship (Rao, 1985). HRD is greatly helpful in vision development consist of the organization's vision, vision content, vision implementation which give organization effectiveness in term of organization development, employee development, communication and controlling (Foster and Akdere 2007). Human Resource Development functions are implemented through sub-system. The HRD sub-system comprises of Compensation system, Performance Appraisal system, Development system, Working environment system and Job Rotation system. The objective of HRD (Rao and Pereira, 1986) may be defined as: (i) to develop capabilities of employees as individual level, (ii) to develop capabilities of employees in term of competency for current job/role or future job/role, (iii) to build up unity in workforce and team spirit for performing jobs/roles, (iv) to create dyadic relationship between superiors and subordinates, (v) to create collaboration among different activities of organization, (vi) to develop capabilities of individuals in respect of organization's health.

4.2. Cooperative Banks

Cooperative banks are the lifeline for rural credit in the Indian financial system. Cooperative banks are key funding agencies, better utilization and mobilization of small savings of their members (Paul and Attri, 2015). Cooperative banks are far reaching rural areas as well as urban areas to fulfill the financial needs of farmers, entrepreneurs and individuals. They provide all types of banking facilities likes deposit, loan, investment etc.

There is a three level structure of Cooperative Banking:

Top Level(apex bank)	:	State Cooperative Bank (SCB)
Middle Level	:	District Central Cooperative Bank (DCCB)
Primary/Block Level	:	Primary Agricultural Credit Societies (PACSs)

4.3. Kangra Central Cooperative Bank (KCCB)

The Kangra Central Cooperative Bank (KCCB) is a central cooperative bank, which founded on March 17, 1920 headquarter at Dharamshala in district Kangra (Himachal Pradesh). Earlier name of the bank was Zamidara Bank, which was constituted by the State Cooperative Societies Act, 1912. Its financial assistance consists of share capital, deposits, loans and overdrafts from NABARD and State cooperative banks. It is working in five districts of Himachal Pradesh i.e. Kangra, Una, Hamirpur, Lahul and Spiti, Kullu with total numbers of 214 branches.

4.4. Literature Review

Mathew (1992) explored that employees in cooperative organizations in Kerala were highly dissatisfied with recruitment, selection, compensation, grievance settlement, feedback system, promotion, career planning and other policies and advised to restructuring the all policies and programs related to human resource development. Purohit (1992) conducted a research on HRD practices and their effectiveness in bank performance, revealed that the bank has maintained proper training programs, appraisal style, working environment and suggested to take advices of HRD professionals. Mahajan (1993) analyzed that employees were satisfied with the organization's structure and policies, but performance appraisal and training program techniques needed improvement.

Kumar (1996) evaluated that most of the employees were not satisfied with their selection for training programs, promotions and transfers but welfare facilities, attitude of management was satisfactory. He further advised that the organization should take consideration of personal variables of employees for their involvement in training, promotion, appraisal, etc. Another study analyzed that bank should allocate more funds for training and welfare programs which will give a positive impact on the performance of employees. (Nainta and Verma, 1997). Singh (2003) measured the impact of human resource development practices on the firm's performance by turnover, productivity, absenteeism, effectiveness, financial performance and suggested that there should be more investment in human development programs to improve firm performance. Managerial employees were having more level of job satisfaction than non-managerial employees relating to human resource development programs (Selvaraj and Deivakani, 2005). If we talk about training programs only, non-executive employees were more satisfied than executive employees (Gupta, 2000).

The district cooperative banks of the Himachal Pradesh are very poor to follow human resource development practices. A study revealed that employees were not satisfied with HRD practices followed by the banks and suggested that banks should make a proper and continuous investment policy for human resource development (Mahajan and Sharma, 2005). Another research work recognized that there was highly dissatisfaction with employee development programs (i.e. Recruitment & selection methods, training, performance appraisal, career planning, transfer & promotion policy, pay scale and participation in decision making, etc.) and advised to re-engineering all policies, models related to employee development (Ranjan, 2012). All employees should be categorized on their job/work basis like as Managerial, Non-Managerial etc. for proper implementation of the HRD subsystem (Joshi and Srivastva, 2012).

4.5. Objective of the Study:

As reviewed the literature, observed that employees were not satisfied with recruitment, selection, training, performance appraisal, compensation, promotion, feedback system and others development functions in the cooperative sector. Although, a very good number of studies have been done, but, a few number of studies are carried on human resource development practices in district co-operative banks. The objective of the present study is followings:

- To describe the Human Resource Development practices followed by the Kangra Central Cooperative Bank.
- To examine the relationship between Human Resource Development subsystem and level of satisfaction of employees.
- To identify the problems existing in HRD practices.
- To provide suggestions relating to HRD practices on the basis of this study.

4.6. Research Design

To study the HRD practices, a Descriptive Research design has used. Primary and secondary, both sources have used for data collection. Interviews and Structured questionnaire tools are used for primary data collection. Annual reports, research articles and publications are used for secondary data collection.

A Descriptive research design has used. For primary source of data collection, Interviews and Questionnaire tools are used, whereas publications and research articles are used for secondary data collection. Sample size of 75 respondents has taken to using Convenience sampling technique for the purpose of this study.

4.7. Data Analysis and Interpretations

This study has conducted with five HRD subsystem named as Compensation Policy, Performance Management, Working Environment, Development Initiatives and Job Rotation & Transfer Policy to examine the HRD practices and their effectiveness in the KCCB. The responses have taken on Five-point Likert scale rating from strongly agrees to strongly disagree from 75 respondents. For data analysis, simple statistics tools (averages, graphs, tables, charts, percentage etc.) are used. Each HRD subsystems are analyzed following:

4.7.i. Compensation Policy

This HRD subsystem measures with components of fair pay policy, the relationship between performance, compensation and economic situation, fringe benefits and health & medical policy.

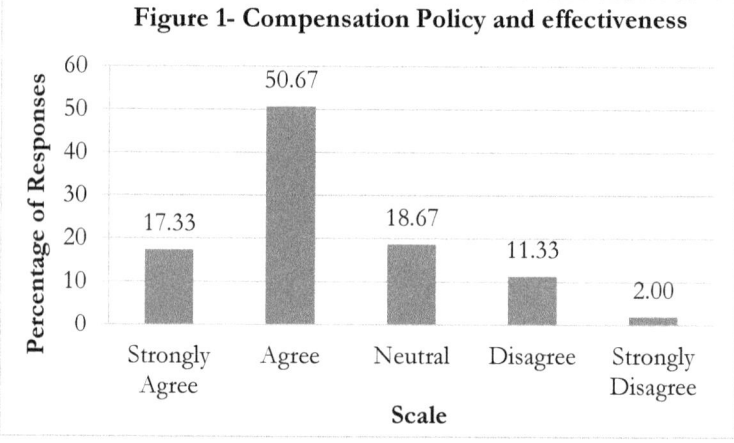

Figure 1- Compensation Policy and effectiveness

The graph above shows that 17.33% of respondents are strongly agreeing and 50.67% respondents are agreeing with the compensation policy in respect of HRD practices. It is reported that 18.67% respondents are neutral and a very less number are disagreeing and strongly disagree which is 11.33% and 2% respectively. Compensation policy has a positive impact on employee's effectiveness.

4.7.ii. Performance Management

Performance management, an HRD subsystem, is a combination of performance appraisal, promotion policy and its implementation.

Performance management is directly linked to effectiveness of outcomes. So, it is a major component for HRD practices.

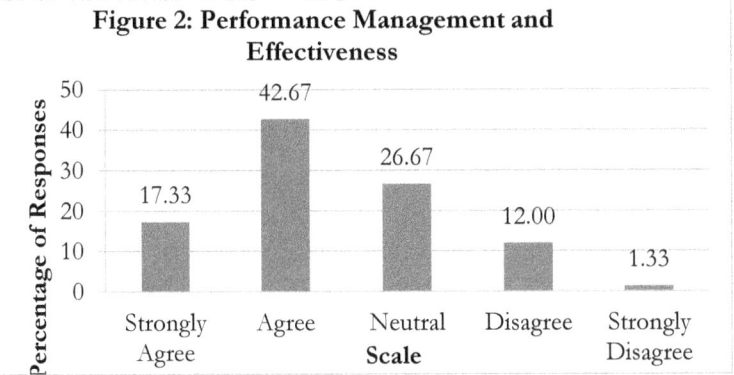

Figure 2: Performance Management and Effectiveness

Above figure states that 17.33 percent employees have strongly agreed and 42.67 percent employees are agreeing in relationship of performance management and its effect as improvement in performance. A big amount, 26.67 percent employees is unable to judge this effectiveness. 12 percent employees are disagreeing and 1.33 percent employee strongly disagrees.

4.7.iii. Working Environment

A healthy working Environment helps to generate positive energy in the workplace. It's an important HRD subsystem to increase effectiveness of the employee's work. This subsystem is a combination of proper lighting, seating arrangements, rest rooms, participation in decision making, morale of employees and grievance settlement.

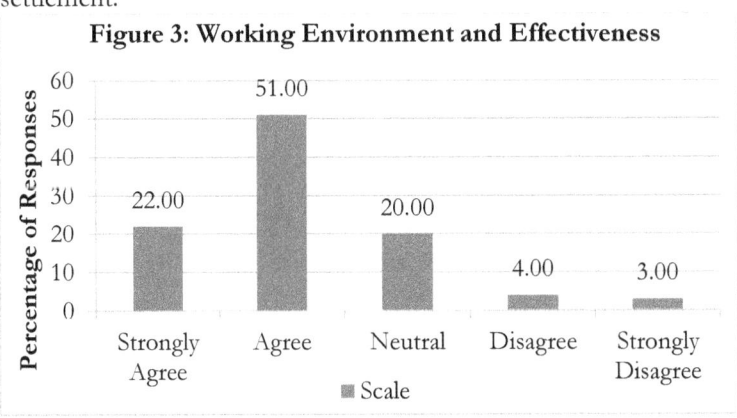

Figure 3: Working Environment and Effectiveness

Above graph reveals that the majority of respondents are satisfied with working Environment. It states that 22 percent respondents are highly satisfied and 51 percent respondents are satisfied. 20 percent respondents are not in a situation to say agreeing or disagree. A few numbers of respondents are disagreeing and strongly disagree with 4 percent and 3 percent respectively.

4.7.iv. Development Initiatives

Employee's development is a key factor of HRD practices. It reflects competency, skills, growth and development of employees. Its major elements are training programs, skills and competency, career development.

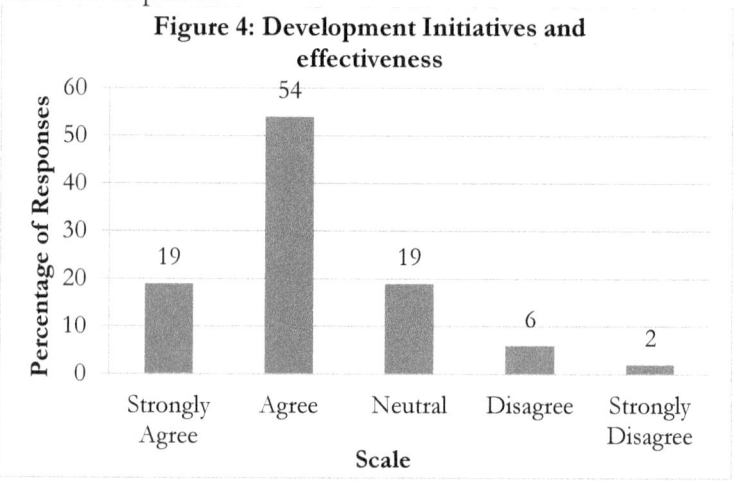

Figure 4: Development Initiatives and effectiveness

Above figure states that majority of the employees' are satisfied with the development initiatives and its effects on their performance. It states that 19 percent employees are strongly agreed and 54 percent is agreed. A less number of employees are disagreeing with 6 percent and strongly disagree with 2 percent only. 19 percent employees are neutral in their development and effectiveness.

4.7.v. Job Rotation & Transfer Policy

To increase the level of efficiencies and skills of employees, job rotation and transfer is a good HRD practice. This HRD subsystem is combing different elements which are fair & transparent job rotation policy, effective transfer policy and both policies helps in performance of employees.

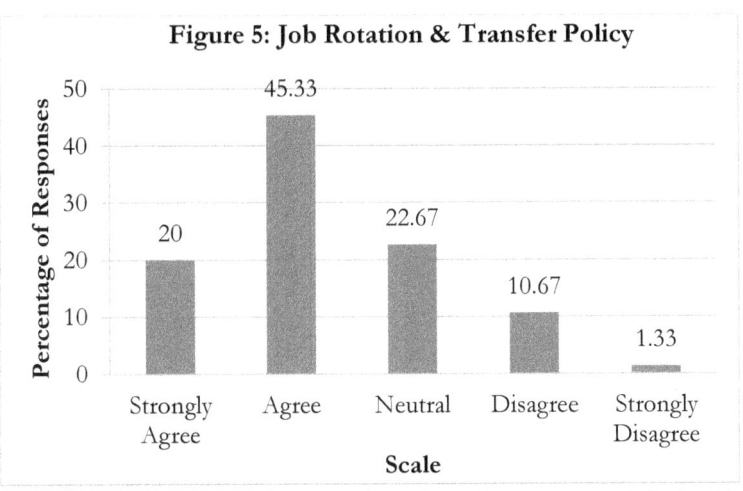

Figure 5: Job Rotation & Transfer Policy

Above graph reveals the majority of employees are satisfied with job rotation and transfer policy. It states that 20 percent employees strongly agree whereas 45.33 percent employees are saying agree. Big ratios, 22.67 percent employees are responses as neutral regarding this policy. But, some negative result is negative with 10.67 percent are disagreeing and 1.33 percent responses are strongly disagreeing.

Suggestions

This study reveals that majorities of employees are satisfied with the exercising different types of HRD practices and their proper implementation in the organization. However, there are some following suggestions, which can be strengthening the HRD practices in the KCCB:

- The main implementation of this research that there is a lot of scope for further investment in development initiatives like training and development for improvement in skills and competencies of employees to perform current or future job with efficiencies.
- This study suggests to establishing an efficient monitoring system for exercising and implementation of HRD practices effectively.
- This research work states to create a mechanism which can recognize the need of individual employees for improvement of skills, competency and career goal and growth time to time.

Conclusion

As per the analysis and result of the study to examine HRD practices with five major HRD subsystems and their effectiveness in KCCB, it concluded that majorities of employees are satisfied with the exercised of HRD subsystems in the organization. Compensation policy of the KCCB is almost good, but some issues are there regarding with employees work performance and reward for that performance. Working environment is good to perform work and highly appreciated by employees. The organization is highly concerned with the career development of employees; so good numbers of employees are satisfied with development initiatives taken by the organization. The KCCB needs to be more focused on performance management practices. At the end, we can say that overall HRD practices in the Kangra Central Cooperative Bank are well designed and practiced; so it has a positive impact on the employee's performance.

References

Foster, Rex D.; and Akdere, M. (2007), "Effective Organizational Vision: Implementation for Human Resource Development", *Journal of European Industrial Training*, Vol. 31, No.2, pp.100-111

Gupta, V.K. (2000), "Human Resource Development and Training in a Corporate Enterprise: A Case Study of BEL", in B.S.Bhatia and G.S.Batra (eds.), *Human Resource Development-Industrial Relations, Labour Management, Organisation Development*, Deep and Deep Publication, New Delhi.

Kumar, R.(2014), *Human Resource Management: A study of Cooperative Bank in Haryana,* Doctoral Thesis, Punjabi University, Punjab

Kumar, S. (1996). *A Critical Study of Human Resource Development in Cooperative Banks of Himachal Pradesh*, Doctoral Thesis, Himachal Pradesh University, Shimla

Kumari, P. A. (2012). "Human Resource Development: A New Roadmap on Success of Industrialization", *Advances in Management*, Vol. 5 No.9, September, pp. 6-11.

Likert, R. (1967). *Human Organisation*, Tata Mcgraw- Hill, New York.

Louma, M. (1999). "The Essence of HRD Orientation: Evidence from the Finnish Metals Industry", *Journal of European Industrial Training*, Vol. 23, No.3, MCB University Press, pp. 113-120.

Mahajan, C. M.(1993). *Human Resource Development in Fertilizer Industry-*

A Case Study of National Fertilizer Ltd. Naya Nangal, Doctoral Thesis, Punjabi University, Patiala

Mahajan, S. K.; and Sharma, I.D. (2005). "Human Resource Development Practices in Cooperative Banks of Himachal Pradesh", in S.L.Goel and P.N.Gautam (eds.), *Human Resource Development in 21 Century*, Deep & Deep Publication, New Delhi

Mathew, P.C. (1992). *Personnel Management Practices in Cooperative Sector in Kerala*, Doctoral Thesis, Cochin University of Science and Technology, Cochin, Kerala.

Nainta, R.P.; and Verma, L.R. (1997), "Human Resource Development in Banking Sector-A Study of Himachal State Cooperative Bank Ltd.", *Indian Cooperative Review*, Vol. XXXIV, No.4, April, pp. 298-307

Purohit, G. N. (1992). *Human Resource Development with Special Reference to Commercial Banks in Rajasthan*, Doctoral Thesis, Jai Narain University, Jodhpur, Rajasthan.

Ramu, N. (2008). "Human Resource Management in Cooperative Banks in India: Issues and Challenges", *CAB CALLING*, July September, pp. 67-72

Ranjan, S. (2012)."Employees Satisfaction with regard to the HRM Practices of Municipal Council Panchkula" in Shalini Gupta (ed), *Human Resource Management: Challenges and Choices*, DBIMCS Publication, Mandigobindgarh, pp.249-260.

Rao, T.V. (1985). Integrated Human Resource Development System. *Goodstein D. Leonard & Pfeiffer J. William, The 1985 Annual: Developing Human Resources, San Diego CA: University Associates*, 227

Rao, T.V. (1991). *Readings in Human Resource Development .Oxford & IBH Publishing Co. Pvt. Ltd.*, New Delhi.

Rao, T.V. and D.F. Pereira (ed). (1986) *Recent Experience in Human Resources Development, Oxford & IBH Publishing Co. Pvt. Ltd.*, New Delhi

Rodrigues Lewlyn L. R. and Chincholkar A. M. (2005). Benchmarking the HR practices of an engineering institute with public sector industry for performance enhancement. *International Journal of Training and Development*, Vol.9, No.1

Selvaraj, V.M.; and Deivakani, M. M. (2005). "Human Resource Development in Cooperative Milk Supply Society", *Management Accountant*, Vol. 2, February, pp.150-154.

Sharma, R.; and Nayyar, S (2005). "Human Resource Development in State Bank of India–A Case Study of Chandigarh Circle", S.L.Goel and P.N.Gautam (eds.), *Human Resource Development in 21 Century*, Deep & Deep Publication, New Delhi.

Singh, K. (2003). "Effect of Human Resource Practices on Firm Performance in India", *Human Resource Development International*, Vol. 6, Issue 1, March, pp. 110-116.

CHAPTER 5
A REVIEW ANALYSIS ON ANTECEDENTS OF ORGANIZATIONAL CITIZENSHIP BEHAVIOUR

Jitendra Singh and Pawan Kumar Chand

Abstract

Present study is an earnest effort to understand the organizational citizenship behaviour among the employees of manufacturing industry at India by recognizing the antecedents such as empowerment, job satisfaction and organizational commitment towards the organizational citizenship behaviour. Review of literature studies were made to stress on research gaps, conclusive hypothesis was framed on the basis of existing literature. Findings of the study give the line of future scope of direction to the researchers on organizational citizenship behaviour with the suggested practical implications. The study will contribute knowledge to the industrialists to manage the work performance of employees at the workplace.

5.1. Introduction

The vital construct of any organization is capable workforce which reflects in good citizens therefore it is critical to engage them to enable them deliver superior performance at the workplace. OCB describes the set of voluntary behaviours demonstrated by the employees during the employment as good citizens of the organization. Apparently, the foundation of OCB can be traced back to the early works of Barnard (1968), who stated that employees should be willing to contribute efforts to cooperative systems for achieving organizational goals. Bateman (1983) and Organ (1983) coined the term 'citizenship' as leading behaviour that propels the social engine of the organization. Because of the importance of good citizenship for organizations, studying the nature and sources of OCB has drawn the attention of many organizational scholars (Organ, 1988). Organizational citizenship behaviour has been one of the most researched employee behaviors in context with organizational perspective for last three decades and the interest continues further. Several studies have inferred that OCB has a significant correlation with organizational success by driving improvements in form of higher productivity, optimal resource utilization, collaboration and team work and ability to adapt to environmental changes. OCB is also described as 'good soldier syndrome' (Organ, 1988) exhibited by the committed employees in the organization.

The focus on OCB or other related constructs have significantly increased from 13 research papers during 1983-1988 to more than 122 papers during 1993-1998 (Podsakoff et al., 2000). This indicates the focus of OCB in the current business world. OCB, which is portrayed as a discretionary behavior, has been the most extensively studied topic in Organizational behavior research in past three decades (Podsakoff, Mackenzie and Fetter, 1993; Emmerik, Hannamn and Jimmieson, 2002; Akbar and Haq, 2004; Lievens and Anseel, 2004; Jahangir, Khalid and Ali, 2005; Chahal and Mehta, 2011) since it continues to tickle interest among researchers during the recent phase therefore, it's recommended to know about the determinants and consequences of this widely investigated variable.

i. Organization citizenship behavior

Organization citizenship behaviour largely includes punctuality, helping others, innovating and volunteering (Organ, 1988). This behaviour also depicts the tendency to refrain from undesirable actions from organization health and conduct viewpoint such as complaining, interfering, demotivating others, arguing and showing fault finding approach with others. Though OCB is not driven by external motivation catalysts like any formal reward system however, it drives the roadmap to an effective organization. Present study is an attempt to understand the affects of empowerment, job satisfaction and organization commitment on organizational citizenship behavior and further building on the lesser explored dimensions.

ii. Employee empowerment

Empowerment includes by definition the involvement and commitment of employees at the workplace. In other words, empowerment can be described as the involvement of employees in the decision making process along with management (Mitchell, 1973; Vroom and Jago, 1988; Cole et al., 1993).

iii. Organization commitment

Allen and Meyer (1996) have prescribed a three -component model of Commitment.

- The 'Affective' component of Organizational Commitment, indicates employees' Emotional attachment towards the organization, this may be tapped as highest form of Commitment vis a vis other components.
- The 'Continuance' component indicates employee's rationale approach of staying with the organization to reap the benefits on comparison to leaving the organization.
- The 'Normative' component revolves around gratitude and feeling factor of employees binding them to remain with the organization.

iv. Job Satisfaction

Job Satisfaction has been studied as one of the components of Organizational Commitment (Kovach, 1977). Job Satisfaction is found to be the state of pleasure achieved by an employee while remaining on the job (Locke, 1969). According to Luthans (1998) three key dimensions of job satisfaction exist:

- Job Satisfaction is the Emotional Quotient, which cannot be expressed but can only be felt.
- Job Satisfaction is a variable of employee meeting or exceeding expectations;
- It has many interwoven factors towards the work itself, pay, promotion opportunities, supervisor and co-workers which are most important characteristics of a job about which people have effective response.

5.2. Review of Literature

The concept of OCB based on the model of Organ and colleagues has been widely accepted. The published literature roams around on the definition of OCB extended by Organ and his colleagues such as Dalton and Cosier (1988), Randall (1994), Love, Pare and Tremblay (2007) and Forret (2008). Few researchers tried to introduce a different perspective however, large difference from already proposed model was not visible to quote a case, Niehoff and Moorman (1993) defined OCB as behavior which is beyond employee's job description. Van Dyne, Graham and Dienesch (1994) proposed the concept of OCB which was developed mainly from multidisciplinary research in the areas of social history, philosophy, political science, and. Civic citizenship means all positive traits and behaviours of a civilized society. (Van Dyne, Graham, and Dienesch, 1994). Based on this body of knowledge, they proposed OCB concept which includes all positive behaviours critical for organizational context (Van Dyne et al., 1994).

The common employee attitudes and behaviours studied in the context include organizational commitment, job satisfaction, organizational citizenship behaviour and job involvement, all of which are regarded as predictors of improved performance. Appelbaum, Bailey, Berg, and Kalleberg (2000). Podsakoff and MacKenzie (1994) state extensive research is not carried out to examine the effects of OCB on individual, group and organizational performance. However, several studies depict that employees receiving supportive HRM practices demonstrate higher levels of organizational citizenship behaviour (Becker and Huselid, 1998; Gong et al., 2010; Snape and Redman, 2010).

Chahal, & Mehta, (2011) described benefits from organizational citizenship behaviour that can be instrumental in organizational success are as follows: increased efficiency of management and employees, releasing organizational resources that can be used for more productive purposes. It also describes improved effectiveness and efficiency of organizational performance, reduced needs to allocate scarce resources for functions that only maintain the status quo, helping coordinating activities within and outside work groups, increased organizational ability to attract and keep efficient employees and increased stability of organizational performance.

Table 1- Various OCB Studies and construct analysis

Researchers	Constructs of OCB
Smith, Organ & Near(1983)	Altruism General Compliance
Organ (1988)	Altruism Conscientiousness Sportsmanship Courtesy Civic Virtue
Lin (1991)	Identification with the organization Assistance to colleagues Harmony Righteous Discipline Self-improvement
Williams & Anderson(1991)	Individual –directed OCB (OCBI) Organization –directed OCB (OCBO)
Van Dyne, Graham &Dienesh (1994)	Obedience Loyalty Participation
Farth, Earley& Lin (1997)	Identification with the company Altruism toward colleagues Conscientiousness Interpersonal Harmony Protecting Company resources
Podsakoff et al. (2000)	Helping behavior Sportsmanship Organizational loyalty Organizational compliance Individual initiative Civic virtue Self-development

5.2.i. Empowerment and OCB

Kanger and Kanongo (1988) observed that the process of employee empowerment is a key step towards organizational effectiveness. Focus of management remains to create a conducive culture which reinforces the employee's behaviour closer to the needs of end user has been studied by Bowen (1992), Ostroff (1992) and to improve the organisation's functioning (Hermel, 1990). However, empowerment does not undermine an initial supervision to coach, train and direct employee, which brings required amount of self-control (Geroy et al., 1998; Lawler, 1993). In another words empowerment is the depiction of employees demonstrating ownership in ensuring organization is able to cater to the needs of the customer (Bowen and Lawler, 1995).

Morrison (1996) found that empowered employees have better ability to invent and demonstrate the organization citizen ship behavior as empowerment enhances the sense of self efficacy amongst employees. Capppelli and Neumark (2001), study infers that work practices transferring autonomy to employees and 'high road practices' do contribute in raising labour cost employees however, it pays back by leading to higher degree of OCB amongst employees. Study also confirms the increase in productivity (sales/employee) however, struggles to prove efficiency.

Today employee empowerment is seen as a one of the best approaches towards organizational success through enhanced employee performance Abdullahi, Noah, Ebrahim, 2007).

5.2.ii. Organizational commitment and OCB

Several theorists have made the proposition that Job satisfaction is a predictor of organizational commitment and organizational citizenship behaviour. (Porter et al, 1974). Commitment is a more global response to an organization and Job Satisfaction is more of a response to a specific job or various facets of the job (Mowday et al., 1982). Wiener (1982) states that job satisfaction is an attitude towards work-related conditions. Therefore, commitment is an attachment to the employing organization as opposed to specific tasks, environmental factors, and the location where the duties are performed which leads us closer to the constructs of OCB. The extent of relationship between organizational commitment and job satisfaction has been studied through correlation analysis and observed that high degree of correlation exists (Monoshree, 2012).

Singh and Gupta (2015) suggested that Indian employees are high on team commitment, job involvement, and on affective commitment to organization. These findings can be interpreted in the light of culture characteristics of Indian work culture which exhibits collectivism and affective reciprocity among Indian managers. Apparently, employees who are more committed to their profession have less attachment to the organization and may depict lesser OCB.

5.2.iii. Job satisfaction and OCB

Bateman and Organ (1983) found a significant correlation between OCB and specific domains of satisfaction (e.g., pay, supervision). Those employees who are satisfied from the organization perspective are more likely to demonstrate better response towards OCB, including helping coworkers or customers and walking an extra mile for the organization (Organ, 1988). Reserchers have carved out a significant statistical relationship between OCB and job satisfaction (Organ and Lingl, 1995). Inother context those who are dissatisfied are more likely to have higher quit intentions, show absentessism from workplace and showcase lesser efforts on the job (Locke and Latham, 1990). There have been various meta-analyses researches supporting the relationship between job satisfaction and OCB (O'Brien and Allen, 2008). To quote few, Organ and Ryan (1995) in their meta analysis review found positive correlations between job satisfaction and OCB. Podsakoff and his colleagues (2000) during his metaanlytical research also showed that there is a significant relationship between job satisfaction and OCB constructs like altruism, courtesy, conscientiousness, sportsmanship, and civic virtue. Apparently, Dalal's (2005) study has also supported the relationship between OCB and job satisfaction. Thus, the empirical studies and metaanlytic reseraches appear to reinforce the relationship between job satisfaction and OCB.

Various researchers have also attempted to establish a correlation amongst OCB, job satisfaction and the hygiene factors of the job according to Herzberg 2 factor theory. Few key studies are as follows:

Herry and Noon (2001) Promotion which is symbol of getting high status in workplace enhances the status, empowerment, entitlements and compensation of employee in the organization. Recognition and promotional opportunities have been found as critical drivers of intrinsic job satisfaction (Robbins, 2001). Pay and promotion are found to be key measures of employee satisfaction (Parvin and Kabir, 2001). Employees were satisfied with their jobs and were not found to be too satisfied with their pay and organizational promotions policies thus their OCB was not able to get established (Togia, Koustelios, Tsigilis, 2004).Yafang and Shih-Wang's (2008) have also witnessed a positive correlation between nurses' job satisfaction and their higher OCB. Catherine (2009), Job satisfaction was found to be predictive of affective commitment, even more strongly in India than in the US. Taken together, affective and normative commitment have been shown to have the greatest degree of desirable outcomes such as reduced stress, absenteeism and turnover and increased organizational citizenship behavior as employees are committed to their organization because they should be, but also do so because they wish to be Indian organizations.Promotion is a structural upliftent in the organization. (Hart, 2010). Recognition means the intangible rewards extended to employees by different status (Danish et al.2010). To further improve the satisfaction and OCB index of employees, organization endeavours to work on multiple areas including fairness on job, good working condition, promotion and rewards to employees which together constitutes to overall employees satisfaction (Parvin and Kabir, 2011).

Frenkel, and Bednall (2012), the results of study indicate that employees who hold a consistent view of the level of support offered by line and senior management will experience greater work satisfaction, and will be less inclined to quit their jobs. These relationships are strengthened when communication between senior managers and HR is frequent. Based on these findings, organizations should ensure that all levels of management demonstrate appropriate and consistent levels of support for employees, enable HR to provide sufficient support to line managers for day-to-day tasks, and facilitate strong communication channels between senior management and HR which is key step towards OCB foundation of the organization. Gupta and Gokhale (2013), Study concludes that employees confirm the support from management, also have been found positively for the 'reporting authority's supporting role'. Employees have been found happy about working conditions and working hours, leave entitlement in the office. Study also shows that the salary level of employees in the scope of industry is directly correlated with their educational qualification. Joji and George (2014), workplace dimensions such as routinisation and job stress factors showed significant influence on job satisfaction, social support factors demonstrated insignificant effect on job satisfaction and OCB. It was expected that the employees would show job satisfaction when the peers and the supervisors were supportive at the workplace which did not come out as the result of investigation. Singh and Gupta (2015) suggested that Indian employees are high on team commitment, job involvement, and on affective commitment to organization. These findings can be interpreted in the light of culture characteristics of Indian work culture which exhibits collectivism and affective reciprocity among Indian managers therefore are expected to show better quotient of OCB.

5.3. Theoretical Framework

From the field of systems theory Michel Saint Germain has linked organization citizenship behaviour of employees with the nature of open systems: The individual as an open system is respected in such organizations; employee is able to transform data into useful decision-making information. There is margin for creativity and autonomy and above all, the decision-making process allows opportunities for a "locus of control" at the individual level. (Germain, 2010). Blue collar employees who are role modelling organization citizenship behaviour together in a way that they reinforce each other will deliver performance outcomes greater than the sum of the outcomes of the individual practices (Purcell 2007). **Labour Process Theory** critiques scientific management as introduced by Frederick W Taylor in the early 1900s and describes core concepts developed by Harry Braverman in the 1970s. Having understood the criticality of human capital at workplace in determining the productivity outcomes, then we must expect an unevenness of outcome disruptive for hypotheses based on common managerial or labour process accounts. Organization citizenship behavior (Ramsay 2000, Dora 2000) precipitate with employee's sense of drive as a partner for organizational performance which leads to organizational success. LP model may be used as a foundation to understand that blue collar employees who have been empowered by organization also tend to demonstrate positive organization citizenship behaviour.

5.4. Research Gaps

There has been fair amount of research around the globe on OCB in various organizational contexts incorporating various cultural dimensions. Most of the researchers have tried to study the positive impacts of organizational citizenship behaviour. Positive side of OCB leads to better organizational performance driven by motivated and agile workforce. Very few studies have attempted to study the rear sight of OCB as mentioned by Bolino and Turnley (2005).

On a critical note, reflecting too much towards organizational citizenship behavior may result in to some personal costs like role overload, job stress and work-life balance issues. Moreover, this may also result in higher turnover in organization if incase employer is not able to manage outperforming employees' aspirations.

5.5. Hypothesis

H1: There will be significant relationship of employee empowerment, job satisfaction and organization commitment with organization citizenship behaviour.

5.6. Practical implications

Research work will be sharing an insight to the industries to unleash the innate potential of the employees for enhancing organization citizenship behavior. The study enlightened the industrialist to foster the right mix of policies and customized organizational development intervention as per different strata of the population.

5.7. Future scope of research

A longitudinal research is further recommended to understand how cultural transformations like organization development interventions play a role in enhancing the organization citizenship behavior on a periodic pattern. Also, other variables such as trust, emotional intelligence may be considered with regards to investigate the pattern of OCB including the implied intensification of the workplace. Further researches may be carried out to evaluate the rear sight impacts of OCB in various industries as the current study focuses only in the manufacturing set up.

References

Allen, J.N., Meyer, P. (1996). Affective, Continuance, and Normative Commitment to the Organization.: An Examination of Construct Validity, *Journal of Vocational Behavior*, Vol.49, Issue 3, December 1996.

Appelbaum, E., Bailey, T., Berg, P. and Kalleberg, A. (2000). Manufacturing Advantage: Why High-Performance Work Systems Pay Off. *Ithaca, NY:* ILR Press.

Barnard C. I. (1968). The Functions of the Executive. *Cambridge, MA*: Harvard University Press.

Bateman T. S. and Organ D. W. (1983). Job Satisfaction and the Good Soldier: The Relationship between Affect and Employee Citizenship‖, *Academy of Management Journal*, Vol. 26 (4): 587-595.

Bateman T. S. and Organ D. W. (1983). Job Satisfaction and the Good Soldier: The Relationship between Affect and Employee Citizenship‖, *Academy of Management Journal*, Vol. 26 (4): 587-595.

Becker, B., Huselid, M. (1998). High Performance Work Systems and Firm Performance: A Synthesis of Research and Managerial Implications. *Research in Personnel and Human Resource Management*, edited by G.R. Ferris. Greenwich, CT: JAI Press.

Bolino, C. M., William, H. T. (2005). The Personal Costs of Citizenship Behavior: The Relationship between Individual Initiative, Role Overload, Job Stress and Work Family Conflict, *Journal of Applied Psychology*, Volume 90, No.4, 740-748.

Bowen, D. E., Ostroff, C. (2000). Understanding HRM-firm performance linkages: The role of the "strength" of the HRM system. *Academy of Management Review*, 29: 203-221.

Bowen, D. E., Ostroff, C. (2000). Understanding HRM-firm performance linkages: The role of the "strength" of the HRM system. *Academy of Management Review*, 29: 203-221.

Cappelli, P., Neumark, D., (2001). Do High-Performance, Work Practices Improve Establishment- Level Outcomes? *Industrial and Labor Relations Review*, Vol. 54, No. 4.

Catherine, T. (2009). Culture, job satisfaction and organizational commitment in India and the United States, *Journal of Indian Business Research*, Vol. 1 Issue: 4, pp.196-212.

Chahal, H & Mehta, S. (2011). Antecedents and consequences of organizational citizenship behavior: A conceptual framework in reference to health care sector, *journal of services research*, 10, 25-44.

Cole, R.E., Bacdayan, P. White, B.J. (1993). Quality, Participation and Competitiveness. *California Management Review*, Vol. 35, No. 3, pp. 68-81.

Dalal, R. S. (2005). A Meta-Analysis of the Relationship between Organizational Citizenship Behavior and Counterproductive Work Behaviorǁ. *Journal of Applied Psychology*, Vol. 90 (6): 1241-1255.

Dalton, D. R., Cosier, R. A. (1988). Psychometric properties of the organizational citizenship scale. *Educational and Psychological Measurement*, *48*, 479-482.

Danish, Q. D., Usman, A. (2001). Impact of reward and recognition on job satisfaction and motivation: An empirical study from Pakistan. *International Journal of Business &Management*, 5(2), 159-167.

Emmerik, H. V., Jawahar, I. M., Stone, T. H. (2005). Associations among altruism, burnout dimensions and organizational citizenship behaviour, *Work and Stress*, *19*, 93-100.

Frenkel,S., Sanders, K. (2012). Tim.Employee perceptions of management relations as influences on job satisfaction and quit intentions. *Asia Pacific Journal of Management*: APJM; Singapore (2013).

Germain, M. (2010). The Results-Oriented Organisations: a Critical Look from a Bertalanffyan Perspective. *In BCSSS Lectures "Uncommon Sense in Thinking Society"*. *Vienna*, 10 December, 2010.

Geroy, G.D., Wright, P.C., Anderson, J. (1998). Strategic performance empowerment model. *Empowerment in Organizations*, Vol. 6, No. 2, pp. 57-65.

Gong, Y., Chang, S., Cheung, S. Y. (2010). High performance work system and collective OCB: a collective social exchange perspective. *Human Resource Management Journal*, 20(2): 119-137.

Gupta, R., Gokhale, H. V. (2013). An Exploratory Study on Job Satisfaction of Employees in Newspaper Industry with Special Reference to Nagpur Region, *Journal of Strategic Human Resource Management; New Delhi 2.1* (2013): 26-36.

Hart, G. (2010). Job satisfaction in a south African Academic Library in Transition. *The Journal of Academic Librarianship*,36(1),53-62.

Hermel, P. (1990). Le management participative. *Paris: Les Editions d' Organisation*.

Herry, E., Noon, M. (2001). A dictionary of human resource management. *New York: Oxford University Press.*

Jahangir, N., Akbar, M. M., & Haq, M. (2004). Organizational citizenship behaviour: Its Nature and Antecedents, *Journal of BRAC University*, 1, 75-85.

Joji A., George, A. P. (2014). The Effects of Workplace Dimensions on Job Satisfaction and Organizational Commitment. *International Journal of Business &Management*, 11(2), 259-267.

Kovach, K. A. (1977). Organization Size, Job Satufaction, Absenteeism and Turnover. *University Press of America*, Washington, DC.

Lievens, F., Anseel, F. (2004). Confirmatory Factor Analysis and Invariance of an organizational citizenship behaviour measure across samples in a Dutch-Speaking Context. *Journal of Occupational and Organizational Psychology*, 77, 299-306.

Locke E A (1969), "What is Job Satisfaction?".*Organization Behaviour & Human Performance*, Vol. 4, No. 4, pp. 309-336.

Locke, E. A., Latham, G. P. (1990). Work Motivation and Satisfaction: Light at the End of the Tunnel, *American Psychological Society*, Vol. 1 (4): 240 – 246.

Love, M. S., Forret, M. (2008). Exchange relationship at work: An examination of the relationship between team-member exchange supervisor reports of organizational citizenship behavior. *Journal of Leadership and Organizational Studies*, 14, 342-352.

Luthans F (1998), "Organisational Behaviour", *Irwin Mc-Graw Hill*, Boston.

Monoshree, M., (2012). Personal Characteristics and Job Satisfaction as predictor of Organizational Commitment: an empirical Investigation, *South Asian Journal of Management*; Oct-Dec 2012; 19.

Morrison, E. W. (1996). Organizational citizenship behavior as a critical link between HRM practices and service quality. *Human Resource Management*, 34, 493–512.

Mowday, R.T., Porter, L.W. and Steers, R.M. (1982), Employee-Organization Linkages. *Academic Press, New York*, NY.

Niehoff, B. P., Moorman, R. H. (1993). Justice as a moderator of the relationship between methods of mentoring and organizational citizenship behavior. *Academy of Management Journal*, *36*, 527-556.

O'Brien, K. E., Allen, T. D. (2008). The Relative Importance of Correlates of Organizational Citizenship Behavior and Counterproductive Work Behavior Using Multiple Sources of Datal, *Human Performance*, Vol. 21: 62 – 88.

Organ, D. W. (1988). Organizational Citizenship Behavior: The Good Soldier Syndrome. *Lexington, MA:* Lexington Books.

Organ, D. W. Lingl, A. (1995) Personality, Satisfaction, and Organizational Citizenship Behavior, *The Journal of Social Psychology*, Vol. 135 (3): 339 – 350.

Parvin, M. M., Kabir, M. M. (2011). Factors Affecting Employee Job Satisfaction of Pharmaceutical Sector. *Australian Journal of Business and Management Research*, Vol.1 No.9 (113-123).

Podsakoff, P. M., MacKenzie, S. B. (1994). Organizational Citizenship Behaviors and Sales Unit Effectiveness. *Journal of Marketing Research*, *31*, 351-363.

Podsakoff, P. M., Mackenzie, S. B., & Fetter, R. (1993). The Impact of Organizationl Citizenship Behaviour on Evaluations of Salespersons Performance. *Journal of Marketing*, *57*, 70-80.

Podsakoff, P. M., MacKenzie, S. B., Paine, J. B., and Bachrach D. G. (2000). Organizational Citizenship Behaviors: A Critical Review of the Theoretical and Empirical Literature and Suggestions for Future Researchl, Journal of Management, Vol. 26 (3): 513–563.

Porter L, Steers R, Mowdey R and Boulian P (1974) , "Organizational Commitment, Job Satisfaction, and Turnover Among Psychiatric Technicians", *Journal of Applied Psychobgy*, Vol. 59, pp. 603-609.

Purcell, J. (2007). Front-line managers as agents in the HRM-performance causal chain: theory, analysis and evidence. *Human Resource Management Journal*, 17(1)

Ramsay, H., Dora, S. (2000). Employees and High-PerformanceWork Systems: Testing inside the Black Box, *British Journal of Industrial Relations*, 38:4 December 2000.

Randall, D. M. (1999). Perceived Organisational Support, Satisfaction with Rewards, and Employee Job Involvement and

Organisational Commitment. *Applied Psychology: An International Review* 48 (2): 197–209.

Robbins, S. P. (2003). Organizational Behavior; Concepts, Controversies and Applications. *10thed. New Jersey: Prentice Hall.*

Singh, A., Gupta, B. (2015). Job involvement, organizational commitment, professional commitment, and team commitment: A study of generational diversity", *Benchmarking: An International Journal*, Vol. 22 Issue: 6, pp.1192-1211.

Singh, A., Gupta, B. (2015). Job involvement, organizational commitment, professional commitment, and team commitment: A study of generational diversity", *Benchmarking: An International Journal*, Vol. 22 Issue: 6, pp.1192-1211.

Snape, E., Redman, T. (2010). HRM Practices, Organizational Citizenship Behaviour, and Performance: A Multi-level Analysis. *Journal of Management Studies* 47(7): 1219–47.

Togia, A., Koustelios, A., Tsigilis, N. (2004). Job satisfaction among Greek academic librarians. *Library & Information Science Research*, 26(3), 373-383.

Van Dyne, L., Graham, J. W., Dienesch, R. M. (1994). Organizational citizenship behavior: Construct redefinition, measurement, and validation. *Academy of Management Journal, 37*, 765-802.

Vroom, V.H. Jago, A.G. (1988). The New Leadership. Managing Participation in Organizations. *New York:* Prentice Hall, Inc.

Wiener, Y. (1982). Commitment in Organization: A Normative View. *Academy of Management Review*, Vol. 7, pp. 418-428.

CHAPTER 6
MAPPING ORGANIZATIONAL CULTURE OF INDIAN BANKS: AN OCTAPACE APPROACH

Mitu Mandal

Abstract

Organizational Culture is one of the most critical components for organizational effectiveness. With the world economy going global, organizational culture has a larger role to play in attaining the competitive advantage of an organization. An organization which promotes a culture of openness, creativity, innovativeness, adaptability can foresee the market demands and can design its strategy accordingly to capture the market. The present study aims to assess Organizational Culture through OCTAPACE approach of public and private sector banks of Delhi-NCR. OCTAPACE stand for Openness, Confrontation, Trust, Autonomy, Proactiveness, Authenticity, Collaboration, and Experimentation. Simple random sampling technique was followed for selecting the bank branches. The sample consisted of 151 employees from clerical cadre. Descriptive statistics, exploratory factor analysis, one-way analysis of variance and independent sample t- test were used for analysis of the data. Exploratory factor analysis revealed six factors naming Openness, Confrontation, Trust, Proactiveness, Authenticity, and Experimentation. Among the OCTAPACE dimensions, proactiveness emerged as the most significant factor having the highest mean score in case of private sector bank and trust emerged as the most significant factor in the case of public sector bank. he study further revealed a significant difference between private sector and public sector banks in all OCTAPACE dimensions except in trust and authenticity. The study has wide managerial implications as it has revealed the existing organizational culture of private and public sector banks which can form the basis for future interventions.

6.1. Introduction

Organizational Culture is one of the most critical components for organizational effectiveness. Numerous studies have highlighted the importance of organizational culture in determining an organization's success (Terblanche & Martins, 2003; Kleijen & et al., 2014; Tameemi & et al., 2014; Pololi et al., 2015). With the world economy going global, organizational culture has a larger role to play in attaining the competitive advantage of an organization. An organization which promotes a culture of openness, creativity, innovativeness, adaptability can foresee the market demands and can design its strategy accordingly to capture the market. Studies revealed that organizational culture plays a significant role in adapting an organization to external environment pressures (Pool, 2000).

In banking context, studies show that organizational culture influences several facets of organization such as adoption of new technology (Daniel, 1999; Twati & Gammack, 2006), customer relationship management, brand management (Mosley, 2007), corporate performance(Ojo, 2010), job satisfaction and turnover intention(Aldhuwaihi, Shee, & Stanton, 2012). The Indian banking sector is in the transition stage. The entire banking industry is going through a wave of technological revolution which has led to dramatic changes in the banking operations. As per the report of Boston Consulting Group (BCG, 2015)-"the power of people in Digital Banking Transformation", banks can only thrive in this digital era, if they are having the supportive organization culture comprising of five important cultural attributes: customer centricity, experimentation, agility, collaboration and continuous innovation. Thus, it is very important that banks are having right organizational culture which can support its strategy to survive and thrive in the competitive turbulent environment. Against this backdrop, the present study has been conducted with following aims (i) to assess the organizational culture of public and private sector banks through OCTAPACE approach (ii) to examine the difference in organizational culture between private and public sector banks (iii) to examine the difference in perceptions of organizational culture of employees of different age groups.

6.2. Theoretical Framework and Literature Review

Organizational culture has been defined differently by multitude of scholars. Robbins (2013) defined organizational culture as "system of shared meaning held by members that distinguish an organization from other organizations". A more elaborative definition of organizational culture was provided by Edgar Schein. Schein (1991) defined organizational culture as "a pattern of shared basic assumptions that a group has learned as it solved its problems of external adaptation and internal integration that has worked well enough to be considered valid and therefore, to be taught to new members as the correct way to perceive, think, and feel in relation to the problems."

Empirical evidence from many countries indicates that organizational culture has a significant effect on performance of an organization. Studies conducted in the West revealed that the shared organizational values and unwritten rules can enhance the profitability of an organization (Kotter & Haskett, 2011). Studies from India too, suggests organizational ethos and values contributes to higher organizational effectiveness (Mufeed & Rafai, 2003). In a study, it was found that OCTAPACE culture implementation increases the performance of the organization (Shrivastava & Srinivasan, 2004).

Pareek (2002) explained organizational culture in terms of organizational ethos. Organizational ethos can be defined as the underlying spirit or character of an entity or group and is made up of beliefs, customs, and practices. Ethos are based on eight important core values. These are openness, confrontation, trust, authenticity, proactivity, autonomy, collaboration, and experimentation. Openness implies free expression of information, openness in receiving and giving feedback both vertically and horizontally; Confrontation means not shying away with problems, deeper analysis of the problems; Trust means maintaining the confidentiality of information and not misusing others; Authenticity means congruence between what one feels, says and does, owing one's actions and mistakes; Proaction means initiative taking, preplanning and taking preventive actions; Autonomy means discretion in doing one's work; Collaboration means helping others, team spirit and solving problem together.; and Experimentation means encouraging creativity and innovation. The present study is based on Pareek's OCTAPACE framework. OCTAPACE has been used in varied contexts to assess the organizational culture. In a study conducted by Purohit et. al (2014), researchers assess the organizational culture of government run primary health centre's in India. Results indicate openness was the most important organizational characteristics followed by confrontation and trust, while autonomy and collaboration were least practiced value. The study also found significantly higher mean scores for the values of Authenticity and Collaboration for the group having more work experience compared to group having less work experience. In a different setting, study was conducted in a software industry; it was found that OCTAPACE value dimensions were lower than the norms especially in terms of collaboration and trust (Subramanium, 2012). Lather. et. al (2010) found that proaction and openness were significantly high whereas autonomy was low the manufacturing organizations. Thus, it can be said that OCTAPACE has been widely used in different settings to assess the organizational culture; and it has revealed varied organizational profile in different settings. Thus, an attempt has been made in the present study to assess the organizational culture of private and public sector banks as well as examine the difference in organizational culture of private and public sector banks.

6.3. Hypotheses

Following hypotheses were formulated:
Hypothesis 1(a): There will be significant difference between private and public sector banks in terms of openness
Hypothesis 1(b): There will be significant difference between private and public sector banks in terms of confrontation
Hypothesis 1(c): There will be significant difference between private and public sector banks in terms of proaction
Hypothesis 1(d): There will be significant difference between private and public sector banks in terms of experimentation
Hypothesis 1(e): There will be significant difference between private and public sector banks in terms of trust.
Hypothesis 1(f): There will be significant difference between private and public sector banks in terms of authenticity

6.4. Method

i. Participants and procedures

The research sample of the present study consisted of 151 employees from two public and two private sector banks, belonging to clerical cadre. Their age ranged from 20 years to 58 years. Out of the total sample, 47% belong to 20-35 age group, 35.8% belong to 36-50 age group and 17.2% belong to above 50 age group. Further, 49% of respondents belong to private sector banks and 51% belong to public sector banks. Table 1 shows the demographic analysis of the participants. Random sampling method was followed for selecting the banks and the bank branches. A total of 25 branches were selected from north, west, and east Delhi region. All respondents of a particular branch participated in the study. Data were obtained by the researcher by personally visiting the bank branches. Permission was taken from each branch manager for distribution of the questionnaires. A sealed envelope containing the questionnaire and rationale of the research study was provided to all the respondents. Respondents were given 1 week time to fill the questionnaire and they were collected back by the researcher after a week. Sample description is placed in table 1

Table 1: Sample descriptions (N = 151)

Variables		Number	Percentage (%)
Age	20-35	71	47.0
	36-50	54	35.8
	Above 50	26	17.2
	Total	151	100
Organization	Private	74	49.0
	Public	77	51.0
	Total	151	100

ii. Measures

Organizational Culture was measured by a standardized tool developed by Udai Pareek(2002) named as OCTAPACE. OCTAPACE measures eight organizational values. 17 items were taken from the original 40 items questionnaire. They are openness, confrontation, trust, authenticity, proactivity, autonomy, collaboration, and experimentation. The instrument is based on 4 point Likert scale, with 4 reflecting high presence of a value in the organization whereas 1 implies low presence of the value in the organization. The instrument had high split half reliability of 0.81 as mentioned by the author (Pareek, 2002).

6.5. Data Analysis

Preliminary Analysis

Since OCTAPACE was originally validated by Udai Pareek(2002) in manufacturing sector, to test its applicability in banking sector, data was subjected to exploratory factor analysis (EFA) using principal component analysis as the extraction method and varimax with Kaiser normalization as the rotation method to reduce the 17 items measuring organizational culture into smaller number of factors.

Table 2: EFA of OCTAPACE Culture

Items	Communalities extraction	1	2	3	4	5	6
Openness_1	0.74	0.80					
Openness_2	0.85	0.90					
Openness_3	0.86	0.91					
Confr_1	0.68		0.80				
Confr_2	0.70		0.79				
Confr_3	0.75		0.78				
Proaction_1	0.62			0.67			
Proaction_2	0.74			0.53			
Experimentation_1	0.71				0.58		
Experimentation_2	0.77				0.55		
Experimentation_3	0.78				0.73		
Experimentation_4	0.80				0.81		
Trust_1	0.71					0.81	
Trust_2	0.62					0.50	
Authenticity_1	0.71						0.45
Authenticity_2	0.80						0.87
% of variance		16.57	14.59	13.23	11.69	8.99	7.66
Eigen values		5.64	2.61	1.74	1.54	1.18	1.09

Notes: Total variance extracted by five factor = 72.76 percent; extraction method, principal component analysis; rotation method, Varimax with Kaiser normalization.

Appropriateness of factor analysis was determined by examining the Kaiser-Meyer-Olkin (KMO) measure of sampling adequacy (0.70) and Bartlett's test of sphericity(sig at0.000). Both tests indicate suitability of performing factor analysis. As shown in table, six underlying factors emerged in the study. The six factors explain 72.76 percent variance with Eigen value greater than 1.The factors are labeled as openness, confrontation, proaction, experimentation, trust, and authenticity. However, two factors naming collaboration and autonomy did not emerge as independent factors and items of these factors were cross-loaded with other factors, hence dropped from the study. After identifying the factor structure, each factor was tested for reliability through Cronbach alpha. All the factors were found to have satisfactory alpha values. The results of EFA and reliability analysis are placed in Table 2and Table 3.

Table 3: Reliability analysis of emerged factors

Serial no.	Name of the Factor	No of items	Cronbach alpha value
1	Openness	3	0.90
2	Confrontation	3	0.80
3	Proaction	2	0.60
4	Experimentation	4	0.82
5	Trust	2	0.63
6	Authenticity	2	0.40

6.6. Results

i. Descriptive Analysis

Mean was computed on all the OCTAPACE dimensions of the total sample. Table 4 depicts the Mean and SD of each OCTAPACE dimensions of the total sample. Among the OCTAPACE dimensions, Confrontation is having the highest mean score (3.18) followed by Proaction (3.16), Trust (3.12), Authenticity (3.06), Experimentation (2.97) and Openness (2.72). Openness is having the lowest mean score. This implies banks need to pay attention to this dimension. Further, mean was also computed as well as compared among different age groups of the total sample. In the age group 20-35 years, highest mean score was in proaction and lowest was in openness.

Table 4: MEAN, SD for OCTAPACE Dimensions (N=151)

Serial No.	OCTAPACE Dimensions	MEAN	SD
1	Openness	2.72	.89
2	Confrontation	3.18	.62
3	Proaction	3.17	.56
4	Experimentation	2.98	.67
5	Trust	3.13	.48
6	Authenticity	3.06	.44

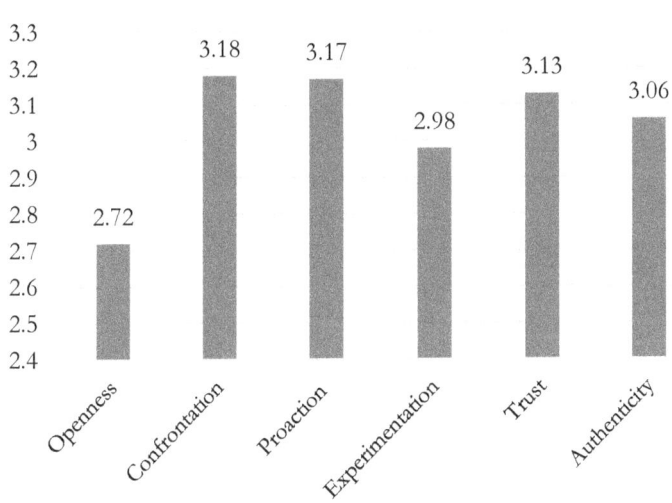

Figure 1: Mean scores of OCTAPACE Dimensions

In the age group 36-50 years, highest mean score was in trust and lowest was in openness. In the age group above 50 years, the highest mean score was in confrontation and lowest was in openness. All the age groups perceived openness as the least present value in the organization. However, significant difference among the age group was found only in case of openness (F=3.78, sig at 0.05 level) and authenticity (F value=3.26, sig at 0.05 level). Mean and F values are placed in Table 5

Table 5: Mean, SD, ANOVA for OCTAPACE dimensions of different age groups (N = 151)

Serial No.	OCTAPACE Dimensions	20-35 MEAN (SD)	36-50 MEAN (SD)	Above 50 MEAN (SD)	F
1	Openness	2.92(.88)	2.61(.89)	2.41(.83)	3.78*
2	Confrontation	3.16(.67)	3.22(.63)	3.15(.47)	.165(NS)
3	Proaction	3.24(.56)	3.09(.59)	3.08(.47)	1.31(NS)
4	Experimentation	3.02(.67)	3.03(.50)	2.74(.67)	1.92(NS)
5	Trust	3.07(.43)	3.23(.50)	3.05(.51)	2.20(NS)
6	Authenticity	3.12(.46)	3.09(.39)	2.87(.45)	3.26*

* $p < 0.05$; ** $p < 0.01$; NS = not significant

Figure 2: Comparison of Mean scores of Public and Private Sector Banks on each OCTAPACE Dimensions

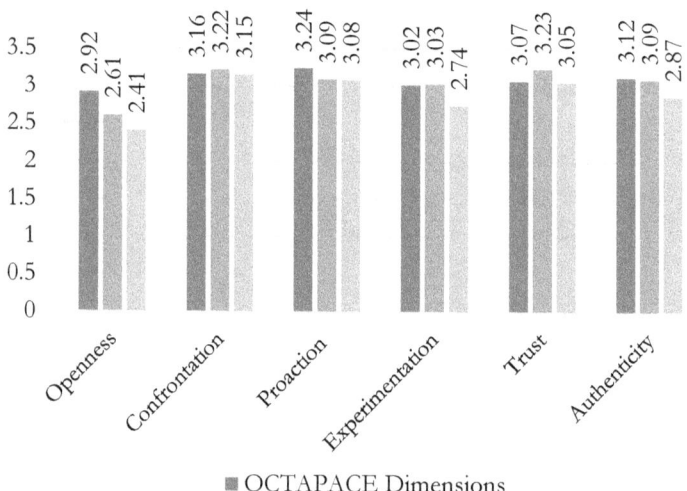

Figure 2: Comparison of Mean scores of Public and Private Sector Banks on each OCTAPACE Dimensions

ii. Testing the Hypotheses

It was hypothesized that there will be significant difference between public and private sector banks in terms of openness, confrontation, proaction, experimentation, trust, and authenticity. Hypotheses 1 (a), 1 (b), 1(c) and 1(d) are proved. Significant mean difference has been found in terms of openness (t=14.72, sig at 0.00 level), confrontation (t=3.25, sig at 0.00 level), proaction (t=8.24, sig at 0.00 level),, experimentation(t=3.73, sig at 0.00 level). T values are placed in table 6.

Table 6: Mean, SD, t values for OCTAPACE dimensions of Public and Private Sector Banks (N = 151)

Serial No.	OCTAPACE Dimensions	Public Sector Banks MEAN (SD)	Private Sector Banks MEAN (SD)	t value
1	Openness	2.04 (.63)	3.42 (.50)	14.72**
2	Confrontation	3.02(.54)	3.34(.66)	3.25**
3	Proaction	2.85(.50)	3.48(.42)	8.24**
4	Experimentation	2.78(.65)	3.17(.65)	3.73**
5	Trust	3.09(.45)	3.15(.50)	.684
6	Authenticity	3.00(.42)	3.13(.45)	1.83

* $p < 0.05$; ** $p < 0.01$; NS = not significant

6.7. Discussion

Organizational values are an important determinant of organizational culture of an organization. Researchers have been conducted on values in various settings but in the banking sector, it is less. There needs to be more focused research on organizational values in banking sector as there is low motivation level found in banking employees, and organizational values play a critical role in determining an employees' behavior. The present study has tried to fill this gap, as it has assessed organizational culture of public and private sector banks. Organizational culture was assessed by a famous tool OCTAPACE developed by Udai Pareek which measures organizational values. Results revealed that openness was perceived as very low followed by experimentation and trust. This implies that culture of the organization is closed and there is restriction in free flow of ideas. Low in experimentation implies employees are not encouraged to think 'out of the box' or work on innovative ideas. Trust has been also found to be low.

Furthermore, it was hypothesized that there will be significant difference between private and public sector in terms of

OCTAPACE dimensions. A significant difference has been found only in case of openness, confrontation, proaction, and experimentation. Public sector banks have been found to have significantly low on the above-mentioned dimensions. Thus, effort should be made by the public sector banks to develop a culture of openness where employees can freely express their ideas, be proactive and can think as well as implement novel ideas. Banking being the most competitive sector, public sector banks can only survive and thrive if it creates a culture of openness and creativity.

Conclusion

In conclusion, it can be said that perception of banking employees for OCTAPACE values namely openness, confrontation, proaction, experimentation, trust, and authenticity are just an average. Openness and experimentation are however significantly low in banks' culture. Interventions are required particularly on these dimensions. Higher management should promote open culture where there is free flow of ideas, expressions, and thoughts. Clerical cadre should be given freedom to experiment with novel ideas. Public sector banks are particularly low in openness and experimentation, and private sector banks are low in authenticity and trust. Authenticity can be improved by encouraging downward communication, and trust can be improved by simplification of work, reduced paperwork and through effective delegation. Thus, the study has wide implication as it has mapped the existing organizational culture of public and private sector banks and revealed the gray areas for interventions for enhancing the effectiveness of banks.

References

Aldhuwaihi, A, Shee, H.K. Stanton, P. (2012). Organizational Culture and the Job Satisfaction-Turnover Intention Link: A Case Study of the Saudi Arabian Banking Sector. *World Journal of Social Sciences*, 2(3) pp. 127 – 141.
Al-Tameemi, Khaldoon S., and Alshawi, Mustafa.(2014). The Impact of Organizational Culture and Leadership on Performance Improvement in Iraq. *The Built & Human Environment Review*, 7, 1-15.
BCG(2015). The power of people in digital banking transformation.

BCG Press.
Daniel, E.(1999).Provision of electronic banking in the UK and the Republic of Ireland. *International Journal of Bank Marketing.* 17(2)72-82.
J.M. Twati, J.G. Gammack, (2006) "The impact of organizational culture innovation on the adoption of IS/ IT: the case of Libya", *Journal of Enterprise Information Management*, 19(2), pp.175-191.
Kleijnen, J., Dolmans, D., Willems, J. & Hans van Hout. (2014).Effective quality management requires a systematic approach and a flexible organizational culture: a qualitative study among academic staff. *Quality in Higher Education*, 20(1), 103-126.
Kotter, J. & J.L. Heskett. (2011). *Corporate culture and performance.* New York: Free Press.
Lather, A., Puskas, J., Singh, A. & Gupta, N. (2010). Organizational culture: A study of selected organizations in the manufacturing sector in the NCR. *Agric. Econ. – Czech*, 56, (8): 349–358.
Martins, E.C. & Terblanche, F. (2003) "Building an organizational culture that stimulates creativity and innovation", *European Journal of Innovation Management*, 6(1), pp.64-74.
Mosley, R. (2007). Customer experience, organizational culture, and the employer brand. *Journal of Brand Management* 15, 123–134.
Mufeed, S.A. & S.N. Rafai. (2003). Need for octapace culture in tourism sector: An instrument for organizational dynamics. *Adopting E-Governance*, 81–94.
Ojo, O. (2010). Organizational Culture and Corporate Performance: Empirical Evidence from Nigeria. *Journal of Business Systems, Governance, and Ethics*, 5, (2), 1-12.
Pareek U. (2002). *Training instruments in HRD and OD.* New Delhi: Tata McGraw-Hill.
Pareek, U. (2011). *Organizational Behaviour.* Oxford University Press: New Delhi.
Pool, S.W. (2000), "Organizational culture and its relationship between job tension in measuring outcomes among business executives", *Journal of Management Development*,19 (1), pp. 32-49.
Purohit, P. & Purohit, S. (2014).A Study of Organizational Values in Government Run Primary Health Centres in India. *Journal of Health Management*, 16(2) 303–313.
Robbins, S.P.(2012). *Organizational Behaviour.* Pearson Education: Delhi.
Schein, E.H. (1990), "Organizational culture", *American Psychologist*,

Vol. 45 No. 2, p. 109.
Srivastava, S.K. & P. Srinivasan (2004). Performance enhancement through continuous improvement. The article presented at second world conference on POM.
Subrahmanian, M.U. 2012. Achieving high involvement & satisfaction through OCTAPACE culture in its companies. *Zenith International Journal of business economics & management research*,2 (5), 131-138.

CHAPTER 7
MICRO AND MACROECONOMIC DETERMINANTS OF CORPORATE FINANCIAL PERFORMANCE: EMPIRICAL EVIDENCE FROM INDIAN TEXTILE FIRMS

Rajneesh Prakash Verma and A.K. Sharan

Abstract

The concept of corporate financial performance has become significant, as most of the companies contemplate corporate financial performance as a measure of its efficiency, growth and development. Prevailing empirical research on the determinants has been largely confined to the overall manufacturing sector and a few specific sub-sectors of manufacturing industry in the Indian context. This paper attempts to explore the empirical corroboration of the extensively held prevailing theories on the determinants of firm's financial performance by using a sample of 297 Indian textile-manufacturing firms. The study uses annual financial statement data over a time span of twelve years from 2002 to 2013 and the sample dataset covers the span of both the pre as well as post-recession of 2008-09. Financial performance is measured by using an accounting measure, i.e., return on assets (ROA) variable. Prevailing literature on the determinants of financial performance suggests that firm's financial performance is significantly swayed by micro-and-macroeconomic variables, i.e., firm's age

(LAGE), *firm's size (LSZ), firm's growth rate (GR), current ratio (CR), leverage ratio (LEV), total asset turnover ratio (TATO), business risk (VROA), inflation rate (IFL), interest rate (ITR), GDP-growth rate (NGGDP) and Lag of return on asset (LROA). The study has employed panel data Fixed-Effect (FE) regression approach with robust estimates for the purpose of empirical investigation. Outcomes show that IFL, LAGE, GR, LEV, TATO, VROA and LROA are the significant determinants of corporate financial performance. However, ITR and LEV are found negatively associated with firm's performance. The findings of the paper would enrich the existing literature on the corporate financial performance and also discusses the relevance of capital structure and micro-and-macroeconomic variables for the Indian textile firms.*

7.1. Introduction

In the background of a dynamic economic condition in which liberalisation and globalization have assumed a noteworthy part in the formulation of the economic policies around the world. Therefore, investment, and additionally financing prospects have intensified and the majority of all, dependence on the capital market has expanded continuously. Financing or capital structure choice is indispensable from the point of view of recently incorporated organisation and for established companies. Capital structure is involved different financial instruments, in particular, preference shares, common shares, and debt instruments. A firm can either utilize one of these instruments or they can utilize the blend of these instruments and this remained as an inquisitive issue for the financial executives. Capital structure choice is an unending procedure and firm's endeavours to achieve ideal capital structure, which inevitably augments its value.

As per the original work of Modigliani and Miller (1958), the decision of capital structure is superfluous under efficient markets with no agency cost, no taxes, no transaction, and there is perfect revelation of all information. Afterward, Modigliani and Miller (1963) facilitated a few circumstances and delineated that interest costs are tax deductible under imperfect capital market, the estimation of the firm value will surge with more leverage. Models grounded on the influence of the tax, suggest that beneficial firms must have more debts and tax administration are more attractive in company's profit for these organizations. Stulz (1990) considers that debts instalment diminishes cash flows accessible for managers, notwithstanding, this diminishing will decrease the possibilities of beneficial investing.

The performance of companies is a crucial reason for sustainable economic growth as these organizations utilize persons, build value and encourage innovation. From the perspective of business executives, the determinants of firm performance may make accessible valuable acumens, which can support the future firm execution and at last to the relating section/division in which the firm is operational. Despite the fact that there has been huge literature accessible concerning capital structure and throughout the years, various studies have investigated a research domain that addresses the effect of capital structure on the firm performance. This aim of the study contributes to the present literature in this area, as it is an endeavour to reveal the capital structure practices of the organizations, particularly about Indian textile manufacturing segment.

7.2. Literature Review

Contemporary literature highlights the well-established determinants of firm's financial performance. Studies advocate that capital structure is one of the significant determinant of financial performance. According to Chadha & Sharma (2016), it focuses on two vital concerns, first is to expand the company's value and second is to limit the cost of capital. It changes from organization to organization and contrasts from industry to industry. Apart from capital structure, there are numerous firm-specific and macro-economic determinants of its performance, such as, firm size, age, growth rate, risk, liquidity, turnover ratio, interest rate, inflation etc. Further, this section briefly discusses about the major studies in the national and international context.

In the International context, McNamara & Duncan (1995) found that GDP growth rate, interest rate, corporate profit and prior-year profitability are the significant determinant of corporate performance. Krishnan & Moyer (1997) empirically determined that leverage itself does not seem to influence corporate performance in case of emerging markets. While, Fama and French (2002) showed that positive relationship exist between leverage and firm's profitability. Zeitun et al. (2007) found negative impact of firm's age and capital structure on performance, while found positive impact of firm's size and growth on performance. Liargovas & Skandalis (2008) reveals that size, location, leverage, effective management and export activity have significant impact on firm performance. Asimakopoulos *et al.* (2009) studied the determinants of profitability and found that sales growth, size and investment have positively affected firm's profitability, while leverage and current assets affected negatively. Gill *et al.* (2011) examined the impact of capital structure on profitability and found positive relationship between "total debt to total assets", "short-term debt to total assets" and "total debt to total asset" with profitability measure. Muritala (2012) found that firm's age, firm's asset turnover, size, and asset turnover are positively associated to firm's performance, and negative relationship between asset tangibility and performance. Kestens *et al.* (2012) showed that the crisis had a negative effect on a firm's performance. Olokoyo (2013) revealed a significant negative influence of leverage on financial performance. Rehman *et al.* (2014) showed that the performance and size of companies both depend upon macroeconomic variables and financial ratios.

In Indian Context, Majumdar (1997) found larger companies were less profitable and more productive, whereas older firms were less productive and more profitable. Kakani *et al.* (2001) found that firm's ownership composition and the leverage were important determinants of firm's financial performance. Bhaduri (2002) found the optimal capital structure choice can be impacted by factors such as size, cash flow, growth, and product as well as industry characteristics. Chander & Aggarwal (2008) revealed that age, past profitability, efficiency ratio, and research and development intensity were statistically significant determinants of profitability of companies. Ghosh (2008) showed that cash flows and corporate profitability lessens as leverage increases. Mahakud & Misra (2009) showed that leverage has the significant negative impact on firm performance, other control variables such as tangibility, firm's size, short-term liabilities, inventory ratio and time dummy also significant impacted performance measures. Bhayani (2010) found that age of the firm, liquidity, operating profit ratio, inflation rate and interest rate has played a significant role in the determination of the firm's profitability. Mistry (2012) found that size, inventory turnover ratio and debt equity ratio are the most significant determinants of the firm profitability. Banerjee & De (2014) found that debt service capacity (interest), firm size and leverage are significant factors effecting that profitability. Chadha & Sharma (2015) revealed that financial leverage has no effect on the financial performance and further found that other independent variables like age, size, asset turnover, sales growth, tangibility, and ownership structure were significant determinants of financial performance

7.3. Sample Selection and Data Description

The data utilized as a part of the empirical investigation of this aim was mined from two distinct sources. The company level data was obtained from the Centre for Monitoring Indian Economy's (CMIE) PROWESS database and the data for macro-economic factors was obtained from Reserve Bank of India's (RBI) "Handbook of Statistics on Indian Economy". From this whole dataset, we have considered a panel dataset of 297 textile-manufacturing firms for the years from 2002 to 2013. Finally, obtained a dataset of 297 companies by arranging all the firm level data series based on data availability. Global financial crises-2008 had an effect at all the spheres of economy. The study has employed a dummy variable (DMY) to find out the effect of financial crises (2008) on the corporate performance of Indian textile manufacturing firms.

For econometric examination, we have obtained "Return on Asset (ROA)" as a dependent variable and, considers it a proxy of companies' financial performance. Eleven independent variables were used in this study, they were further classified into the following two sets (1) Macroeconomic factors (2) Microeconomic factors to have more prominent understanding about the degree of relationship at macro and as well as micro level. The study uses three macro-economic independent variables data, namely, "Inflation Rate (IFL)", "Interest Rate (IT)" and "GDP-Growth Rate (NGGDP)". Alongside these macro-economic variables, we have considered seven micro-economic independent variables, to be specific, "Firm Age (LAGE)", "Firm Size (LSZ)", "Firm Growth Rate (GR)", "Current Ratio (CR)", "Leverage Ratio (LR)", "Total Asset Turnover Ratio (TATO)" and "Business Risk (VROA)". The model also considers "Lag of return on asset (LROA)" as a significant independent variable, as earlier year profitability impacts the companies' financial performance.

7.4. Variables Specifications

This section of the study briefly discusses about the dependent and independent variables, along with their definition.

7.4.i. Dependent Variable

Literature suggests numerous accounting measures to gauge financial performance. The empirical model has considered "Return on asset (ROA)" as a dependent variable and, it is the proportion of "net income (NI) to total asset (TA)".

7.4.ii. Independent Variables

a) Macro-economic Variable

Inflation (IFL)
The proxy variable used for measuring inflation is the growth rate of "Wholesale Price Index (WPI)" for manufacturing products.

Interest Rate (ITR)
The study considers "Weighted Average Call Money Rate" as a gauge for interest rate.

Gross Domestic Product-Growth Rate (NGGDP)
The percentage change in nominal GDP for manufacturing sector is a proxy used for measuring the current growth prospect in an economy for textile/manufacturing companies.

Firm Age (LAGE)

b) Micro-economic Variable

Firm Age (LAGE)
It is measured as the natural logarithm of the number of years since the firm's incorporation.

Firm Size (LSZ)
Size is evaluated as the natural logarithm of the total assets.

Firm Growth Rate (GR)
Here, we have considered "compounded annual growth rate (CAGR) of total assets" as a proxy of company's growth.

Current Ratio (CR)
Is the ratio of "current asset and current liability of a firm".

Leverage Ratio (LR)
Capital structure of a company is one of the significant determining factor that influences performance. It is obtained as the ratio of "total debt and total assets of a firm".

Total Asset Turnover Ratio (TATO)
Is the ratio of "net sales and total assets of a firm".

Business Risk (VROA)
Finally, considered "coefficient of variation of ROA for the past four years" as a proxy for business risk.

7.5. Empirical Methodology

The investigation considers panel data system with the purpose of empirical examination as it considers cross-sectional and time series properties. For the preliminary analysis, the study evaluated descriptive statistics such as Average, Minimum, Maximum and Standard Deviation. Next, the study used "Karl Pearson correlation", which determines the "degree of association" among variables. Further, we employ numerous panel data unit root test for assessing the stationarity property of panel data series. Assessment of the Baseline regression model possibly performed with various panel data—econometric techniques and, it is important to determine best-fit model between "Fixed-Effect (FE) and Random Effect (RE)". We employ "Hausman test" to select between FE and RE.

7.5.i. Specification of Empirical Model

This section discusses about the baseline regression models, which represents the relationship among firm performance, micro-economic variables and macro-economic variables. Initially, we study the influence of "macro-economic variables on firm performance variable". Next, we study the influence of "micro-economic variables on firm performance variable"; and finally we determine the combine influence of "both micro-economic and macro-economic variables on firm performance variable".

The baseline models framed for empirical estimation of the study are as follows:

Model 1 (Macro-economic Model)
$$ROA_{it} = \beta_0 + \beta_1 IFL_{it} + \beta_2 ITR_{it} + \beta_3 NGGDP_{it} + \beta_4 L\_ROA_{it} + \varepsilon_{it} \quad \ldots (1)$$

Model 2 (Micro-economic Model)
$$ROA_{it} = \beta_0 + \beta_1 LAGE_{it} + \beta_2 LSZ_{it} + \beta_3 GR_{it} + \beta_4 CR_{it} + \beta_5 LEV_{it} + \beta_6 TOTA_{it} + \beta_7 VROA_{it} + \beta_8 L\_ROA_{it} + \varepsilon_{it} \quad \ldots (2)$$

Model 3 (Combined Macro-economic and Micro-economic Model)

$$ROA_{it} = \beta_0 + \beta_1 IFL_{it} + \beta_2 ITR_{it} + \beta_3 NGGDP_{it} + \beta_4 LAGE_{it}$$
$$+ \beta_5 LSZ_{it} + \beta_6 GR_{it} + \beta_7 CR_{it} + \beta_8 LEV_{it} + \beta_9 TOTA_{it}$$
$$+ \beta_{10} VROA_{it} + \beta_{11} L_{ROA_{it}} + \varepsilon_{it}$$

Here,
α_0 =   intercept
β_0, β_1 = Coefficients
ε_{it} =   error term for firm i at time period t.

7.6. Empirical Results

7.6.i. Descriptive Analysis

Table 1 depicts overall descriptive statistics of all the variables. For the complete sample, lowest value of average ROA was -81.11 percent, highest value of average ROA was 35.04 percent and overall value of ROA is measured as 3.63 percent with standard deviation of 10.17 percent for the duration of the study. Overall sample's LAGE is 3.2698 and, it's minimum and maximum values were 1.3863 and 7.6074 respectively. We obtained 6.7248 as the average log value of size for the complete sample, its minimum and maximum values were 2.3321 and 11.7812 respectively over the duration of the study. We found average value of business risk (VROA) was 0.3382, its minimum and maximum values were -72.4503 and 86.4422 respectively. GR was 9.00 percent for the whole sample with minimum and maximum values of -68.62 percent and 253.45 percent respectively. GR was having a standard deviation of 27.48 percent. We obtained 1.4636 as the CR value for the whole sample, its minimum and maximum values were 0.0000 and 16.3300 respectively along with 1.4265 standard deviation. LEV value for the whole sample was 0.6562, its minimum and maximum values were 0.0003 and 9.3729 respectively with 0.8458 standard deviation. For the whole sample, TATO was 1.0169, its maximum and minimum values were 0.0000 and 4.6300 respectively together with a standard deviation of 0.6694. LROA was 0.0355 for whole sample, its minimum and maximum values were similar to that of ROA variable in conjunction with a standard deviation of 0.1036. In the context of macro-economic variables from 2002-2013, we found that IFL for manufacturing industry was 4.67 percent and its minimum value was

1.83 percent. Maximum value of IFL was 7.23 per cent and its standard deviation was 1.78 percent. We obtained 6.14 percent as the ITR, its minimum and maximum were 3.24 percent and 8.22 percent respectively with 0.0143 standard deviation. Lastly, we observed that NGGDP of manufacturing sector was 13.04 percent. Minimum and maximum NGGDP values were 3.98 percent and 21.69 percent respectively along with a standard deviation of 4.51 percent.

7.6.ii. Correlation Analysis

At the subsequent stage, we used correlation method to determine the degree of relationship among the dependent and independent variables (see, Table 2). Correlation analysis is significant for the reason that before executing the econometric model, it is better to confirm whether multi-collinearity issue exist among variables or not. Correlation of ROA is found highest with LRAO (i.e., r = 0.6177) at one percent significance level. ROA is found negatively allied with LEV at one percent significance level, IFL and ITR with at ten percent significance level. It is found positively linked with all the other independent variables used in the study at one and ten percent significance level.

We found significant association among most of micro-and-macro-economic variables at one, five and ten percent significance level, and within these variables. ITR is found having positive association with IFL (r = 0.4550) at one percent significance level. At last, we can conclude from the correlation matrix that none of the correlation coefficient (r) value among all is having value larger than 0.80. No sign of multicollinearity is detected in the sample.

7.6.iii. Panel Unit Root Test

The study employed panel-unit root test to ascertain the stationary property of the variables. We adopted "Levin et al. (2002)", i.e. the LLC statistics and, this test is based on the null hypothesis that a unit root exists in the panels. The test "with intercept" and "with intercept and trend" showed the nonexistence of unit root in the data series in all cases. Finally, we conclude that all the examined variable series shows stationary characteristics (see, Table 3), as they reject null hypothesis of containing unit root at one and ten percent level of significance. At the consequent stage, we can conduct multiple regression analysis.

Table 1
Summary Statistics on Dependent, Macro-and-Micro-economic variables of Indian Textile Firms
(Sample size, 2002 – 2013, N = 297)

Variable	Return on Asset (ROA)				Firm Age (LAGE)				Firm Size (LSZ)				Business Risk (VROA)			
Statistics	Avg.	Min.	Max.	Std. Dev.	Avg.	Min.	Max.	Std. Dev.	Avg.	Min.	Max.	Std. Dev.	Avg.	Min.	Max.	Std. Dev.
Overall	0.0363	-0.8111	0.3504	0.1017	3.2698	1.3863	7.6074	0.6494	6.7248	2.3321	11.7812	1.6716	0.3382	-72.4503	86.4422	5.2868

Variable	Firm Growth Rate (GR)				Current Ratio (CR)				Leverage (LEV)				Total Asset Turnover Ratio (TATO)			
Statistics	Avg.	Min.	Max.	Std. Dev.	Avg.	Min.	Max.	Std. Dev.	Avg.	Min.	Max.	Std. Dev.	Avg.	Min.	Max.	Std. Dev.
Overall	0.0900	-0.6862	2.5345	0.2748	1.4636	0.0000	16.3300	1.4265	0.6562	0.0003	9.3729	0.8458	1.0169	0.0000	4.6300	0.6694

Variable	Return on Asset (LROA)				Inflation Rate (IFL)				Interest Rate (ITR)				GDP-Growth Rate (NGGDP)			
Statistics	Avg.	Min.	Max.	Std. Dev.	Avg.	Min.	Max.	Std. Dev.	Avg.	Min.	Max.	Std. Dev.	Avg.	Min.	Max.	Std. Dev.
Overall	0.0355	-0.8111	0.3504	0.1036	0.0467	0.0183	0.0723	0.0178	0.0614	0.0324	0.0822	0.0143	0.1304	0.0398	0.2169	0.0451

Source: Evaluated Estimated using Stata 14.
Note: (1) All the macroeconomic series are compiled from RBI's "*Handbook of Statistics on Indian Economy*" database.
(2) For WPI, 1993-94 base year was considered. (3) All values in the table depicted in absolute term

Table 2
Correlation matrix among the dependent and independent variables (Sample size, 2002 – 2013, N = 297)

	ROA	LAGE	LSZ	VROA	GR	CR
ROA	1					
LAGE	0.0305* (0.0691)	1				
LSZ	0.1909*** (0.0000)	0.2040*** (0.0000)	1			
VROA	0.0949*** (0.0000)	0.0019 (0.9102)	0.0257 (0.1244)	1		
GR	0.3434*** (0.0000)	-0.0009 (0.9579)	0.1635*** (0.0000)	0.0457*** (0.0064)	1	
CR	0.1103*** (0.0000)	-0.0483*** (0.0039)	-0.0816* (0.0000)	0.0187 (0.2631)	0.0338** (0.0435)	1
LEV	-0.3608*** (0.0000)	-0.0020 (0.9068)	-0.1166* (0.0000)	-0.0655*** (0.0001)	-0.1785*** (0.0000)	-0.2375*** (0.0000)
TATO	0.2063*** (0.0000)	0.0471*** (0.0049)	-0.1952*** (0.0000)	0.0338** (0.0439)	-0.0025 (0.8830)	-0.0962*** (0.0000)
IFL	-0.0326* (0.0518)	0.1182*** (0.0000)	0.0722*** (0.0000)	-0.0405** (0.0156)	-0.0122 (0.4679)	0.0281* (0.0935)
ITR	-0.0321* (0.0556)	0.0636*** (0.0001)	0.0472*** (0.0048)	-0.0090 (0.5931)	-0.0723*** (0.0000)	0.0451*** (0.0071)
NGGDP	0.0585*** (0.0005)	0.0664*** (0.0001)	0.0489*** (0.0035)	-0.0063 (0.7089)	0.1617*** (0.0000)	0.0013 (0.9363)
LROA	0.6177*** (0.0000)	0.0134 (0.4236)	0.2247*** (0.0000)	0.0547*** (0.0011)	0.2426*** (0.0000)	0.1228*** (0.0000)

Source: Estimated using Stata 14.
Notes: (1) Figures in square brackets are probability values (*p*-Values) and all *p*-Values are two-tailed
(2) Subsequent asterisks (***), (**) & (*) denotes rejection of the null hypotheses at 1%, 5% & 10% significance level, respectively.

Cont......

	LEV	TATO	IFL	IT	GGDP	LROA
LEV	1					
TATO	-0.1508*** (0.0000)	1				
IFL	0.0065 (0.6971)	0.0286** (0.0875)	1			
ITR	-0.0124 (0.4589)	0.0585*** (0.0005)	0.3596*** (0.0000)	1		
NGGDP	0.0288** (0.0854)	-0.0518*** (0.0020)	0.4550*** (0.0000)	-0.1516*** (0.0000)	1	
LROA	-0.3731*** (0.0000)	0.1572*** (0.0000)	0.0707*** (0.0000)	0.0667*** (0.0001)	0.0725*** (0.0000)	1

Source: Estimated using Stata 14.
Notes: (1) Figures in square brackets are probability values (p-Values) and all p-Values are two-tailed
(2) Subsequent asterisks (***), (**) & (*) denotes rejection of the null hypotheses at 1%, 5% & 10% significance level, respectively.

Table 2
Panel Unit Root Test Results (Sample size, 2002 – 2013, N = 297)

Variables	ROA	LAGE	LSZ	VROA	GR	CR
Intercept	-14.9035**	-87.0959**	-17.4799**	-49.7271**	-32.9062**	-36.7776**
	(0.0000)	(0.0000)	(0.0000)	(0.0000)	(0.0000)	(0.0000)
Intercept + Trend	-21.5009**	-1.1e+02**	-34.2535**	-36.8490**	-30.9517**	-65.7941**
	(0.0000)	(0.0000)	(0.0000)	(0.0000)	(0.0000)	(0.0000)
Variables	LEV	TATO		IFL	ITR	NGGDP
Intercept	-17.5750**	-16.6357**		-56.3766**	-11.9749**	-1.5064*
	(0.0000)	(0.0000)		(0.0000)	(0.0000)	(0.0660)
Intercept + Trend	-25.1663**	-21.6821**		-59.5913**	-26.8625**	-14.7194**
	(0.0000)	(0.0000)		(0.0000)	(0.0000)	(0.0000)

Source: Estimated using Stata 14.
Note: Subsequent asterisks (**) & (*) denotes rejection of the null hypotheses at 1% & 10% significance level, respectively

7.6.iv. Hausman Tests

The study determine the best-fit model between panel Fixed Effect (FE) and Random Effect (RE) by using "Hausman-test (1978)". The resulting Hausman-tests $\chi 2$ statistics are found significant for all models, i.e. all $\chi 2$ values and their respective p-values shows the rejection of null hypothesis for Hausman-test estimates (see, Table 4). Hence, using the FE estimator outcomes is more efficient outcomes than the RE estimator. Finally, we conclude that FE models are better than RE models in all cases.

Table 3: Hausman Test Results

Model 1		Model 2		Model 3	
F-stat & Chi-square Value ($\chi 2$)	Probability value (p-Value)	F-stat & Chi-square Value ($\chi 2$)	Probability value (p-Value)	F-stat & Chi-square Value ($\chi 2$)	Probability value (p-Value)
516.0200*	0.0000	488.5200*	0.0000	497.9100*	0.0000

Source: Estimated using Stata 14.
Note: Asterisk (*) denotes rejection of the null hypotheses at 1% significance level,

7.7. Results and Discussions

The detailed description about the baseline models and best-fit models starts in the following section.

i) Panel Fixed Effects (FE) Estimates

Results of the FE estimates with clustered standard errors for Model 1 shows that coefficients of the IFL (-0.5531), NGGDP (0.1682), L_ROA (0.3677) and Intercept (0.0320) are statistically significant at one percent level. However, the coefficient of ITR (-0.1272) is statistically not significant. (see column 2, Table 5).

The estimates of the FE estimates for Model 2 indicates that coefficients of GR (0.0705), TATO (0.0338), VROA (0.0008) and L_ROA (0.2958) are statistically significant at one percent level. The coefficients of LAGE (0.0333), LEV (-0.0158) and Intercept (-0.0878) are also statistically significant but at five percent level. However, the coefficient of LSZ (-0.0037) and CR (0.0018) are statistically not significant. (see column 3, Table 5).

The assessments of the FE estimates for Model 3 depicts that coefficients of IFL (-0.5322), NGGDP (0.0999), LAGE (0.0467),

GR (0.0659), TATO (0.0358), L_ROA (0.3031) and Intercept (-0.1148) are statistically significant at one percent level. The coefficients of LEV (-0.0158) and VROA (0.0007) are statistically significant at five percent level. The coefficient of ITR (-0.2088) is statistically significant at five percent level. While, LSZ (-0.0031) and CR (0.0020) are statistically not significant. (see column 4, Table 5).

Table 4: Panel Fixed Effects (FE) Results (2002-2013)

Variables	Model 1	Model 2	Model 3
IFL	-0.5531***		-0.5322***
	(0.0951)		(0.0911)
ITR	-0.1272		-0.2088*
	(0.1026)		(0.1084)
NGGDP	0.1642***		0.0999***
	(0.0364)		(0.0367)
LAGE		0.0333**	0.0467***
		(0.0133)	(0.0144)
LSZ		-0.0037	-0.0031
		(0.0039)	(0.0039)
GR		0.0705***	0.0659***
		(0.0099)	(0.0099)
CR		0.0018	0.0020
		(0.0016)	(0.0016)
LEV		-0.0158**	-0.0162**
		(0.0080)	(0.0079)
TATO		0.0338***	0.0358***
		(0.0079)	(0.0078)
VROA		0.0008***	0.0007**
		(0.0003)	(0.0003)
L_ROA	0.3677***	0.2958***	0.3031***
	(0.0336)	(0.0343)	(0.0338)
DMY	0.0069**	-0.0064	-0.0031
	(0.0032)	(0.0043)	(0.0049)
Intercept	0.0320***	-0.0878**	-0.1148***
	(0.0072)	(0.0400)	(0.0433)
N	3564	3564	3564
R^2	0.3884	0.3547	0.3301
F-value	33.1100***	45.1300***	37.6600***

Source: Estimated using Stata 14.
Notes: (1) Figures in square brackets are standard errors.

(2) Subsequent asterisks (***), (**) & (*) denotes rejection of the null hypotheses at 1%, 5% & 10% significance level, respectively.

The FE estimates of Model 1, Model 2 and Model 3 shows that NGGDP, LAGE, GR, TATO, VROA, and L_ROA have a significant positive relationship with firm's performance. LEV, IFL and ITR is negatively associated relationship with firm's performance. A dummy variable (DMY) was used to compare the Pre- (2008) crises and Post- (2008) crises financial performance of the Indian textile industry. DMY is significant for Model 1 of FE estimates, but not significant for Model 2 and Model 3.

The FE estimates of the models shows that R^2 values of Model 1, Model 2 and Model 3 are 0.3882, 0.3547 and 0.3301 respectively, and these implies that 38.82 percent, 35.47 percent and 33.01 percent variation of dependent variables is explained by independent variables. The F-statistic are 33.1100, 45.1300 and 37.6600 for Model 1, Model 2 and Model 3 respectively, and these are found statistically significant at one percent level and hence, rejects the null hypothesis of joint insignificance of coefficients for all cases. Eventually, we conclude that all the FE regression models are well-specified.

Discussions and Conclusion

This study examined the relationship among the financial performance, micro-and-macro-economic variables by using a sample of 297 textile manufacturing firms in India between 2002 and 2013. Analysis had been done in different stages to ensure that no indistinctness remains in the final models. We applied Fixed Effect and Random Effect model, to identify the best fit models. Model 1 of the study captures the impact of macro-economic variables on firm performance. Similarly, Model 2 relates the firm performance to the micro-economic variables. Finally Model 3 captures the combine impact of macro-micro variables on financial performance. Results of all FE models suggested that IFL, ITR and NGGDP are significant for all the models except one case (FE Model 1) in which ITR is not significant. Both IFL and ITR have negatively influenced firm performance, while NGGDP has positively affect firm performance. Most of the micro-economic variables, namely, LAGE, GR, LEV, TOTA, VROA and LROA are found significant for all FE models. All the micro-economic variables are found positively associated with firm performance except LEV. Capital Structure (LEV) has negative relationship with the performance measure. The empirical contribution of the current study to the financial performance literature is in the distinctiveness of considering both macro-micro factors.

References

Asimakopoulos, I., Samitas, A., & Papadogonas, T. (2009). Firm-specific and economy wide determinants of firm profitability: Greek evidence using panel data. Managerial Finance, 35(11), 930-939.

Banerjee, A., & De, A. (2014). Determinants of Corporate Financial Performance Relating to Capital Structure Decisions in Indian Iron and Steel Industry An Empirical Study. Paradigm, 18(1), 35-50.

Bhaduri, S. N. (2002). Determinants of capital structure choice: a study of the Indian corporate sector. Applied Financial Economics, 12(9), 655-665.

Bhayani, S. J. (2010). Determinant of profitability in Indian cement industry: an economic analysis. South Asian Journal of Management, 17(4), 6.

Chadha, S., & Sharma, A. K. (2015). Capital Structure and Firm Performance: Empirical Evidence from India. Vision: The Journal of Business Perspective, 19(4), 295-302.

Chadha, S., & Sharma, A. K. (2015). Capital Structure and Firm Performance: Empirical Evidence from India. Vision: The Journal of Business Perspective, 19(4), 295-302.

Chadha, S., & Sharma, A. K. (2016). An Empirical Study on Capital Structure in Indian Manufacturing Sector. Global Business Review, 17(2), 411-424.

Chander, S., & Aggarwal, P. (2008). Determinants of corporate profitability: an empirical study of Indian drugs and pharmaceutical industry. Paradigm, 12(2), 51-61.

Fama, E. F., & French, K. R. (2002). Testing trade-off and pecking order predictions about dividends and debt. The review of financial studies, 15(1), 1-33.

Ghosh, S. (2008). Leverage, foreign borrowing and corporate performance: firm-level evidence for India. Applied Economics Letters, 15(8), 607-616.

Gill, A., Biger, N., & Mathur, N. (2011). The effect of capital structure on profitability: Evidence from the United States. International Journal of Management, 28(4), 3.

Hausman, J. A. (1978). Specification tests in econometrics.

Econometrica: Journal of the Econometric Society, 1251-1271.

Kakani, R. K., Saha, B., & Reddy, V. N. (2001). Determinants of financial performance of Indian corporate sector in the post-liberalization era: an exploratory study. National Stock Exchange of India Limited, NSE Research Initiative Paper, (5).

Kestens, K., Van Cauwenberge, P., & Bauwhede, H. V. (2012). Trade credit and company performance during the 2008 financial crisis. Accounting & Finance, 52(4), 1125-1151.

Krishnan, V. S., & Moyer, R. C. (1997). Performance, capital structure and home country: an analysis of Asian corporations. Global Finance Journal, 8(1), 129-143.

Levin, A., Lin, C. F., & Chu, C. S. J. (2002). Unit root tests in panel data: asymptotic and finite-sample properties. Journal of econometrics, 108(1), 1-24.

Liargovas, P., & Scandalidis, K. (2008). Factors affecting firms' financial performance: the case of Greece No 12. Working Papers from University of Peloponnese, Department of Economics.

Mahakud, J., & Misra, A. K. (2009). Effect of Leverage and Adjustment Costs on Corporate Performance: Evidence from Indian Companies. Journal of Management Research, 9(1), 35.

Majumdar, S. K. (1997). The impact of size and age on firm-level performance: some evidence from India. Review of industrial organization, 12(2), 231-241.

McNamara, R., & Duncan, K. (1995). Firm Performance and Macroeconomic Variables. School of Business Discussion Paper No. 66. Retrieved from http//epublications.bond.edu.au/discussion papers/66

Modigliani, F., & Miller, M. H. (1958). The cost of capital, corporation finance and the theory of investment. The American economic review, 261-297.

Modigliani, F., & Miller, M. H. (1963). Corporate income taxes and the cost of capital: a correction. The American economic review, 53(3), 433-443.

Muritala, T. A. (2012). An empirical analysis of capital structure on firms' performance in Nigeria. International Journal of Advances in Management and Economics, 1(5), 116-124.

Olokoyo, F. O. (2013). Capital structure and corporate performance of Nigerian quoted firms: A panel data approach. African Development Review, 25(3), 358-369.

Rehman, R. U., Zhang, J., & Ali, R. (2014). Firm Performance And

Emerging Economies. Journal of Applied Business Research, 30(3), 701.

Stulz, R. (1990). Managerial discretion and optimal financing policies. Journal of financial Economics, 26(1), 3-27.

Zeitun, R., Tian, G. G., & Keen, S. (2007). Macroeconomic determinants of corporate performance and failure: evidence from an emerging market the case of Jordan. Corporate Ownership and Control, 5(1), 179.

CHAPTER 8
FACTORS RESPONSILBE FOR SHARE PRICE FLUCTUATIONS WITH SPECIAL REFERENCE TO INFRASTRUCTURE SECTOR IN INDIA

Amit Kumar and Deepika Jhamb

Abstract

Share market is considered to be one of the important drivers for economic growth of the country. Indian share market may not be the largest share market but it is attracting eyes of every investor and is considered to move far ahead of most other stock markets around the world in coming years. As we know that share price movement mainly depends on the demand and supply concept of any company but what drive this demand and supply is important to know. There are various factors responsible to drive this demand and supply concept. Fundamental and Technical analysis are the two concepts which is studied by the various investors to predict the movement of the market and every time single or mix of two or more factors responsible for this price movement. There are very few investors which exactly know the concept of fundamental and technical analysis. It is important to know how this share movement is related with different factors which are associated with this. The main objective of this paper is to analyze the factors responsible for share price fluctuations with special reference to the infrastructure sector of India (Considering top two companies of infrastructure sector).The results of this research paper portrait that Company related news, Dividends Paid, Industry P/E, Earning per shares (EPS), profitability and government policies are main drivers of share prices fluctuations and how much these factors have impact on the share price movement. We have tried to keep our research and its results as simple as possible with latest market examples and it also include how much share movement is based on these factors which can easily be studied and understand by any investors.

8.1. Introduction

It has been said that Risk will always be directly proportional to Rate of return. Investments in Stock Market are considered to be risky yet providing more rates of returns than any other mode of investment. With total value of little more than $3.0 trillion, NSE and BSE are in top 20 share market of the world (Source: Wikipedia, List of stock exchanges). Infrastructure is also a key driver for the Indian Economy. In 2014, when BJP government took political control, their main focus was to strengthen the infrastructure sector of the India with the help of Introduction of Foreign Direct Investments (FDIs).After this type of strong and steady step not only local investors but also FII's (Foreign Institute investors) also show deep interest in investments in Indian Market and closely watching movements of stock trading in different share market of India. As political power play an important role in growth of any country's economy and there is lots of talk regarding strengthen the infrastructure sector so, we have taken Indian infrastructure sector and its two top giants companies (i.e., Larsen & Toubro and Adani ports & Special Economic Zone) to analyzing impact of every single factor on these two companies share price movement. As news plays an important role in share prices fluctuations so we also tried to analyzed the impact of different news of the company on its share price fluctuations.

Government policies also an important driver for any economy of the country so we also analyzed the impact of recent Indian government policy like demonetization on the index (Nifty 50) and reality sector of the country (because real estate is the one of the sector which is majorly effected by demonetization) .

8.2. Literature Review

Prediction of share prices is very difficult task because many market forces make it more difficult to understand its behavior, yet many studies conducted showing the relationship between stock prices change and fundamental variables. India Brand Equity Foundation (IBEF), 2016 has thrown light on the importance of the infrastructure sector in Indian Economy and funding to the infrastructure sector by the government of India. According to Kumar and Mohan (1975), retained earnings and dividend yield are the main drivers of stock prices in India. Fama and French (1989) pointed out that the stock price will fluctuate with changes in expected dividends, expected future price of stocks and expected variance of return on stocks. Paulo and Pensiri (2002) analyzed the relationship between economy news (like foreign direct investment, Budgets, inflation, Gross domestic product, profitability of governments bonds) and share market. Reilly and Brown (2003) describe that factors like expectation of earnings, dividends and interest rates have effect over stock prices. And they also highlighted that growth rate of money supply is a main indicator of stock price changes.

Chen, Roll and Ross (1986) Highlights the economic variables have a systematic effect on the stock market fluctuations. They tried to explain the stock price volatility with the help of changes in fundamentals. DeBondt and Thaler (1985) Highlights the stock price fluctuations are mainly due to the overreaction of the market participants on the news. Palomino (1996) Highlights about imperfect information that all agents have can influence the stock prices and Noise traders could dominate the market for certain time with high utility. Fisher (1961) portrait that four variables are important for share prices fluctuation for different companies. These variables are: The last declared dividends per shares, the last declared undistributed profit per share, the past average annual growth in dividends per share and the size of companies to which the share corresponds. Every variable have significant influence on stock prices volatility.

King (1966) Highlighted argument against the hypothesis that market and industry factors explain co-movement in stock prices. The conclusion drawn from this is that stock prices of similar industry category will move at somehow in related direction. Harkavy (*1955*) highlights that tendency of fluctuation of share prices is directly proportional to earning distributed over a given period of time. Udegbunam and Oaikhenan (*1999*) studied the stock market of Nigeria by annual data covering the period *1979-1999*. And there findings provided conclusion that output, growth, interest rate, Inflation, industrial production and money growth are the main drivers for generating share prices fluctuations in Nigeria.

8.3. Objective Of The Study

1. To analyze the factors responsible for fluctuations of the share prices with special reference to infrastructure sector of India.
2. To study whether the factors like News, Dividend yields, Industry P/E, Earning per share (EPS), and profitability of the company are responsible for Fluctuations of the share prices of any company.

8.4. Research Methodology

The present study is purely based upon secondary data analysis which has been collected from various annual reports of the company and articles reviewed thoroughly for understanding the nature of news and effect of that news on share prices of the company.

The present study is taking into consideration the two major giants of infrastructure sector for further analysis. Top two companies of Infrastructure on the basis of Market Capitalization are as follows:

COMPANY	MARKET CAP (In Cr) (Updated 31 Jan 2017)
LARSEN & TOURBO	*1,40,210.77*
ADANI PORTS	*62,925.87*

There are different types of investors in the stock markets like Short-Term or Long-Term or Active or Passive. Every investors use different techniques for investing in stock market. Short-term investors who trade on daily basis or maximum by weekly basis are mostly depends over important news displaying related to the company or related to sector and for long-term investors they mainly focus on technical charts of the company. A proper look over the factor responsible for the fluctuations of the share price holds the key of success for investors.

8.5. Results Finding And Discussion

1) **Company News and Political interference effect on share prices**

News are the important source for investors to check the real information related to company which helps in fluctuations of share prices a lot. We are considering only that news which has large effect on share prices.

INFRA INDEX

When Modi's Government came into throne then there were lots of conversations regarding infrastructure sectors and all of views are positive towards relation between Infrastructure sector and Modi's Government. And this relation can be seen on numbers, Infra sector of India have seen some positive trends and made new high of *3483.80* on *7 July 2014*. And this shows that how political behavior can affect the share prices and growth of the sector. Following table showing the High and Low numbers of Infra Index (Studying Last *5* Years Data):

	LOW PRICE (*3 Sep 2013*) Before NDA Government	High Price (*9 Jun 2014*) After NDA Government
INFRA INDEX	*1896.15*	*3499.75*

From above table we can easily conclude that NDA Government came into existence on *12 May 2014*, the afterwards there was upwards and positive mood of Infrastructure Sector. Low price level touched before NDA government.

Recently *1 February 2017*, Union Budget is declared and due to this there is hike of 50 points in infrastructure sector within 2 days. From last three years this sector has seen the growth of *34.50%*.

A. Larsen And Toubro

Larsen is the largest company of India in infrastructure sector with around rupees *1, 40,210.77* Cr of Market capitalization. It is one of most important company in this sector.

Now let's look at the news affect on its share prices. Few news considered to show there affect either positive or negative on the share prices. (Updated Till Jan *2017*).

NEWS	SHARE FLUCTUATIONS WITH DATES
L&THydrocarbon-led consortium bags orders from Saudi Aramco	Positive trend for next four days with fluctuation of 40 points above (2 Jan 2017 – 5 Jan 2017)
Government awards L&T multi-modal terminal contract at Sahibganj (19 Oct 2016)	Positive trend with having growth of 35 points (17 Oct 2016 – 21 Oct 2016)
Larsen & Toubro sets Rs Two lakh cr revenue target by 2021(26 Aug 2016) L&T bags Rs 864 crore order from Qatar's KAHRAMAA (26 Aug 2016) L&T wins Rs 1,489 crore water supply project (31 Aug 2016)	Positive trend with having growth of 63 Points (26 Aug 2016 – 1 Sep 2016)
Larsen & Toubro bags orders worth Rs 1,509 cr in September (28 Sep 2016) Carnival Group acquires LT's realty projects for 1,785 cr (01 Oct 2016) Will save Rs 100 cr on RBI policy, but need bigger cuts: L&T (01 Oct 2016) Adani Ports inks pact with L&T for Kattupalli Port operations (03 Oct 2016) L&T dispatches first consignment of ITER cryostat (19 Oct 2016)	Positive trend with having growth of 185 Points (28 Sep 2016 – 19 Oct 2016)
Larsen & Toubro drops port development project in Gujarat (21 Aug 2015)	Negative trend with having decline of 155 Points (20 Aug 2015 – 24 Aug 2015)

B. Adani Ports And Special Economic Zone

Adani Ports is the second largest infrastructure company of India with market capitalization of Rs *62,925.87* Cr. Now let's look at the news effects on its share prices. Again little news considered to show the effect of the news.

NEWS	SHARE FLUCTUATIONS WITH DATES
Adani Ports raises USD 500 million via bonds (19 Jan 2017)	Next day of this news, share price was Ten points down
Adani Ports to develop 3rd phase of Mundra Port for Rs 6,000 cr (13 Jan 2017) Adani Ports raises $500 mn via foreign currency bonds (13 Jan 2017)	There was mix news on this day so as same seen on the fluctuation of the share prices. Not much movement seen in share prices.
Notice to Adani Port and SEZ, GMB on alleged damage to ecology (6 Dec 2016)	News came around 9:52 am and there was decline of 4 points from previous day's closing.
Adani Ports to deleverage further: Fitch (31 Oct 2016)	There was downtrend after this news and stock shed around 19 points from 308 to 289.
RBI allows foreign investors to raise stake in Adani Ports (1 Oct 2016)	Share price increased after this news and even share price opened was showing a gap from previous day closing.
Adani Food's pulses processing unit proposal in SEZ rejected (25 Aug 2016)	After this negative news for the company, share prices of the company suddenly came down around Ten points from opening price of that day.
'Govt never imposed penalty of Rs 200 cr on Adani port, SEZ' (8 Aug 2016)	After this news, share prices increase around Five points from the opening price of that day.
Moody's lowers Adani Ports ratings outlook to negative (19 May 2016)	On this day, company's share prices down by 15 points.
APSEZ to seek shareholders nod to raise up to Rs 10,000 cr (4 May 2016)	After this news, company's share price was down by 26 points from the opening price of the company on same day.
Adani Ports & SEZ raises Rs 500 cr via issue of securities (12 April 2016)	Due to affect of this news company's share price increased by Five points from the opening price.
Adani Ports raises Rs 750 crore through debentures (17 Feb 2016)	Due to this news company's share price closed above 11 points from the opening price of that same day.
APSEZ says no impact of NGT order on operations at Hazira (19 Jan 2016)	After this positive news for the company share prices showing positive trend with around Ten points above the opening price of that day.

2) Dividend Payment effect on share prices

Now we will look into the dividend paid by the company and their effect on share price fluctuations. Dividend paid by the company in last five years, we will look Impact on share prices after announcement date and effective date of the dividends.

A) Larsen and Toubro

DIVIDEND PAID (%)	ANNOUNCEMENT DAY	IMPACT	EFFECTIVE DAY	IMPACT
Rs.18.2500 per share (912.5%) Dividend	25-05-2016	Share price closed above 31.60 points from opening.	18-08-2016	On effective day share prices are down and closed 9 points below the opening price of the stock.
Rs.16.2500 per share (812.5%) Dividend	01-06-2015	Showing more bulls as the share price closed above 31.55 points from the opening price.	01-09-2015	On this day, stock sheds 23 points from the opening price.
Rs.14.2500 per share (712.5%) Dividend	30-05-2014	Share price closed below 13 points from opening price but very next day share price showing positive trend and there was increase of 31.10 points.	13-08-2014	Share price closed 24.20 points below that of opening price.
Dividend per share taken as Rs. 12.33 per share (616.5%)	22-05-2013	There was huge downtrend of points in a single day with around 99.15 points.	13-08-2013	Share price showing uptrend with having 13.75 points above from opening price of same day.
Rs.16.50 per share (825%) Dividend	14-05-2012	Share price increased by 12.50 points on same day and its impact can also be seen on next day with increase of 74.25 points.	14-08-2012	Share price increased by 20.60 points.

B) Adani Ports and SEZ

DIVIDEND PAID (%)	ANNOUNCEMENT DAY	IMPACT	EFFECTIVE DAY	IMPACT
Rs.*1.1000* per share(*55%*)Interim Dividend	*09-03-2016*	Share prices decline and closed Two points below of the opening price.	*22-03-2016*	Share prices showing negative trend and there was *2.45* points decline in the share prices.
Rs.*1.1000* per share(*55%*)Dividend	*04-05-2015*	Positive trend with rise in *22.35* points on the same day.	*22-05-2015*	Share price closed *1.40* above than that of opening price.
Rs.*1.0000* per share(*50%*)Dividend	*15-05-2014*	There was not much movement in the share price; there were low price movement with *0.90* rises in the share price.	*31-07-2014*	Decline in Share price with *1.50* points. But this decline was not much.
Rs.*1.0000* per share(*50%*)Final Dividend	*15-05-2013*	Rise in share price with *1.8* points above than that of opening price.	*30-07-2013*	Decline in share price with 2.4 points and also this negative effect can be seen in next few days.
Rs.*0.70* per share(*35%*)Final Dividend	*14-05-2012*	Little Rise in the share price with *0.70* points, not much impact seen by this.	*30-07-2012*	Rise in the share price with *4.45* points.

From above table, we can easily analyze that dividend payments plays an important role in share price fluctuations, mostly good dividend payments leads to rise in share prices but sometime when dividend paid is not up to mark of the expectation of the investors then dividend also plays negative role in the share price movements. Dividend shows the potential of the company's earning so it is an important driver for price movements.

3) EPS (Earning Per share) affect on share prices

Earnings Per share show the profit of the company but alone it will not affect in the fluctuations of the share prices. Now we will consider the following charts for this relation of EPS and Share Prices of different companies.

A) LARSEN

We have taken the average of share prices of last Five years and average EPS of last five years (*2012-2016*). (For making it more comfortable to understand in chart, we have decided to divided the share prices by *100*).

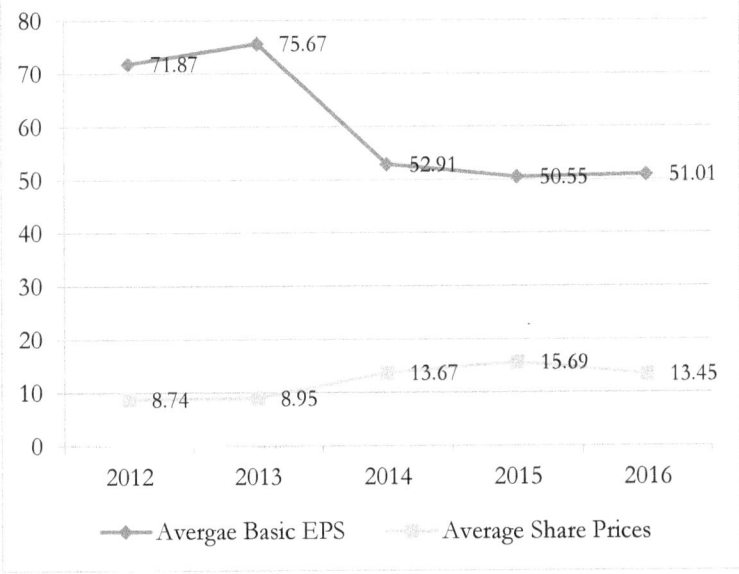

From above chart we can easily conclude that as the EPS increased from *2012* to *2016* so as the prices of the Larsen also increased from *2012-2016*. Except in the year *2016*, average EPS is increasing but average share prices decreasing.

B) Adani Ports and SEZ

Again, We have taken the average of share prices of last Five years and average EPS of last five years (*2012-2016*). (For making it more comfortable to understand in chart, we have decided to divided the share prices by *100*).

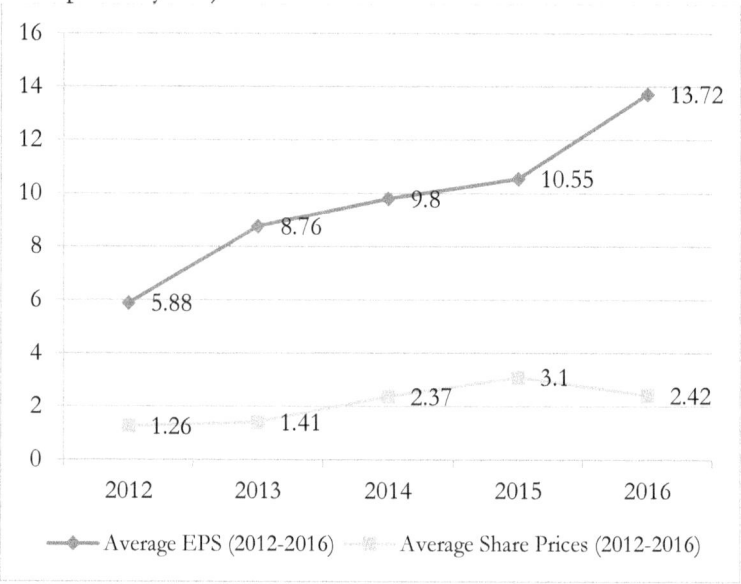

From above chart we can see that EPS increases and somehow same uptrend can also be seen in share prices except year *2016* (EPS increased much but average share price falls). So from this, we come to a conclusion that EPS alone is not good indicator of share price fluctuations. The main false thing with EPS is buyback of the shares by the company. Buyback of shares may increase EPS but not always buyback of shares helps in increasing of share prices.

4) Industry P/E Affect on Share Prices

P/E ratio is mainly indicating us about the value of the stock and some selector saw this indicator in the process of stock selection. It is always considered that high P/E means over valued of a company and low P/E means undervalued of a stock. So we will look the past performance of P/E ratio and how stock price movement is related with this (*2012-2016*).

We are taking high price of that stock in the respective year. **(For making it more comfortable to understand in chart, we have decided to divided the share prices by 100)**

A) LARSEN

Average P/E (Yearly) (2012-2016)	24.1	19.5	19.6	27.5	33.9
Share Price (Yearly) (2012-2016)	8.74	8.95	13.67	15.69	13.45

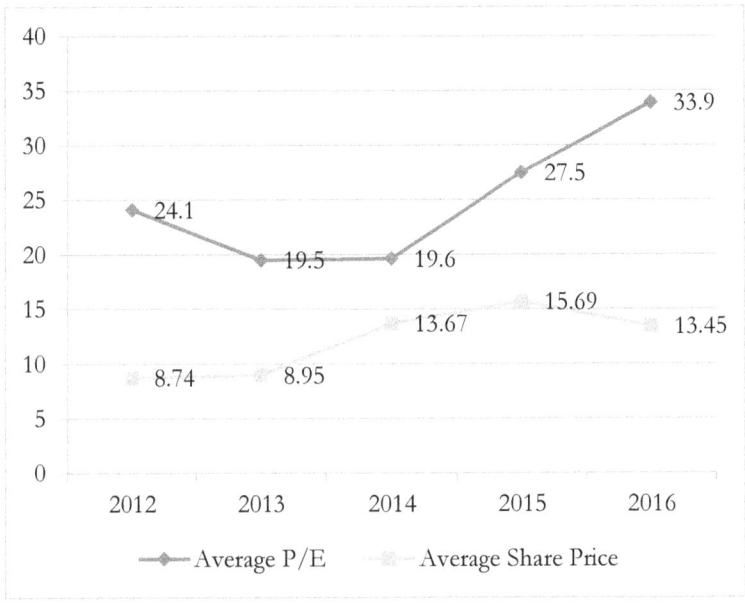

B) Adani Ports

Average P/E (Yearly)(2012-2016)	25.5	16.8	18.5	23.8	19.7
Share Price (Yearly)(2012-2016)	1.26	1.41	2.37	3.1	2.42

As we know that Industry P/E is the indicator for understanding the value of the stock. So from above analysis of two companies we can conclude that when the P/E ratio is low then there will be growth in share prices which can be seen from the same year or from next year and so on. So from this we can also add one more point that if P/E ratio is lower than it is good for stock because it tell us that stock is undervalued and have all the ability to grow. But still this is not only reason for price movements and investor need to look over other indicator too. Still P/E ratio is good for understanding valuation of the stock.

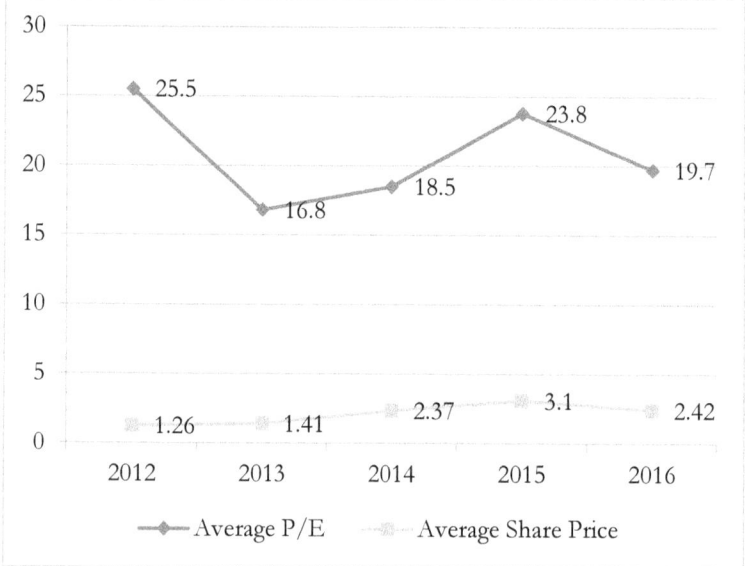

5) Profitability of the Company affects on Share Prices

As profit and loss account of a company matters a lot in the business because profit maximization is the ultimate goal of any company. So profitability of the company plays an extremely important role in price movement of any stock.

So now we will study the effect of quarterly results of Larsen and Toubro and Adani Ports and Special Economic Zone on their share price fluctuation.

A) LARSEN

We will study the price fluctuation on the same day and the day after Quarterly results and yearly audited results declaration (Based on last 2 Years consolidated data).
(A-Annual result, Q-Quarterly result)

Results Declaration date and Time	Conclusion of Result	Share Movement on Same day of results declaration (based on Adjusted Closing of that day)	Share Movement on next day of results declaration (Based on Adjusted Closing of that day)
28th Jan 2017 (2:20 Pm)(Q3)	L&T Q3 profit up 39%	Holiday on that Day	Up by 2.9 points
22nd Nov 2016(4:20 Pm)(Q2)	L&T Q2 profit up 84%	Down by 18.35 Points	Up by 27.7 points
29th July 2016 (7:42 Pm)(Q1)	L&T Q1 Profit up 46%	Up by 32.3 Points	Up by 16.15 Points
25th May 2016(A)	L&T annual profit up by 5.05% as com-pare to previous year on yearly basis	Up by 49.45 Points	Up by 182.55 Points
29th Jan 2016 (6:46 Pm)(Q3)	L&T Q3 net up 19%	Up by 27.15 Points	Up by 20.4 Points
30th Oct 2015 (2:13 Pm)(Q2)	Profit after tax increased 15.5 percent year-on-year to Rs 996 crore in July-September quarter and Adjusted profit fell 20 percent to Rs 686 crore Y-o-Y	Trading was off on that day for L&T	Down by 82.1 Points
31st July 2015 (5:04 Pm)(Q1)	Profit is expected to grow 4.5 percent Y-o-Y on adjusted basis and consolidated (reported) profit is seen falling 14.1 percent year-on-year	Up by 17.5 Points	Down by 11.85 Points
30th May 2015(A)	L&T annual profit down by 7.95% as com-pare to previous year on yearly basis	No trading on that day	Up by 51.1 points
9th Feb 2015(3 Pm)(Q1)	Q3 Profit down by 14.6% y-o-y	Down by 111.1 Points	Down by 1.15 Points

B) Adani Ports And Special Economic Zone

We will study the price fluctuation on the same day and the day after Quarterly results and yearly audited results declaration (Based on last 2 Years consolidated data). (A-Annual Result, Q-Quarterly Result)

Results Declaration date and Time	Conclusion of Result	Share Movement on Same day of results declaration (based on Adjusted Closing of that day)	Share Movement on next day of results declaration (Based on Adjusted Closing of that day)
14th Feb 2017(Q3)(5:52 Pm)	Adaniports Q3 profit up 25% on y-o-y basis	Down by 2.55 Points	Down by 7.05 Points
25th Oct 2016(Q2)(2:40 Pm)	Adaniports Q2 profit up 61% on y-o-y basis	Up by 27.15 Points	Down by 7.7 Points
9th August 2016(Q1)(3:20 Pm)	Adaniports Q1 profit up 31% on y-o-y basis	Down by 0.9 Points	Up by 18.7 Points
3rd May 2016(A)	Annual profit up by 21.74% on y-o-y basis	Up by 2.55 Points	Down by 27.25 Points
12th Feb 2016(Q3)(8:27 Pm)	Adaniports Q3 profit up 26% on y-o-y basis	Down by 8.8 Points	Up by 13.1 Points
2nd Nov 2015(Q2)(3:21 Pm)	Adaniports Q2 profit up 16% on y-o-y basis	Down by 0.7 Points	Down by 4.35 Points
10th Aug 2015(Q1)(3:31 Pm)	Adaniports Q1 profit up 12.8% on y-o-y basis	Down by 1 Points	Down by 6.75 Points
1st May 2015 (A)	Annual Profit up by 33.57% on y-o-y basis	Not traded	Up by 29.65 Points
28th Jan 2015(Q3)(1:37 Pm)	Adaniports Q3 profit up 13.7% on y-o-y basis	Down by 5.9 Points	Up by 4.9 Points

From above studies, we can easily predict that profit and loss of the company is the main base of price movement. And it also totally depend on the sentiments of the investor how they will consider profit and loss of the company. If the company results matches with the expectation of the investor then the price movement can be seen on positive side.

6) Government Policies

We know that authorities of any country plays an important role in the growth of economy by taking various steps in favor of the companies or few hard steps for better future of the country. So, our next factor is to basically check how much government policies have affect on the share price movement. For this we are taking a recent example i.e., **Demonetization**. On *8 November 2016 (20:15* IST), the Government of India announced the demonetization of all ₹*500* and ₹*1,000* banknotes. This was the sudden action taken by Government of India. Now we will studies the Demonetization affect on various indices of the Indian share market.

NIFTY50

Date	Open	High	Low	Close	Shares Traded	Turnover (₹ Cr)
07-Nov-2016	8535.75	8535.85	8481.45	8497.05	178070534	8436.70
08-Nov-2016	8540.00	8559.40	8480.10	8543.55	201759648	8515.57
09-Nov-2016	8067.50	8476.20	8002.25	8432.00	323968654	15536.37

As the announcement made after closing of the market, so its effect clearly seen on next day opening price which is around *500* points below then closing price of *8*th November *2016* and moreover there is huge increase in the turnover of *7020.8* Cr.

NIFTY REALITY

Date	Open	High	Low	Close	Shares Traded	Turnover (₹ Cr)
07-Nov-2016	198.25	199.95	197.90	198.60	31911057	246.88
08-Nov-2016	199.25	200.45	196.40	198.20	23908723	178.93
09-Nov-2016	175.45	177.55	164.50	175.20	145979327	966.12

As this step was taken to control the flow of black money, and real estate is the main source where black money was stored in different ways so it's important to studies the effect of Demonetization on real estate indices.

And from above table we can conclude that this sector also opened below from the previous day's closing.

And also look at the share traded number there is huge difference in the share traded between 8th November 2016 and 9th November 2016.

From above studies we can easily conclude that single policy made by the authority of any nation can be a reason for share price fluctuation.

Conclusion

Share price shows the value of the stock. And after analyzing the various factors involved in our study, we can say that share price fluctuation either depends on various factors or alone single factor is also responsible for share price movement. It's all depends on the sentiments of investor that what information matters them more.

We have taken six factors in our studies and all these factors somehow play an important role in share price fluctuations.

Every factor has its own importance in the way of price movement.

References

Larsen & Toubro and Adani ports & SEZ (Annual Reports, 2012-2016).

Kumar, S., & Mohan, M. *(1975)*. Determinants of share prices in India. Indian Economic Journal, *23(1)*, *23*.

Fama, E. F., & French, K. R. *(1989)*. Business conditions and expected returns on stocks and bonds. Journal of financial economics, *25(1)*, *23-49*.

Gillam, L., Ahmad, K., Ahmad, S., Casey, M., Cheng, D., Taskaya, T., & Manomaisupat, P. *(2002)*. Economic News and Stock Market Correlation: A Study of the UK Market. In Conference on Terminology and Knowledge Engineering.

Chen, N. F., Roll, R., & Ross, S. A. *(1986)*. Economic forces and the stock market. Journal of business, *383-403*.

Bondt, W. F., & Thaler, R. *(1985)*. Does the stock market overreact? The Journal of finance, *40(3)*, *793-805*.

Palomino, F. *(1996)*. Noise trading in small markets. The Journal of Finance, *51(4)*, *1537-1550*.

Fisher, G. R. *(1961)*. Some factors influencing share prices. The Economic Journal, *71(281)*, *121-141*.

King, B. F. *(1966)*. Market and industry factors in stock price behavior. The Journal of Business, *39(1)*, *139-190*.

Udegbunam, R. I., & Oaikhenan, H. E. *(1999)*. Fiscal Deficits and the Nigerian Stock Market: Theory and Empirical Evidence. Journal of Economic Management, *6(1)*, *41-69*.

CHAPTER 9
MOTIVE FOR MERGERS AND ACQUISITIONS IN THE INDIAN BANKING INDUSTRY

Tirth Raj, Shrekant Sharma and Pinky

Abstract

This research paper looks at Mergers and Acquisitions (M&A's) that have happened in Indian banking sector to understand the resulting synergies and the long term implications of the merger. Companies have been actively involved in mergers and acquisitions domestically as well as internationally. It is influence banks to gain global reach and effective synergy and allow banks to acquire the emphasize assets of weaker banks. A complete combination of two separate organization involving in a business is referred as business merger. Acquisitions on the other hand are take-over. In this case one company actually buys another company. Through Mergers and Acquisitions (M&A's) banks not only get established brand names, new geographies, complementary product offerings but also opportunities to cross sell to new accounts acquired. The process of Mergers and Acquisitions is not a new to the Indian Banking. The main objective of this paper is to assess the impact of Mergers and Acquisitions in Indian Banking Industry, their position before and after Mergers & Acquisitions and finding out the reasons behind these Mergers & Acquisitions (M&A's). Mergers & Acquisitions (M&A's) are the strategic growth devices in the hands of more and more Companies not only to stay in the competition but also to extend their margins, market share and dominance globally. The scale and the pace at which merger activities are coming up are remarkable. In the sense, mergers and acquisitions has become a strategic concept to grow quickly for a number of leading companies' world over. The booms in mergers and acquisitions suggest that the organizations are spending a significant amount of time and money either searching for companies to acquire or worrying about whether some other company will acquire them.

9.1. Motive for Mergers and Acquisitions in the Indian Banking Industry

Mergers and acquisitions (M&A's) are defined as consolidation of companies. It is differentiating the two terms, **Mergers** is the combination of two companies to form one, while **Acquisitions** is one company taken over by the other. M&A's is one of the major aspects of corporate finance world. Today, the banking industry is counted among the rapidly growing industries in India. In the last two decades, there has been paradigm shift in banking industries. A relatively new dimension in the Indian banking industry is accelerated through (M&A's). In order to attain the economies of scale and also to combat the unhealthy competition Consolidation of Indian banking sector through (M&A's) on commercial considerations and business strategies are the essential pre-requisite. Latest example of State Bank of India (SBI) 1 April was merger of State Bank of India (SBI) with five of its associate banks. The associate banks are State Bank of Bikaner and Jaipur (SBBJ), State Bank of Mysore (SBM), State Bank of Travancore (SBT), State Bank of Hyderabad (SBH) and State Bank of Patiala (SBP). After the merger, SBI set to be among the top 50 large banks of the world. SBI was ranked 52 in the world in terms of assets in 2015, according to Bloomberg, and a merger will see it break into the top 50. In India, the provisions relating to mergers and amalgamation and other schemes, Companies Act, 1956 and specifically, in sections 391to 395 of the companies Act, 1956 and in the rules 67 to 87of the companies (court) Rules, 1959.

9.2. Literature Review

Under this study an extensive review of literature has been carried out for the purpose of providing an insight into the work related to Mergers and Acquisitions (M&A's). Several studies have been conducted to examine the impact of M & A on different aspects of the banking sector.

Mehta Jay, Kakani Ram Kumar (2006) probed into various motivations behind mergers and acquisitions in the Indian Banking sector. The paper also looked at the international mergers and acquisition scenario and compared it with the Indian scene. **Anand Manoj & Singh Jagandeep (2008)** studied the impact of merger announcements of five banks in the Indian Banking Sector these mergers were the Times Bank merged with the HDFC Bank, the Bank of Madurai with the ICICI Bank, the ICICI Ltd with the ICICI Bank, the Global Trust Bank merged with the Oriental Bank of commerce and the Bank of Punjab merged with the centurion Bank. **Kuriakose Sony & Gireesh Kumar G.S (2010)** in their paper, assessed the strategic and financial similarities of merged Banks, and relevant financial variables of respective Banks were considered to assess their relatedness. The result of the study found that only private sector banks are in favor of the voluntary merger wave in the Indian Banking Sector. **Khan Azeem Ahmad (2011)** evaluated the performance of banks after merger in terms of Gross Profit Margin, net profit margin, operating profit margin, return on capital employed, debt equity ratio and return on equity. The results of the study suggested that after the merger the efficiency and performance of banks has improved. **Gupta Himani (2013)** analyzed the impact of mergers and acquisition on financial efficiency of banks in India by comparing selected pre and post-merger indices..

9.3. Merger And Acquisition Strategies

Acquisition or takeover is a popular strategic alternative adopted by Indian companies. For more than three decades after Independent, the normal route of growth was through licensing and setting up new project. The post- liberalization period has seen an increasing use of takeover strategies as the means of rapid growth. The real impetus for M&A strategies arose after the liberalization measures of 1991. The Monopolies and Restrictive Trade Practices (MRTP) Act was amended and no prior government permission was required to carry out M&A's. The securities Exchange Board of India (SEBI) introduce the substantial Acquisitions of share and Takeovers Regulations, 1994 that provided hostile takeovers. Another committee set up in 1996 known as the Bhagwati Committee, went into the issue of rationalizing the takeover.

9.4. Research Methodology

Primary and secondary data collection tools are used for the study. In the primary data collection direct observation has been used. Various web sites have been studied and observed and in the secondary data collection various study material (Books, Magazines, journals) and research works which have been done on mergers and acquisitions have been studied. Important and related data has been gathered and used for this research work the purpose of evaluation, investigation data is collected from Merger and Acquisitions (M&A's) of the Indian banking industry. The financial and accounting data of banks is collected from companies Annual Report to examine the impact of M&A's on the performance of banks. Financial data has been collected from National Stock Exchange (NSE), Securities and Exchange Board of India (SEBI), Bombay Stock Exchange (BSE) and other websites.

9.5. Objective

1. To Study The Trends Of (M&A's) in Indian banking sector.
2. To understand the purpose of mergers and acquisitions.

9.6. Sample Selection

The study analyses two major Banks undergone Mergers and acquisition (M&A's) these are:-
1. ICICI BANK
2. STATE BANK OF INDIA

9.7. Sources Of Data

The secondary data is collected for the study. The required data for the study were collected and compiled from the CMIE data base and the annual reports of the banks. The study covers a period from 2008-2017. In addition, the other required data were collected from various journals and magazines.

9.8. Merger And Acquisition In Indian Banking: Present Scenario

In the past three decades, India's banking system has earned several outstanding achievements to its credit. It is no longer confined to metropolises or cities in India. The first banks were Bank of Hindustan 1770-1829 and The General Bank of India, established 1786 and since defunct. The largest bank, and the oldest still in existence, is the State Bank of India, which originated in the Bank of Calcutta in June 1806, which almost immediately became the Bank of Bengal. This was one of the three presidency banks, the other two being the Bank of Bombay and the Bank of Madras, all three of which were established under charters from the British East India Company. The three banks merged in 1921 to form the Imperial Bank of India, which, upon India's independence, became the State Bank of India in 1955. The Government of India issued an ordinance and nationalized the14 largest commercial banks in 1969. These banks have 85 per cent of bank deposits in the country. A second round of nationalization of 6 more commercial banks took place in 1980. Later on, in the year 1993, the government merged New Bank of India with Punjab National Bank. On 1st April, 2017, State Bank of India, which is India's largest Bank merged with five of its Associate Banks (State Bank of Bikaner & Jaipur, State Bank of Hyderabad, State Bank of Mysore, State Bank of Patiala and State Bank of Travancore) and Bharatiya Mahila Bank with itself.

9.9. Reasons For Bank Merger

1) **Merger of weak banks**
   Practice of merger of weak banks with strong banks was going on in order to provide stability to weak banks. Mergers can diversify risk management.

2) **Reduce competition**
   Innovation of new financial products and consolidation of regional financial system are the reasons for merger. Markets developed and became more competitive and because of this market share of all individual firm reduced so mergers and acquisition started.

3) **New services and Products**
   Introduction of e- banking and some financial instruments. Removal of entry barrier opened the gate for new banks with high technology and old banks can't compete with them so they decide to merge.

4) **Skill & Talent**
   Transfer of skill takes place between two organization takes place which helps them to improve and become more competitive.

Table 1: List of Mergers And Acquisitions In Indian Banking Industry

Year in which the (M&A'S) took place	Name of the acquiring Bank	Bank targeted	Motive/Types
1996	State Bank of India	Kashinath Seth Bank	Forced Merger
2001	ICICI Bank	Bank of Madura	Voluntary Merger
2002	ICICI Bank	ICICI Limited	Voluntary merger
2006	ICICI Bank	Sangli Bank	Voluntary Merger
2008	State bank of India	State bank of Saurastra	Voluntary merger
2010	ICICI Bank Ltd	The Bank of Rajasthan	Acquisition
2010	State bank of India	State bank of Indore	Acquisition
2017	State Bank of India	State Bank of Bikaner & Jaipur (SBBJ) State Bank of Mysore (SBM), State Bank of Travancore (SBT), State Bank of Hyderabad (SBH) State Bank of Patiala (SBP)	Forced Merger

9.10. ICICI Bank

Industrial Credit and Investment Corporation of India Bank (ICICI) was originally promoted in 1994 by ICICI Limited, an Indian financial institution, and was its wholly-owned subsidiary. ICICI's shareholding in ICICI Bank was reduced to 46% through a public offering of shares in India in fiscal 1998, an equity offering in the form of ADRs listed on the NYSE in fiscal 2000, ICICI Bank's acquisition of Bank of Madura Limited in an all-stock amalgamation in fiscal 2001, and secondary market sales by ICICI to institutional investors in fiscal 2001 and fiscal 2002. ICICI was formed in 1955 at the initiative of the World Bank, the Government of India and representatives of Indian industry. ICICI Bank (Industrial Credit and Investment Corporation of India) is an Indian multinational banking and financial services company headquartered in Mumbai, Maharashtra, India, with its registered office in Vadodara. In 2014, it was the second largest bank in India in terms of assets and third in term of market capitalization.

Table 2: Key Financial Indicators of ICICI Bank
(In billion except per share data)

ICICI BANK	Mar 2017	Mar 2016	Mar 2015	Mar 2014	Mar 2013	Mar 2012	Mar 2011	Mar 2010	Mar ' 2009	Mar ' 2008
Net Interest income	217.37	164.75	190.40	212.24	138.66	107.34	90.17	81.14	83.67	73.04
Earnings per share (Diluted)	16.77	16.65	9.13	16.93	14.39	11.19	9.01	7.20	6.74	7.83
Earnings per share (Basic)	16.84	16.75	19.32	17.00	14.44	11.22	9.05	7.23	6.75	7.88
Total assets	7,717.91	7,206.95	6,461.29	5,946.42	5,367.95	4,890.69	4,062.34	3,634.0	3,79301	3,997.95
Equity capital &Reserves	999.51	897.36	804.29	732.13	667.06	604.05	550.91	516.18	495.33	464.71
Total capital adequacy ratio	17.4%^{2}	16.6%^{2}	17.0%^{2}	7.7%^{2}	18.7%^{1}	18.5%^{1}	19.5%^{1}	19.4%^{1}	15.5%^{1}	4.0%^{1}
Profit after tax	98.01	97.26	111.75	98.10	83.25	64.65	51.51	40.25	37.58	41.58
Dividend per share	2.50	5.00	5.00	4.60	4.00	3.30	2.80	2.40	2.20	2.20
Deposits	4,900.39	4,214.26	3,615.63	3,319.14	2,926.13	2,555.0	2,256.02	2,020.17	2,183.48	2,444.31
Advances	4,642.2	4,352.64	3,875.22	3,387.03	2,902.49	2,537.28	2,1636	1,812.06	2,183.11	2,256.16

Source- Bank Annual Report

9.11. Analysis And Interpretation

ICICI bank had undergone M&A four times and is now one of the leading bank in India with increasing financial status.Net interest income, earnings per share, total assets, total capital adequacy ratio, reserves & equity capital, profits after tax are showing a continuous increasing trend throughout ten years. Deposits reduced marginally from year 2009- 2011 but again increased in 2013.similarly advances also showed declining trend for year 2009-2011, but again increased in year 2013. Performance Review Quarter ended March 31, 2014 Consolidated profit after tax crosses the 10,000 crore milestone 18% year-on-year increase in standalone profit after tax to 9,810 crore (US$ 1.6 billion) for the year ended March 31, 2014 (FY2014) from 8,325 crore (US$ 1.4 billion) for the year ended March 31, 2013 (FY2013). 15% year-on-year increase in standalone profit after tax to 2,652 crore (US$ 443 million) for the quarter ended March 31, 2014 (2014) from 2,304 crore (US$ 385 million) for the quarter ended March 31, 2013 (2013) 15% year-on-year increase in consolidated profit after tax to 11,041 crore (US$ 1.8 billion) for FY 2014 from 9,604 crore (US$ 1.6 billion) for FY2013 Operating profit increased by 24% to 4,454 crore (US$ 743 million) for -2014 from 3,605 crore (US$ 602 million) for 2013. The Bank, whose financial statements reflect total assets of 1,407,430 million as at 31 March 2017, total revenues of `65,406 million for the year ended 31 March 2017 and net cash outflows amounting to `58,032 million for the year ended 31 March 2017. Total capital adequacy of 17.70% and Tier-1 capital adequacy of 12.77% as per Reserve Bank of India's guidelines on.

9.12. State Bank Of India

The roots of the State Bank of India lie in the first decade of the 19th century, when the Bank of Calcutta, later renamed the Bank of Bengal, was established on 2 June 1806. The Bank of Bengal and two other banks (Bank of Madras on 1 July 1843 and Bank of Bombay on 15 April 1840)) were amalgamated to form the Imperial Bank of India. On 1 July 1955, the Imperial Bank of India and SBI was created by an act of Parliament to succeed the Imperial Bank of India. State Bank of India (SBI) is an Indian multinational, **public sector** banking and **financial services** company.

Table 3: Key Financial Indicators of SBI Bank
(In billion except per share data)

SBI	2017	2016	2015	2014	2013	2012	2011	2010	2009	2008
Net Interest income	61,860	57,195	55,015	49,282	44,329	43,291	32,526	23,671	20,873	17,021
Return on Average Assets	0.41	0.46	0.68	0.65	0.97	0.88	0.71	0.88	1.04	1.01
Net profit	10,484	9,950	13,101	10,891	14,104	11,707	8,265	9,166	9121	9121
Return on Equity (%)	7.25	7.74	11.17	10.49	15.94	14.36	12.84	14.04	15.07	17.82
Earnings Per Share	13.15	12.98	17.55	145.88	206.20	184.31	130.16	144.37	143.77	126.62
Dividend Per SBI Share (Price)	2.60	2.60	3.5	30.00	41.50	35.00	30.00	30.00	29.00	21.50
Capital Adequacy Ratio	2,06,685	1,81,800	1,54,491	1,45,845	1,29,362	1,16,325	98,530	90,975	85,393	85,393
SBI Share (Price	293.40	194.25	267.05	1,917.7	2,072.75	2,096.35	2,765.3	2,078.2	1,067.1	1,600.25

Source- Bank Annual Report

9.13. Analysis And Interpretation

SBI is the first leading bank in India. The financial indicators like net interest income, earnings per share ,net profit were on increasing trend till year 2009-10 then it declined marginally during 2010-11.But after 2011-12 it shows a rising trend. The decline may be due to the cost of M&A during the year 2008 and 2010. FY14 OVER FY13- Operating Profit increased from Rs.40, 922 crores in FY13 to Rs.42, 097 crores in FY14 (2.87% YoY growth). Net Profit (after minority interest) decreased from Rs.17,916 ccrores in FY13 to Rs.14,174 crs in FY14(-20.89% YOY growth). Earnings per Share declined by 23.54% from Rs.267 in FY13 to o Rs.204 in FY 14.The Operating Profit of your Bank for FY2017 was at `50,847.90 crore as compared to `43,257.81 crore in FY2016. Your Bank posted a Net Profit of ` 10,484.10 crore for FY2017, as compared to ` 9,950.65 crore in FY2016, i.e. an increase of 5.36% even after higher provisioning requirements on NPAs. Previous year had resulted in significant rise in Non-Performing Assets (NPA) of the Bank. This increase during FY2017, was much lower from ` 98,173 crore to ` 1,12,343 crore The Gross NPA thus stood at 6.90% as on March 2017, up by 40 bps.

9.14. Suggestions

1. There is also a need that merger or large size is just a facilitator, but no guarantee for improved profitability.
2. The thrust should be on improving risk management capabilities, corporate governance and strategic business planning.
3. The strong banks should be merged with strong banks to compete with foreign banks and to enter in the global financial market.
4. The strong banks should not be merged with weak banks, as it will have adverse effect upon the asset quality of the stronger banks.

Conclusion

Merger is the useful tool for growth and expansion in Indian Banking Sector. There is also a need to note that merger or large size is just a facilitator, but no guarantee for improved profitability on a sustained basis. Hence, the thrust should be on improving risk management capabilities, corporate governance and strategic business planning. In the short run, attempt options like outsourcing, strategic alliances, etc. can be considered. Findings of this study suggest that trend of merger in Indian banking sector has so far been restricted to restructuring of weak and financially distressed banks. The Indian financial system requires very large banks to absorb various risks that have been emerged from operating in local and global market. The Government and policy makers should be more cautious in promoting merger as a way to reap economies of scale and scope. As a result, M&A's are considered as most strategic concepts to make sure growth for the companies in the corporate world.

References

Azar Kazmi (2011), "Merger and Acquisitions (M&A's) sin the strategic Management and Business Policy" pages no. 187-190.

Azeem Ahmad Khan (2011), "Merger and Acquisitions (M&As) in the Indian Banking Sector in Post Liberalization Regime", International Journal of Contemporary Business Studies.

Dr. Goyal K.A. & Joshi Vijay (2011), "Mergers in Banking Industry of India: Some Emerging Issues", Asian Journal of Business and Management Sciences, Issn: 2047-2528, Vol. 1 No. 2.

Gupta, Himani (2013) "Impact of Merger and Acquisitions on Financial Efficiency of Banks of India", MAIMS Journal of Management, Vol. 8 (1) April 2013, pp. 38-43.

Murthy, G. K. (2007). Some Cases of Bank Mergers in India: A Study. In Bose, J. (Ed.), Bank Mergers: The Indian Scenario. (244-259). Hyderabad.

www.wikipedia.com
www.investopedia.com
www.sbi.in
www.icicicom
www.moneycontrol.com
www.nseindia.com

CHAPTER 10
AWARENESS REGARDING LIFE INSURANCE: A CASE STUDY OF SHIMLA TOWN

Leena Devi and Ranjana

Abstract

Insurance is perceived by the common man as a risk protection measure. It is an arrangement by which individuals expose to certain contingencies get compensated financially when there is a loss. Life Insurance companies play an vary important role in the welfare of human well-being by providing protection to millions of people against life risk such as uncertain death or accident. Reforms in life insurance sector have opened up growth of private players but still their reach in rural market is comparatively nascent. The potential exist in the rural market is a great opportunity for the existing players. Few measures have been taken but with a population of 1.3 billion as on May 10, 2017 there is a huge gap between insurable population and insured population. At present 8-10% rural household are covered under life insurance schemes and remaining 90% can be targeted for the new innovative insurance schemes. The policies of life insurance are intangible in nature companies have to identify the means to make their services more tangible. There is a need to create a broader awareness about life insurance in all geographic areas in India through specific collective campaign.The success of the insurance companies depends on the awareness among policyholders about insurance products and satisfaction of the policyholders regarding services rendered by the insurance companies. This study is descriptive study. Data has been collected from a sample of 200 policyholders of various companies with the help of Questionnaire. This study mainly focuses on to the awareness level of the people of Shimla town, Himachal Pradesh. It also discusses various factors which may have any impact on awareness level. This study included various demographic and economic factors namely age, gender, marital status, level of education, household annual income and occupation. Results of analysis show that Education level and income has significant relationship with awareness level of people of Shimla whereas age, gender, marital status and occupation have no significant impact on awareness level.

10.1. Introduction

The origin of the concept of insurance is adumbrated in antiquity. Independent of its origin and antecedents, insurance today occupies an important place in the socio-economic life of all civic societies. The primary function of insurance is providing protection by assessing the risk and sharing the same with many by the process of sharing and thus, minimizing individual risk and its impact. Human life is a most pivotal asset and life insurance is generally considered as most important means of protecting one's family against the unforeseeable circumstance of the death of earning member. So, Life insurance is a must for everyone because life is very precious (NCAER,2011,sponsored by IRDA).Life insurance primarily deals with the death and its economic consequences.

Insurance sector is a booming sector and the penetration in Indian is quite low. Since the penetration of private companies and policies is low among the consumer, it is necessary to create awareness about life insurance policies and satisfaction among consumer. The Indian life insurance industry has achieved only a little because of the lack of insurance awareness, poor affordability and low investment in the life insurance products(Kathirvel and Radhamani 2014). The huge and ever rising population levels in our country provide an attractive opportunity but still nearly 70% Indian lives are un-insured. Hence present study is an attempt to find out the awareness level of people of Shimla (C. Balaji 2015).There is tremendous growth potential for life insurance sector in India as we have population and still the Indian life insurance market is untapped. Further, it indicates the growth prospects and a huge potential for life insurance business in country (vikas Gairola 2016).

10.2. Review of Literature

C. Balaji, (2015) in his study has discussed that the insurance sector is one of the most booming sector in India. He explains that penetration level of insurance in India is quite low when as compared to developed nations. Kathirvel and Radhamani (2014) believe that in spite of the healthy growth witnesses in the insurance sector in recent years and expansion of market, the inroad that life insurance has made into market remains lower in India than in many parts of world. The study has noted that improving insurance awareness requires both structuring and enhancing the penetration of an appropriate awareness creation campaign with a regional and spatial focus. Narender and Sampath (2014) also advocate the improvement of marketing strategies of Indian insurance companies as insurance is one of the leading sector in world economy. Jain and Goyal (2012) concluded that although uninsured might have heard of life insurance, there is a lack of knowledge about the various aspect of insurance even among policy holders. They also suggest that the government needs to create appropriate awareness and take necessary steps to protect the poor households. A Survey conducted by NCAER(2011), also reveal that only 38% among the uninsured households are unaware about life insurance and the awareness is lower among rural uninsured households (56.5%) as compared with urban uninsured households(66%).

10.3. Objectives

The objectives of the study are:
1. To understand and determine the awareness of people under study on insurance
2. To identify the factor that influences the responses of policyholders.

10.4. Research Methodology

The study is concluded using the following research

methodology:

The present study has been undertaken in Shimla Town. Selection of sample of respondents was made by following random sampling and on the whole a sample size of 260 respondents was planned from general public. The questionnaire were got filled from 260 respondents, out of which 200 was found to be suitable for the purpose of analysis. The data has been collected by administering the self-structured questionnaire. The analysis of the data collected has been carried out by using statistical tools like descriptive statistics, percentage and chi-square test to identify the factor determining the awareness of the life insurance.

10.5. Data Analysis And Interpretation

Table 1: Demographic Characteristic of Respondents

S.No	Factor	Demographics	No. of respondents	Percentage
1.	Gender	Male	121	60.5
		Female	79	39.5
		Total	200	100
2.	Age	Up to 30	55	27.5
		31 to 45	51	25.5
		46 to 60	56	28.0
		Above 60	38	19.0
		Total	200	100
3.	Education	Up to primary	25	12.5
		Up to secondary	32	16.0
		Up to Graduation	73	36.5
		Post graduation and above	70	35.0
		Total	200	100
4.	Occupation	Agriculture/Labour	22	11.0
		Business	60	30.0
		Govt. Employee	62	31.0
		Private Employee	56	28.0
		Total	200	100
5.	Annual Income	Less than 100000	84	42.0
		100000 to 300000	75	37.5
		Above 300000	41	20.5
		Grand Total	200	100

Source: primary probe

The profile of the respondents is shown in the above table. The profile focuses on the demographics of the respondents. It shows that Male constituted 60.5% and female 39.5% of the total respondents. 53% of the respondents belong to the age group of 31 to 60 years. As far the education level of the respondents is concerned, the highest education levels attained by most of respondents were educated with graduation degree qualification followed by master degree qualification. As per the classification occupation is concerned, the majority of policyholder are government employees. Based on family incomemost of respondents had annual income of less than 100000 42 %.

Table 2: Association between demographic factors and whether respondents are Aware about life insurance

S. No	Factor	Demographics	Awareness Yes	Awareness No	Total	
1.	Gender	Male	102 (84.2%)	19 (15.8%)	121	$P > .05$
		Female	62 (78.4%)	17 (21.6%)	79	χ^2-2.055
	Total		164	36	200	
2.	Age	Up to 30	44 (80%)	11 (20%)	55	$P > .05$
		31 to 45	38 (74.5%)	7 (24.5%)	51	χ^2-3.629
		46 to 60	44 (78.5%)	12 (21.5%)	56	
		Above 60	24 (63.1%)	14 (36.9%)	38	
	Total		164	36	200	
3.	Education	Up to primary	13 (52%)	12 (48%)	25	$P < .01$
		Up to secondary	19 (59.3%)	13 (40.7%)	32	$\chi^2$46.434
		Up to Graduation	63 (86.3%)	10 (13.7%)	73	
		Post graduation and above	69 (98.5%)	1 (1.5%)	70	
	Total		164	36	200	
4.	Occupation	Agriculture/Labor	13 (59%)	6 (41%)	22	$P > .05$
		Business	45 (75%)	15 (25%)	60	χ^2-4.533
		Govt. Employee	53 (85.4%)	9 (14.6%)	62	
		Private Employee	50 (89.2%)	6 (10.8%)	56	
	Grand Total		164	36	200	
5.	Annual Income	Less than 100000	59 (70.2%)	25 (29.8%)	84	$P < .01$
		100000 to 300000	65 (86.6%)	10 (13.4%)	75	$\chi^2$16.154
		Above 300000	40 (97.5%)	1 (2.5%)	41	
	Total		164	36	200	

Source: primary probe

Table 2 shows that majority of people in both gender are aware of life insurance i.e. Male (84.3%) and Female (78.5%). It is clear that males are more aware than females in Shimla although the difference is marginal. The awareness level is highest in young people and least in people above age 60 The chi-square value is insignificant at 5% level of significance for Age, occupation and Gender, which shows that there is no association between awareness level with age and gender factor. The rest other factor shows that there is a positive association with the awareness level.

Table 3: Association between demographic factors and whether respondents are insured or not

S.No	Factor	Demografics	Insured Yes	Insured No	Total	
1.	Gender	Male	72 (59.5%)	49 (40.5%)	121	$P > .05$
		Female	49 (62%)	30 (37.9%)	79	$\chi^2 - .127$
	Total		121	79	200	
2.	Age	Up to 30	27(49%)	28(51%)	55	$P > .05$
		31 to 45	36(70.5%)	15(29.4%)	51	$\chi^2 - 10.629$
		46 to 60	40(71.4%)	16 (28.5%)	56	
		Above 60	20(52.6%)	18(47.3%)	38	
	Total		121	79	200	
3.	Education	Up to primary	6 (24%)	19 (76%)	25	$P < .01$
		Up to secondary	12 (37.5%)	20 (62.5%)	32	$\chi^2 - 39.117$
		Up to Graduation	44 (60.2%)	29 (39.8%)	73	
		Post graduation and above	59 (84.3%)	11 (15.7%)	70	
	Total		121	79	200	
4.	Occupation	Agriculture/Labour	8 (36.3%)	14 (63.7%)	22	$P > .05$
		Business	33 (55%)	27 (45%)	60	$\chi^2 - 8.752$
		Govt. Employee	42 (67.7%)	20 (32.3%)	62	
		Private Employee	38 (67.8%)	18 (32.2%)	56	
	Total		121	79	200	
5.	Annual Income	Less than 100000	35 (41.7%)	49 (58.3%)	84	$P < .01$
		100000 to 300000	48 (64%)	27 (36%)	75	$\chi^2 - 30.645$
		Above 300000	38 (92.6%)	3 (7.4%)	41	
	Total		121	79	200	

Source: primary probe

In study, it was found out that majority of both groups in gender category are insured under life insurance policies i.e. female 62% and male 59.5%. The chi-square value shows that gender has no association with the taking up of life insurance policies. The difference in insurance level is on account of sampling fluctuations. Whereas rest of the demographic factors shows that there is a positive association with tendency of acquiring insurance policies. As the age and income increases, the tendency to take an insurance policy increases. Similarly higher the education level, there is much more chance that the individual will have a life insurance policy.

Table 4: Association between demographic factors and their opinion about necessity of life insurance

S. No	Factor	Demografics	Is Life insurance necessary Yes	No	Total	P value
1.	Gender	Male	77(63.6%)	44 (36.3%)	121	$P > .05$
		Female	43 (54.4%)	36 (45.6%)	79	$\chi^2 - 1.688$
		Total	120	80	200	
2.	Age	Up to 30	35 (63.6%)	20 (36.3%)	55	$P > .05$
		31 to 45	34 (75.5%)	11 (24.5%)	45	$\chi^2 - 9.32$
		46 to 60	26 (46.4%)	30 (53.6%)	56	
		Above 60	25 (56.8%)	19 (43.2%)	44	
		Total	120	80	200	
3.	Education	Up to primary	5 (20%)	20 (80%)	25	$P < .01$
		Up to secondary	13 (40.6%)	19 (59.4%)	32	$\chi - 34.56$
		Up to Graduation	45 (61.6%)	28 (38.3%)	73	
		Post graduation and above	57 (81.4%)	13 (18.6%)	70	
		Total	120	80	200	
4.	Occupation	Agriculture/Labour	8 (36.3%)	14 (63.6%)	22	$P > .05$
		Business	34 (56.6%)	26 (43.3%)	60	$\chi^2 - 7.376$
		Govt. Employee	42 (67.7%)	20 (32.3%)	62	
		Private Employee	36 (64.2%)	20 (35.8%)	56	
		Total	120	80	200	
5.	Annual Income	Less than 100000	39 (46.4%)	45 (53.6%)	84	$< .01$
		100000 to 300000	50 (66.6%)	25 (33.3%)	75	$\chi^2 - 12.252$
		Above 300000	31 (75.6%)	10 (24.4%)	41	
		Total	120	80	200	

Source: primary probe

Table 4 shows that majority of people in both gender are agreed with the statement that life insurance is necessary for everyone. Data also shows that Age and opinion regarding the necessity of life insurance for every human being are negatively associated means mostly young people agreed with this statement as compare to those with the higher age group. There is wide difference in the opinion of the respondents about this statement on the basis of their education level. The occupation is not associated with opinion whereas annual income is positively associated with the statement.

Table:5 shows that similarly majority of people among all age groups and both genders are unaware of IRDA and they are not independent and not associated with awareness of IRDA. Whereas, Education and Income shows a positive association with awareness level. No doubt, the awareness about IRDA and its role is low in each type of occupation yet the knowledge about it varies significantly among these occupations. So, the two attributes are not associated with each other.

Table 5: Association between demographic factors and whether respondents are aware about IRDA

S.No	Factor	Demografics	Awareness about IRDA Yes	Awareness about IRDA No	Total	P value
1.	Gender	Male	52 (42.9%)	69 (57.1%)	121	P >.05
		Female	30 (37.9%)	49 (62.1%)	79	χ^2 -.494
	Total		82	118	200	
2.	Age	Up to 30	25 (45.4%)	30 (54.6%)	55	P >.05
		31 to 45	24 (53.3%)	21 (46.7%)	45	χ^2 -6.958
		46 to 60	16 (28.5%)	40 (71.5%)	56	
		Above 60	17 (38.6%)	27 (61.4%)	44	
	Total		82	118	200	
3.	Education	Up to primary	3 (12%)	22 (88%)	25	P <.01
		Up to secondary	5 (15.6%)	27 (84.4%)	32	χ^2 -34.21
		Up to Graduation	28 (38.4%)	45 (61.6%)	73	
		Post graduation and above	46 (65.7%)	24 (34.3%)	70	
	Total		82	118	200	
4.	Occupation	Agriculture/Labour	5 (22.7%)	17 (77.3%)	22	P >.05
		Business	22 (36.6%)	38 (63.3%)	60	χ^2 -5.151
		Govt. Employee	28 (45.1%)	34 (54.9%)	62	
		Private Employee	27 (48.2%)	29 (51.8%)	56	
Total			82	118	200	
5.	Annual Income	Less than 100000	23 (27.3%)	61 (72.7%)	84	P <.01
		100000 to 300000	34 (45.3%)	41 (54.7%)	75	χ^2 -14.43
		Above 300000	25 (60.9%)	16 (39.1%)	41	
	Total		82	118	200	

Source: primary probe

Conclusion

The insurance sector has come into sharp focus in India in the recent years due to the phenomenal changes taking place in tern of new private companies entering and offering new products. Even among uninsured, 58.2% have heard of life insurance. Although many might have heard regarding life insurance, there is lack of knowledge about various aspect of insurance even among policy holders (Jain & Goyal, 2012). An analysis based on demographic and economic parameters enable an understanding of the categories of people which are aware and insured with insurance. Study shows that Education and Income Level have significant association with awareness and getting insurance policy. That throw light on the fact that companies should make insurance easy to understand and affordable for people with lower education and lower income. The success and overall growth potential of the insurance business depends on the efforts being made by insurance companies, to come up with new range of policies which suits lower income group.

References:

Arunajatesan,(2001) Risk management & Insurance: Concept and Practices of Life and General Insurance,pp-3,

Balaji, C., (2015) customer awareness and satisfaction of life insurance policy holders with reference to Mayiladuthurai town, International Journal of Multidisciplinary research and Development,2(1), 145-147.

chaudhary, S., (2016). Consumer perception regarding Life Insurance Policies: A Factor Analytical Approach, Pacific Business review International, 9(6), 42- 48.

Jain, D., & Gayal, N.,(2012).An Empirical Study of the level of Awareness Toward Various Rights And Duties Among The Insured Households in Rajasthan, India, Journal of Arts, Science & Commerce, 3(2), 40-49

Kathirvel, N., & Radhamani, S., (2014). Policyholder's awareness of LIC's services with reference to Tirupur District, Tamilnadu, International Journal Of Engineering inventions, 17-22.

Narender, S., & Sampath, L., (2014). Consumer Awareness toward life insurance sector in India, 3(3), 45-51.

Murthy, S., R., & Kumar, N., P., (2015). Agent' Perception towards Life Insurance Corporation of India, International Journal of Multidisciplinary Advanced Research Trends, 2(2), 35-41.

Reddy, P., R., & Jahangir, Y.,(2015). Customer perception toward life insurance services in rural market, Indian Journal of applied Research, 1(1), 272-275.

Saxena, G., & Sharma, P., (2017) Penetration of life insurance sector in India, IJERMT, 6(4), 239-241.

Unas, A., W., & Kumar, S., R., (2015). A study on policyholders Satisfaction On service Of LIC: reference to Coimbatore District, International journal of Informative and futuristic research. 2(10), 3620-3626.

CHAPTER 11
KNOWLEDGE AND CONCERNS AMONG MILLENNIALS OF NORTH INDIA REGARDING ONLINE ADVERTISING

Sahil Gupta and Rajesh Kumar

Abstract

Purpose – *This article studies the knowledge about Online advertising among the millennials of North India, as with the increase in mobile and Internet penetration in every corner of the country, the online space is within the reach of every individual specially the youth which are more Tech-savvy. Even with this rapid growth India is still lagging behind in the cyber space, so this study explores the knowledge and the concerns specially the privacy related concerns among the users.*

Design/methodology/approach – *Data from a survey of 278 online consumers were used to study the knowledge about online advertisement and privacy concerns. Using a 5 point Likert scale respondents submitted their responses on a standardized scale. With the help of appropriate tools ranks and importance of various privacy concerns are measured and knowledge about online advertising was rated.*

Findings – *Findings of the study results reveal that the awareness level and knowledge is still inadequate to attain understanding of this new advertising technique. Also from the findings shows that youth despite of the fact is exposed to latest tools and technique still is not fully aware in terms of privacy concerns.*

Research limitations/implications – *Future research can be conducted using different methodologies, such as interviews, focus groups discussion and expert talks to study the knowledge and various privacy concerns among the users as the results are indicating that youth is still unaware of various loophole and privacy issues.*

11.1. Introduction

"We have technology, finally, that for the first time in human history allows people to really maintain rich connections with much larger numbers of people." – Pierre Omidyar, founder, eBay. This involvement of technology into marketing and its sub dimensions has change the world tremendously. Peng et. al., 2014 revels that with the growth of new information sources and channels and devices people are shifting towards new mediums for the information now a day. Nowadays, advanced technology allows for the tracking of customer's shopping behaviour in browsing websites by using 'cookies'(Alreck et al. 2007). Then the advertisement of the products or services that users had browsed will be displayed on other websites. This advertising method is called online behavioural targeting.

Online behavioural advertising empowers the company to showcase the advertisement to the target population and it enable to extract the information about these consumers. However, it can be seen as an invasion of people's privacy. There are also some privacy worries in the context of behavioural targeted advertising (Alreck et al. 2007; Goldfarb & Tucker 2011).

Online behavioural advertising involves the collection and analysis of information about consumers' online behaviour for marketing-related purposes such as serving targeted ads or developing purchase propensity models (Sotto, L. J., & McLellan, M. J. ,2012).

With the increase in the sales of smartphone handset and increasing penetration of internet specially the way private player like Reliance JIO, Airtel and even Indian government has taken various initiative of "Digital India" people specially the youth is now more diverted to online environment. In recent years we have seen a huge increase in the usage of Smart phone, in many parts of globe this increase is rapid due to high penetration of new technology in communication.

Statistics shows, children in United States now are more likely to own a mobile phone than a book, with 85% of kids owning a phone as to only 73% owning books while in India mobile Internet users are expected to cross the 300 million mark by 2017 from 159 million users at present (IAMAI,2015). Looking at this massive opportunity the marketer is using this space to advertise their products in more customise and lucrative manners. They are advertising to various website with different formats, which in result leads to behavioural advertising. Indians are not behind in using Twitter and Facebook, showing the highest growth in social networking of about 37.4 per cent in 2016.

The other side leads to privacy concern among the users where are concerns whether the information taken in online environment will be misused. Akhter, S. H. (2014) Says that Although privacy concern is considered a serious dimension for online consumer behaviour, a review indicates that very less studies are conducted to measure its psychological antecedents.

Barwise and Strong (2002), Tsang, Ho, and Lian (2004), and Rettie, Grandcolas, and Deakins (2005) examine consumers' reception of permission-based advertising in the form of SMS; as it has seen that unknown messages sent to consumers likely irritate receivers (Okazaki and Taylor 2008).

Okazaki, S., Li, H., & Hirose, M. (2009)., suggests marketers should also bring in a technology to enhance their spam blocking mechanism because these spam may be harmful in legal issues also.

Phelps et al. (2001), in the direct marketing context, found that with positive attitudes the privacy concern is reduced, while desire gas increased for information control. With growth of social networking websites, like Twitter and Facebook, it individual prerogative that what amount of information he/she wants to share with the world. These websites earn high commercial profits by using the information shared by user on their profile and updates (Quinn 2009). However, Yang, H. (2012). States its inappropriate to use, sneak the personal data shared on these social websites.

11.2. Objective Of The Study

The objective of the study is to measure and study the awareness level of security concerns and knowledge levels towards online advertising among the millennials of North India. We all are exposed to various types of advertisement in our day to day life and too in various forms, these days along with traditional medias online media and online environment is playing a crucial role as technology has reaching in every corner of the country. With increase in mobile user and Internet penetration the online advertising is reaching in everyone reach along with it has certain security concerns. So this study tries to capture the knowledge levels and awareness regarding various security issues.

11.3. Methodology

A comprehensive study has been conducted to capture the knowledge level and concerns in online advertising. Theoretical foundation of the study is based on secondary sources such as research papers, articles, magazines and articles on consumer buying behaviour, for this purpose databases like EBSCO, ProQuest were used.

The Study is both exploratory and descriptive in nature. A questionnaire has been designed in which questions related awareness, behavioural security and privacy. In total 278 questionnaires were distributed in Tricity i.e. Panchkula, Chandigarh, and Mohali districts but only 226 could be filled in with response rate of 82%.

The data was collected from the universities in the Tricity and adjoining area i.e Punjab University, Chandigarh University, Chitkara University, Punjab Engineering Collage, Government collage Panchkula, DAV collage, Elante Mall and through social networking website like Facebook also. Our target population was majorly youth of age between 18-30 years. The respondents were approached randomly initially in offline mode and in online mode questioner was circulated in communities.

Eight variables related to awareness and behavioural and Ten variable related to security variables rated from 1 to 5 by respondents according to their importance. 'Totally Disagree' variables were rated 5, while 'Totally Agree' variables were rated

11.4. Results And Discussion

11.4.i. Frequency of Internet Usage

The collected data shows that the on an average 57 % percent of the respondents are using internet quite frequently ie they are spending more than 6 hours on internet. This is may be due to the respondents of this age bracket is high on social networking, chatting, surfing. About 37% percent users are using internet between 2-4 hours daily and about 6 percent of respondents are using internet less than 2 hours daily. This data itself supports to type of internet services available in last 6 months and due to high increase in the no of smartphone users.

11.4.ii. Preferred usage Type

After analysing the responses, the usage of internet among the respondents were found to be, Social Networking website, Search Engine, Video portals (YouTube etc.), blogs were found to be 83 %, 72 % 48% and 23% respectively. The role of mobile based apps seen quite crucial as apps of social networking sites and video portals are easily available which directly impacts the usage patterns and frequency of a particular type of site.

11.4.iii. Importance of Different Attributes:

Respondents rated twenty attributes from 1-5 according to their importance. Descriptive statistics show that the attributes with higher mean are perceived to be more important by respondents.

11.4.iv. Awareness and Behaviour towards Online advertisement

The responses were collected on the standardized scale given by McDonald and Cranor (2010) and by Turow et al. (2009).

Table 1 represents that respondents in high numbers are not aware companies are collected and storing information but yes the mean score of 3.8 shows respondents agree to this that websites are customizing the advertisement as per the user. Respondents are agree on to punishing the company for gathering and storing the user information.

Table 1: Awareness and Behaviour towards Online advertisement.

Sr. No	Variables	Mean Score
1	When I visit a website, I see the same ads as someone else visiting that website	2.1

2	Companies should only gather and store information about my Internet use (such as search terms, visited sites, online purchases) when I give them permission to do so (reverse Coded)	4.2
3	The ads that appear on a website differ per visitor	3.8
4	It is punishable for companies to gather and store information about the Internet use of individuals.	4.7
5	Your browsing history determines which ads you are going to see during your next visit	2.8
6	Companies are allowed to store information about Internet use, provided that it is not traceable to a person	2.1
7	Companies create different user segments based on their Internet behaviour, and they show these groups targeted ads	1.8
8	Online content and services can be offered for free because of online advertising revenues	3.2

11.4.v. Awareness towards privacy and security concerns

The result regarding respondent's awareness towards security and privacy table 2 shows the result. The responses are collected on the scale given by Baek and Morimoto (2012) and McDonald and Cranor (2010).

Above table shows respondents are highly unaware of the role of cookies and what potential harm it can does to user and user are quite sensitive to information sharing too. Respondents believes that personal data gat misused, while they also fear for them to be saved securely.

Table 2: Awareness towards privacy and security concerns

Sr. No	Variable	Mean Score
1	Cookies collect browsing history; they save the websites you visited	3.1
2	A virus scanner prevents companies from storing information based on search behaviour, visited	4.2

	websites and online purchases	
3	My browsing history is being saved by means of cookies	2.8
4	Cookies are used to place ads based on your Internet behaviour	2.1
5	Software can ensure that cookies are automatically removed	1.2
6	Cookies ensure, for instance, that your passwords are being store	1.5
7	Cookies are person-based; it is possible to relate the stored information to an individual	1.7
8	I believe that personal data have been misused too often	3.6
9	I worry about receiving ads in which I am not interested	3.9
10	I am concerned about the potential misuse of personal data	4.5
11	I fear that information has not been stored safely	3.6
12	I feel uncomfortable when data are shared without permission	4.6

Conclusion

The study conducted to check the awareness level among the millennials shows people are still highly unaware about the new technique used in the online advertising and also highly unaware about the cookies stored in their own PC, which store several type of information. Although with increase in the reach of smartphone and high speed internet in India people are getting used to latest technology but this lack of awareness can be dangerous sometimes.

Future research can be carried out while including other factors to check the awareness among their various left over dimensions in online advertisement.

References

Akhter, S. H. (2014). Privacy concern and online transactions: The impact of internet self-efficacy and internet involvement. *The Journal of Consumer Marketing, 31*(2), 118-125. doi:http://dx.doi.org/10.1108/JCM-06-2013-0606

Alnahdi, S., Ali, M., & Alkayid, K. (2014). The effectiveness of online advertising via the behavioural targeting mechanism. Paper presented at the, 5(1) 23-31. Retrieved from https://search.proquest.com/docview/1558853925?accountid=147490

Alreck, PL & Settle, RB 2007,'Consumer reactions to online behavioural tracking and targeting', Journal of Database Marketing & Customer Strategy Management, vol. 15, pp. 11-23.

Baek, T. H., & Morimoto, M. (2012). Stay away from me: Examining the determinants of consumer avoidance of personalized advertising. Journal of Advertising, 41(1), 59–76.

Barwise, P., & Strong, C. (2002). Permission-based mobile advertising. *Journal of interactive Marketing, 16*(1), 14-24.

Hsin Chang, H., Rizal, H., & Amin, H. (2013). The determinants of consumer behavior towards email advertisement. *Internet Research, 23*(3), 316-337.

McDonald, A. M. & Cranor, L. F. (2010). American's attitudes about internet behavioral advertising practices. In Proceedings of the 9th workshop

Okazaki, S., Li, H., & Hirose, M. (2009). Consumer Privacy Concerns And Preference For Degree Of Regulatory Control: A study of mobile advertising in japan. *Journal of Advertising, 38*(4), 63-77. Retrieved from https://search.proquest.com/docview/236467131?accountid=147490

Peng, J., Zhang, G., Zhang, S., Dai, X., & Li, J. (2014). Effects of online advertising on automobile sales. *Management Decision, 52*(5), 834-851.

Peng, J., Zhang, G., Zhang, S., Dai, X., & Li, J. (2014). Effects of online advertising on automobile sales. *Management Decision, 52*(5), 834-851. Retrieved from https://search.proquest.com/docview/1633967290?accountid=147490

Phelps, J., Nowak, G., & Ferrel, E. (2000). Privacy concerns and consumer willingness to provide personal information. Journal of Public Policy & Marketing, 19(1), 27–41

Quinn, L. (2009), "Market segmentation in managerial practice: a qualitative examination", Journal of Marketing Management, Vol. 25 Nos 3/4, pp. 253-72.

Ratten, V. (2015). Social Cognitive Theory and the Technology Acceptance Model in the Cloud Computing Context: The Role of Social Networks, Privacy Concerns and Behavioural Advertising. In *Adoption of Innovation* (pp. 43-56). Springer International Publishing.

Rettie, R., Grandcolas, U., & Deakins, B. (2005). Text message advertising: Response rates and branding effects. *Journal of targeting, measurement and analysis for marketing, 13*(4), 304-312.

Smit, E. G., Van Noort, G., & Voorveld, H. A. (2014). Understanding online behavioural advertising: User knowledge, privacy concerns and online coping behaviour in Europe. *Computers in Human Behavior, 32*, 15-22.

Sotto, L. J., & McLellan, M. J. (2012). Online behavioral advertising: A user's guide. *The IP Litigator : Devoted to Intellectual Property Litigation and Enforcement, 18*(6), 1-5. Retrieved from https://search.proquest.com/docview/1239269255?accountid=147490

Turow, J., King, J., Hoofnagle, C. J., Bleakley, A., & Hennessy, M. (2009). Americans reject tailored advertising and three activities that enable it. Annenberg School of Communication, Departmental Papers. <http://ssrn.com/abstract=1478214>.

Yang, H. (. (2012). Young American Consumers' Prior Negative Experience Of Online Disclosure, Online Privacy Concerns, And Privacy Protection Behavioral Intent. *Journal of Consumer Satisfaction, Dissatisfaction and Complaining Behavior, 25*, 179-202. Retrieved from https://search.proquest.com/docview/1288743191?accountid=147490

CHAPTER 12
FINANCIAL INCLUSION THROUGH PRADHAN MANTRI JAN DHAN YOJANA – AN EMPERICAL ANALYSIS

Rajneesh Kumar Sharma

12.1. Introduction

Financial inclusion enables improved and better sustainable economic and social development of the country. It helps in the empowerment of the underprivileged, poor and women of the society with the mission of making them self-sufficient and well informed to take better financial decisions. The financial inclusion takes into account the participation of vulnerable groups such as weaker sections of the society and low income groups, based on the extent of their access to financial services such as savings and payment account, credit insurance, pensions etc. Also the objective of financial inclusion exercise is easy availability of financial services which allows maximum investment in business opportunities, education, savings for retirement, insurance against risks, etc. by the rural individuals and firms. Chakraborty (2011), define the financial inclusion is the process of ensuring access to appropriate financial products and services needed by all sections of society including vulnerable groups such as weaker sections and low income groups at an affordable cost in a fair and transparent manner by mainstream institutional players. This issue started gaining importance recently in the news media.

The Pradhan Mantri Jan Dhan Yojana is an ambitious scheme that will provide a host of benefits including a bank account, insurance and a debit card for all. It is a mega financial inclusion plan under which bank accounts and RuPay debit cards with inbuilt insurance cover of Rs 1 lakh will be provided to crores of persons with no access to formal banking facilities. The ambitious scheme aims to bring poor people into the ambit of the Government's financial programme. It will cover both urban and rural areas and those who open account would get Domestic Debit Card (Ru-pay card). The long term vision of the Jan Dhan Yojana is to lay the foundation of a cashless economy and is complementary to Narendra Modi's Digital India Scheme. Planning Commission (2009), financial inclusion refers to universal access to a wide range of financial services at a reasonable cost. These include not only banking products but also other financial services such as insurance and equity products. The household access to financial services includes access to contingency planning, credit and wealth creation. Access to contingency planning would help for future savings such as retirement savings, buffer savings and insurable contingencies and access to credit includes emergency loans, housing loans and consumption loans. On the other hand, access to wealth creation includes savings and investment based on household's level of financial literacy and risk perception.

12.2. Review of Literature

The achievement of objectives of the study, the related literature has been reviewed because no research can be completed in itself without its scientific analysis of literature. The review of concerned literature has been completed by taking the help of journals, abstracts, books, web-sites and reports etc. the number of studies related to the PMJDY have been analyzed to identify main gaps in literature.

A group of studies undertaken by **Rajnikanta (2014), Harpreet and Nain (2014), Achala and Getanjali (2015), Shanti (2015) and Bijoyata (2016),** concluded that the PMJDY was a National Mission on financial inclusion which was concentrated on individual household with an aim to provide formal financial support through the organized financial system.

The studies undertaken by **Brij (2014), Ashish and Amrita**

(2014), Sanjay Tiwari (2015), K. K. Tripathy (2015) and Rajesh & Sarvesh (2016) observed that the PMJDY has created a positive environment and has provided a big push to the government's objective of universal financial inclusion. The success of this Yojana will be judged on the basis of (a) expanding formal banking up till the doorsteps of the rural borrowers (b) making the financing in rural areas profitable and viable.

12.3. Objectives of the Study

The main objectives of the study as under:
1. To Study the Awareness of the Respondents about the PMJDY in Himachal Pradesh.
2. To Analyze the Respondents Opinion Regarding Benefits Available under PMJDY.
3. To find out the problems faced by the beneficiaries of the PMJDY and advanced suggestions overcome such problems.

12.4. Methodology Adopted

In order to study the performance of PMJDY and to know the accrued benefits, a sample of 100 customers have been taken. Since the study is based on Hamirpur district of Himachal Pradesh, the sample for the study has taken from the customers who have opened their accounts under the PMJDY scheme in different branches consisting of five commercial banks and one cooperative bank operating in the district. In all, a sample of 100 customers has taken with the help of convenience sampling from the banks selected for study. While selecting the sample, an utmost care was taken that the respondents of all ages, qualifications, sex and occupation were taken into consideration and regional and geographical variations are also duly represented. Consistent with the objective of the study, different techniques like the simple percentage, mean, standard deviation, skewness, kurtosis and chi-square have been used for the analysis of the collected data.

12.5. Result And Discussion

12.5.i. Awareness of PMJDY among Respondents

Table observed that 88 percent of respondents are aware about the PMJDY, out of which maximum number of respondents fall under semi urban area i.e. 95.5 percent, followed by 91.7 percent respondents from urban area and 81 percent respondents are rural area that aware about the PMJDY. It reveals that 19 percent respondents of rural area are not aware to PMJDY, and 8.3 percent of respondents of urban and 4.5 percent of respondents under semi urban reports that they don't know PMJDY. The mean value of the opinion of the respondents is more than the average standard score, which also supports the above opinion. The negative values of skewness also depict that the opinion of the respondents is scattered more towards the higher side of the standard average score 2. The calculated value of kurtosis also supports the above opinion.

Table 1: Awareness of PMJDY among Respondents

Residential Background	Responses			Total	Mean	σ	SKW	Kurtosis
	Yes	No	Do not know					
Rural	34 (81.0)	8 (19.0)	0 (0.0)	42 (100.0)	2.810	0.3974	-1.635	0.706
Semi-urban	21 (95.5)	0 (0.0)	1 (4.5)	22 (100.0)	2.909	0.4264	-4.690	22.00
Urban	33 (91.7)	0 (0.0)	3 (8.3)	36 (100.0)	2.833	0.5606	-3.148	8.371
Total	88 (88.0)	8 (8.0)	4 (4.0)	100 (100.0)	2.840	0.4654	-2.996	8.323

Chi – Square (d.f = 4) Value = 14.865 Table Value = 9.48 P Value = .005

Source: Field Survey

Note: Figure in brackets shows percentage

The computed value of the chi-square is 14.865 and table value is 9.48 (P-value 0.005) which is found less than table value at 5% level of significance. Therefore null hypothesis is rejected and there is found significant relationship between the residence place of respondents and their awareness about PMJDY.

12.5.ii. Respondents Opinion Regarding Benefits Available under PMJDY

In the following paragraph, an attempt has been made to analyse the account holder's views and their awareness about the benefits available under PMJDY on the basis of educational qualification.

12.5.iii. Benefits Available to Account Holders under PMJDY- Interest on Deposit

Table 2 shows that there are 62 percent respondents replied 'yes' about the benefits available to account holder under PMJDY – interest on deposit, out of which,72.7 percent respondents are qualified up to matric, 54.5 percent respondents are graduate and above and 50 percent respondents are illiterate. It shows that majority of the respondents are of the opinion that they know that account holder under PMJDY will get benefit in the form of interest on deposit amount.

Table 2: Benefits Available to Account Holders under PMJDY- Interest on Deposit

Education on level	Responses			Total	Mean	σ	SKW	Kurtosis
	Yes	No	Do not know					
Illiterate	6 (50.0)	2 (16.7)	4 (33.3)	12 (100.0)	2.167	0.938	-0.383	-1.931
Up to Matric	32 (72.7)	8 (18.2)	4 (9.1)	44 (100.0)	2.636	0.650	-1.599	1.348
Graduation and Above	24 (54.5)	10 (22.7)	10 (22.7)	44 (100.0)	2.318	0.829	-0.668	-1.212
Total	62 (62.0)	20 (20.0)	18 (18.0)	100 (100.0)	2.440	0.608	-0.590	-0.557

Chi – Square (d.f = 4) Value = 5.847 Table Value = 9.48 P Value = .211
Source: Field Survey
Note: Figure in brackets shows percentage

While, 22.7 percent respondents comes under the group of graduation and above, Nearly 18.2 percent respondents of up to matric, about 16.7 percent respondents among the illiterate did not know about the PMJDY that the benefits available to account holder under PMJDY – interest on deposit account. Almost 33.3 percent respondent's are illiterate, nearly 22.7 percent respondents come under graduation and above and 9.1 respondents under up to matric are replied don't know about it. The values of mean, skewness and kurtosis also support the above analysis. The computed value of chi-square is 5.847 at and table value is 9.48 which have found less than table value therefore null hypothesis is accepted and there is found insignificant relationship at 5% level of significance. So it is concluded that there is found insignificant relationship between the education level of respondents and their awareness about PMJDY that the benefits available to account holder under PMJDY – interest on deposit account.

12.5.iv. Benefits under PMJDY to Account Holders - Accidental Insurance of Rs 1 Lakh

Table 3 observed that 74 percent of respondents are aware to PMJDY, out of which, majority of respondents 81.8 percent come under the group of up to matric followed by 72.7 percent from graduation and above, 50 percent among illiterate are aware about the benefits available to account holders under PMJDY – accidental insurance of Rs.1 lakh.

Table 3: Benefits Available to Account Holders under PMJDY- Accidental Insurance of Rs 1 Lakh

Education level	Responses			Total	Mean	σ	SKW	Kurtosis
	Yes	No	Do not know					
Illiterate	6 (50.0)	0 (0.0)	6 (50.0)	12 (100.0)	2.000	1.044	0.000	-2.444
Up to Matric	36 (81.8)	6 (13.6)	2 (4.5)	44 (100.0)	2.770	5.522	-2.307	4.683
Graduation and Above	32 (72.7)	8 (18.2)	4 (9.1)	44 (100.0)	2.636	0.650	-1.599	1.348
Total	74 (74.0)	14 (14.0)	12 (12.0)	100 (100.0)	2.262	0.693	-1.557	0.918

Chi – Square (d.f = 4) Value = 20.329 Table Value = 9.48 P Value = .000
Source: Field Survey

Note: Figure in brackets shows percentage

While 18.2 percent of respondents under graduation and above, 13.6 percent of respondents up to matric, are not aware about that benefits available to account holders under PMJDY – accidental insurance of Rs.1 lakh. Almost 50 percent of the respondents' among illiterate, 9.1 percent respondents among graduate and above, 4.5 percent respondents among up to matric are replied don't know. The mean scores of the respondents of each qualification level shows that it is above the mean standard score. The negative values of skewness also point out that the majority majority of the opinions of the respondents are highly concentrated towards the higher side on the three point scale.

The values of mean, skewness, standard deviation and kurtosis also support the above analysis. On application of chi-square test it has been found to be 20.329 at corresponding P-value 0.000 is less than the 0.050. It is significant at 5% level of significance. So it is concluded that there is significant relationship between the education level of respondents and their awareness about the benefits available to account holders under PMJDY – accidental insurance of Rs.1 lakh.

12.5.v. Views of Account Holders under PMJDY- Overdraft Limit upto Rs 5000/- After 6 Months

It is reveals from the table that majority of respondents i.e. 86.4 percent up to matric, 77.3 percent respondents' come under graduate and above, nearly 33.3 percent are illiterate respondents aware about the benefits available to account holders under PMJDY – overdraft limits upto Rs.5000 after 6 month. While 22.7 percent respondents come under graduation and above, approximately 16.7 percent respondents' are illiterate and 9.1 percent respondents up to matric do not aware about the benefits available to account holders under PMJDY – overdraft limits upto Rs.5000 after 6 month. Almost 50 percent respondents among the illiterate respondents followed by 4.5 percent respondents' among the up to matric are replied don't know about it.

The individual mean score of each educational group depicts that it is above the mean standard score. It supports the above analysis. The negative values of skewness of each group of educational level also support the above finding. The computed value of chi-square test is 36.703 and value is 9.48 which are found less than the calculated value therefore null hypothesis is rejected and there is found significant relationship at 5% level of significance.

Table 4: Views of Account Holders under PMJDY- Overdraft Limit upto Rs 5000/- After 6 Months

Education level	Responses			Total	Mean	σ	SKW	Kurtosis
	Yes	No	Do not know					
Illiterate	4 (33.3)	2 (16.7)	6 (50.0)	12 (100.0)	1.833	0.937	-0.383	-1.931
Up to Matric	38 (86.4)	4 (9.1)	2 (4.5)	44 (100.0)	2.818	0.495	-2.805	7.312
Graduation and Above	34 (77.3)	10 (22.7)	0 (0.0)	44 (100.0)	2.772	0.424	-1.348	-1.194
Total	76 (76.0)	16 (16.0)	8 (8.0)	100 (100.0)	2.680	0.618	-1.771	1.919

Chi – Square (d.f = 4) Value = 36.703 Table Value = 9.48 P Value = .000

Source: Field Survey
Note: Figure in brackets shows percentage

So it is concluded that there is found significant relationship between the education level of respondents and their awareness about the benefits available account holders under PMJDY – over draft limits up to Rs.5000 after 6 month.

Conclusion And Suggestions

The main findings of the study are spelled out as follows:

The major chunk of the respondents aware about Pradhan Mantri Jan Dhan yojana.

The majority of the respondents know that account holder will get benefit in the form of interest on deposit amount, accidental insurance of Rs.1 lakh, life insurance of Rs.30000/-, overdraft limit up to Rs.5000/- after 6 month.

It is observed that 64% respondents are of the opinion that accidental insurance, life insurance and overdraft facility is enough for promotion of scheme.

By inference from the study, the following recommendations and suggestions are made with regard to the improvement and development of the PMJDY:

Benefits of the scheme should be explained to every person in the country. Pradhan Mantri Jan Dhan Yojana through entitles of an accidental insurance of Rs. 1 lakh, life insurance of Rs. 30000/- and overdraft limit up to Rs. 5000/- after 6 months.

Financial literacy, awareness should be created about use of RuPay card at least once in 90 days, to get benefits of accidental insurance cover.

Survey shows that some people still have no bank account. So there is needed to make efforts through government agencies and also through banks for 100% financial inclusion.

BC's are not fully involved because of less compensation. Being scattered area, BC found difficult to locate customers to earn lively hood so, BCs should be suitably compensated to work whole heartedly.

Rate of interest on deposit should be increased gradually and rate of interest on loans should be decreased gradually.

Life insurance coverage to be implemented to all account holders irrespective of family head or earning hand of the family under the scheme. Accidental insurance coverage of 1 lakh and life insurance coverage of Rs. 30000/- should be increased, speedy settlement and less condition at the time of claim settlement be applicable.

Majority of the respondents are of opinion that Pradhan Mantri Jan Dhan Yojana put an additional pressure on banks account of overdraft facility in the accounts especially when banks are already reeling under rising NPAs, so for availment of overdraft limit of 5000/- in the account under the scheme, seeding of Aadhaar card number and linking of DBT should be compulsory to avoid account becoming NPA and inoperative.

Proper mechanism should be developed for controlling overlapping of accounts and seeding of Aadhaar card number should be compulsory in each account for availment of benefits of the scheme, which will help government for keeping proper control and for transparent data for future planning.

References

Ahmed (2015), *"Pradhan Mantri Jan Dhan Yojana: A swot analysis"*
    Journal for advanced research in commerce and management studies, Vol.2, Issue-2.

Amit (2015), *"Pradhan Mantri Jan Dhan Yojana: A Right Path towards*

Poverty Alleviation in India", IISN, Vol.1, Issue 2-3, PP. 1-11.
Ashish, Amrita, B.P, and A.B (2014), *"Pradhan Mantri Jan Dhan Yojana for weaker section – An evaluation*", Shabd Brahan – International research journal of Indian languages, Vol.2, Issue-12.Oct, PP.69-70.
Brij (2014), *"Pradhan Mantri Jan-Dhan Yojana: Features Needs and Challenges"*, International Journal of Marketing, Financial Services, Vol. 3 (12), PP. 111-117.
Deepa. (2014), *"Spreading financial literacy in rural India: An overview of HDFC bank's initiative in Kerala"*, Europeon journal of applied social science research, Vol.1, Issue-2, PP.101-105.
Jaspreet (2016), *"A Review Study on Pradhan Mantri Jan Dhan Yojana – A New Scheme towards Financial Inclusion"*, International Journal of Business Management and Scientific Research, Vol. 18, Issue June.
Jitender and Rashmi (2015), *"Pradhan Mantri Jan Dhan Yojana (PMJDY): An innovative scheme for financial inclusion in India"*, TIJ's research journal of social science, Vol.4, Issue-9.Jan.
Kumar Divyesh, Venkatesha H R (2014), *"Financial Inclusion Using Pradhan Mantri Jan- Dhan Yojana- A Conceptual Study"*, A Peer Reviewed International Journal, Vol.1, Issue.XX.Dec, PP.38-39.
Pathak Ashish, Soni Amrita, Agrwal .B.P, Vajpayee A.B.(2014). *"Pradhan Mantri Jan Dhan Yojana for weaker section – An Evaluation,"* Shabd Braham – International Research Journal of Indian Languages, Vol.2, Issue12. Oct, PP.69-70.

CHAPATER 13
CRITICAL APPRAISAL OF DISASTER PREVENTION PREPAREDNESS AND MITIGATION MANAGEMENT IN HIMACHAL PRADESH

Kewal Ram and S.S. Chauhan

Abstract

This study examined the disaster prevention preparedness and mitigation management in Himachal Pradesh. The Disaster Management is a process of involving all stakeholders with a continuous and integrated process of planning, organizing coordinating and implementing measures for minimizing the loss of human and properties. Hence, the role of culture of prevention, preparedness and mitigation are imperative. The sample was drawn from the rural as well as urban population on the basis of purposely randomly from the Panchayati Raj Institutions and urban local bodies of Municipal Corporation Shimla and Mandi, besides principal stakeholder's political, administrative officers, judges, NGOs, Professionals and Media. Total 302 respondents were interviewed. It was hypothized that the State and District Administration have had failed to tackle the disaster like situation in Himachal Pradesh. In this study, the primary data was collected and field based survey was conducted. An interview schedule containing a set of questions were prepared and asked the respondents and they have replied in written. The data was further consolidated and *analyzed accordingly. The hypotheses of this study proved beyond all doubts, as the prevention preparedness and mitigation measures were not taken seriously. The majority of the line departments did not bother to prepare their departmental disaster management plan and also failed to launch special campaign for awareness among the communities. The Administration has also failed to involve all stakeholders like media, NGOs, Professional, rural and urban communities in the process of Disaster Management. In conclusion, we would recommend that all stakeholders must be participated in the prevention, preparedness and mitigation management, so that, a safe and disaster resilient communities could be transformed through a culture of prevention, preparedness and mitigation management and apparently disaster damages and losses of human and properties could be minimized, if disaster/ incident occurred.*

13.1. Introduction

Quarantelli says, "Disaster" is certainly the key concept in the area. Yet even what is assumed in the subtitle of the roundtable-namely, different social constructs of the concepts, is not fully agreed upon or used. A hazard may be regarded as the pre-disaster situation, in which some risk of disaster exists, principally because the human population has placed itself in a situation of vulnerability. This can be defined as, "the degree of loss to a given element or set of element at risk resulting from the occurrence of natural phenomenon of a given magnitude. (Alexander, 1999)

The hazard has a potential threat to human and their welfare arising from a dangerous phenomenon or substance that may cause loss of life, injury, property damage and other community losses or damage. Then risk-the likely consequence-becomes the combination of the probability of a hazardous event and its negative consequences (Smith, 2013). The energy, ability and patriotic sentiment back of the campaign for "preparedness" would certainly be most praiseworthy, were they exerted for a truly purpose. It is an excellent thing to prepare, with energy, ability and love of country, provided that we prepare for the right thing and by the right means.(Hull,1916)

What is necessary is to educate the public on what needs to be done during and after an earthquake as well as teach them methods of simple retrofitting of non-engineered structures, so that damage due to earthquake could be reduced considerably. Time and again it has been demonstrated that it is Not Earthquakes But Buildings That Kill People (Gupta, 2003). The previous research studies (Hull et al., 1916, Quarantelli et al., 1998, Alexander et al., 1999,Sinha and Sharma,1999, Pant, 2001, Fernando et al., 2001, Gupta et al., 2003, Wisner et al., 2003, Pelling et al, 2003, Bankoff et al., 2006, Cartar et al., 2008, Arthur et al., 2011, Smith et al., 2013, Singh et al., 2013, Thomas and Phillips et al., 2013, on the disaster prevention, preparedness and mitigation management and suggested number of remedial measures on these issues, but huge gaps are still prevalent in the Administrative mechanisms in India. Therefore, this empirical study has been taken to pursue in Himachal Pradesh.

13.2. Concept in Disaster Management

a) Hazard

Hazards are defined as phenomena that pose a threat to people, structure, environmental resources and economic assets and which may cause disaster. They could be either man-made or naturally occurring in our environment.

b) Disasters

"A disaster is a sudden, calamitous event that seriously disrupts the functioning of a community or society and causes human, material and economic or environmental losses that exceed the community's or society's ability to cope using its own resources". As per the Disaster Management Act, 2005, disaster means a catastrophic mishap, calamity or grave occurrence in any area, arising from natural or manmade causes, or by accident of negligence which results in substantial loss of life or human suffering, damage to and destruction of property, or damage to or degradation of environmental and is of such a nature or magnitude as to be beyond the coping capacity of the community of the affected area.(Arthur,2011)

c) Vulnerability

Physical Vulnerability: vulnerability in the built environment. Social vulnerability experienced by people and their social, economic and political systems (Peeling). The word vulnerability is used in the English hazards and disaster management literature in a large number of ways. Ben Wisner has classified the vulnerability into

seven:
  i. Structural engineering vulnerability
  ii. Lifeline infrastructural vulnerability
  iii. Macro-economic vulnerability
  iv. Regional economic vulnerability
  v. Commercial vulnerability (including insurance exposure)
  vi. Social vulnerability

d) Risk Assessment

Risk is a measure of the expected losses (deaths, injuries, property, economic activity etc.) due to a hazard of a particular area over a specific time period. There are four most important factors like hazards, location, exposure and vulnerability which contribute to risk.

i) Hazards (physical effects generated in the naturally occurring event)
ii) Location of the hazard relative to the community at risk
iii) Exposure
iv) Vulnerability of the exposed structure and system to the hazards expected to affect them during their useful life.

Alexander (1999) distinguished between risk and vulnerability, nothing that "vulnerability refer to the potential for casualty, destruction, damage, disruption or other form of loss in a particular element; risk combines this with the probable level of loss to be expected from a predictable magnitude of hazard (which can be considered as the manifestation of the agent that produces the loss). A disaster occurs when a significant number of vulnerable people experience a hazard and suffer severe damage in such a way that recovery is unlikely without external aid. Risk is defined as the probability of meeting danger or suffering harm or loss. In relation to disaster, risk has been more specifically described as the probability that a disaster will occur, using relative terms such as high risk to indicate the degree of probability. Risk assessment includes on evaluation of all the elements that are relevant to an understanding of existing hazards and their effects on a specific environment. (Carter, 2008).

e) Prevention and Preparedness

Prevention is better than cure. The HPC (2001) also pointed out about the culture of prevention. A growing shift in approach to disaster management is the initiative for prevention and preparedness rather than relief. Preparedness includes the formulation of viable emergency plan, the development of warning systems, the maintenance of inventories and the training of personnel. It may also embrace search and rescue measures as well as evacuation plan for areas that may be at risk from a recurring disaster. Preparedness, therefore, encompasses those measures taken before a disaster event which are aimed at minimizing loss of life, disruption of critical services, and damage before the disaster occurs. Prevention and preparedness are the key elements of mitigation for the Disaster Management.

f) Mitigation

Mitigation refers to efforts for reducing the actual or probable effects of a disaster on people, structures, economic and social systems and the environment. Mitigation seeks to reduce risk that is vulnerability to damages or losses. Mitigation focuses on the hazard that causes the disaster and attempts to minimize the adverse impacts of the hazard on communities. The reasons to focus on mitigating disaster impacts include rising economic and social costs of disasters, existence of technical know-how to reduce disaster impacts and costs, and the fact that mitigation is an integral component of sustainable development.(Fernando,2001)

The comprehensive emergency management is a widely used approach at all levels of government to deal with the inevitability of natural hazards and their potential to cause disaster in a given community. The components of a comprehensive emergency management system include:
1. Preparedness activities
2. Response activities
3. Recovery activities
4. Mitigation activities

According to Wisner, there are two approaches for mitigation:
i) Structural Approach
ii) Non-Structural Approach

13.3. Rationale of the Study

Himachal Pradesh is situated in the North-West India and it lies between 30°22'40" degree to 33°12'40" North altitude and 75°47'55" to 79°04'22" East longitude. Himachal Pradesh is prone to various hazards both natural and man-made. The main hazards consist of earthquakes, landslides, floods, flashfloods, snowstorms and Avalanches, drought, dam failure, fire (domestic and forest fire) road accidents, stampede, boat capsizing, cold waves, lighting, biological industrial and chemical hazards. Therefore, the risk for human and property losses are always on the rise and Himachal Pradesh also lies in the seismic zone V & IV for earthquake i.e. Seismic Hazard.

13.4. Objectives of the Study

This study conducted in district Shimla and Mandi and covered the critical analysis of the disaster prevention, preparedness and mitigation management in Himachal Pradesh. The main objectives of the empirical study were the following:

1) To assess the preparedness activities in the State of Himachal Pradesh with special reference to prevention, preparedness and mitigation for disaster risk reduction measures.
2) To suggest appropriate strategies and action plan for improvising the Administrative System.

This paper highlights the shortcomings and gaps in the implementation of National Policy on Disaster Management, State Policy on Disaster Management and the Disaster Management Act, 2005.

13.5. Hypotheses

This study conducted in district Shimla and Mandi and covered the critical analysis of the disaster prevention, preparedness and mitigation. The main hypotheses of the empirical study were the following:

1) Whether the preparedness activities in the state of Himachal Pradesh with special reference to prevention, preparedness and mitigation for disaster risk reduction measures were taken vigorously?
2) To suggest appropriate strategies and action plan for improvement in the Administrative System.

13.6. Methodology (Sample Size)

In this study, primary data was collected and interpreted. The primary data was collected through a structured questionnaire and interviewing. The questions were required to be replied by the respondents i.e. 150 Administrative and Political stakeholders, 40 Rural stakeholders, 40 urban stakeholders, 72 stakeholders from communities, NGOs, Media and professionals. Hence, total 302 respondents were interviewed in Shimla and Mandi district of Himachal Pradesh.

13.7. Significance

The findings of the paper will facilitate to improve the administrative preparedness for tackling the impending disasters in the state of Himachal Pradesh in future with utmost care, efficiency and effectiveness for minimizing the human and property losses in disaster like situation.

Table 1: Opinion of Respondents Regarding the Preventive Initiative and Special Campaign for Hazards Mitigation Management in the State of Himachal Pradesh

Sr. No.	Description	Total	Yes		No		Can't say	
			Nos.	%	Nos.	%	Nos.	%
1	Admin. Stakeholders	150	62	41.33	67	44.67	21	14.0
2	Rural Stakeholders	40	8	20.0	32	80.0	-	-
3	Urban Stakeholders	40	6	15	33	82.5	1	2.50
4	Communities, NGO's, Media & Professionals	72	13	18.06	54	75.0	5	6.94
5	Grand Total	302	89	29.47	186	61.59	27	8.94

The above table depicts the preventive initiatives and special campaign held for hazard mitigation in the state of Himachal Pradesh. The eighty nine respondents i.e. 29.47 percent have appreciated the mitigation management but an overwhelming majority of respondents i.e. one hundred eighty six comprising of sixty seven administrative stakeholders, thirty two rural stakeholders, thirty three urban stakeholders and fifty four communities, NGOs,

Media and professionals i.e. 61.59 percent negatively responded and remaining twenty seven respondents i.e. 8.94 per cent did not say anything about the hazard mitigation management in the state of Himachal Pradesh. Hence, the overall preventive and mitigation management campaign could not be successful.

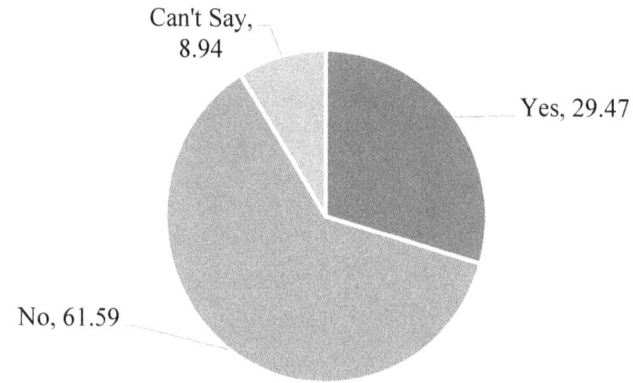

Table 2: General Awareness and Preparation of Family Disaster Management Plan

Sr. No.	Description	Total	Yes		No		Can't say	
			Nos.	%	Nos.	%	Nos.	%
1	Admin. Stakeholders	150	74	49.33	71	47.33	5	3.34
2	Rural Stakeholders	40	2	5.0	37	92.5	1	2.50
3	Urban Stakeholders	40	4	10.0	35	87.5	1	2.50
4	Communities, NGO's, Media & Professionals	72	21	29.17	46	63.89	7	9.72
5	Grand Total	302	101	33.44	189	62.58	14	4.63

The table 2 depicted the general awareness of the respondents and their preparation for family disaster management plan. One hundred and one respondents i.e. 33.44 per cent had revealed that they have had prepared their family level disaster management plan, but actually they prepared First Aid Medical Kit whereas an overwhelming majority i.e. 189 respondents (62.58) percent opined that they did not prepare any plan so far, and remaining respondents i.e. 4.63 said nothing about such preparation.

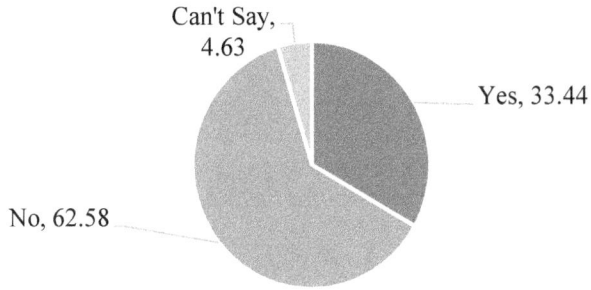

The above table clearly highlights the lackadaisical attitude of the authorities about any special campaign for prevention and preparedness at the level of individual and family as well as at the State/ District/ Sub-Division/Tehsil/ Block/MC/PRIs and communities level too. Even the media, NGO and professional were not involved in special campaign for disaster preparedness activities.

Table 3: Opinion of respondents about the status of preparation of State Disaster Management Plan, District Disaster Management Plan, Departmental Plan, Block MC & PRI Level DMPs in the State of Himachal Pradesh

Sr. No.	Description	Total	Yes		No		Can't say	
			Nos	%	Nos	%	Nos	%
1	Admin. Stakeholders	150	59	39.33	77	51.33	14	9.33
2	Rural Stakeholders	40	5	12.5	32	80.0	3	7.50
3	Urban Stakeholders	40	9	22.5	28	70.0	3	7.50
4	Communities, NGO's, Media & Professionals	72	19	26.39	47	65.28	6	8.33
5	Grand Total	302	92	30.47	184	60.93	26	8.60

The above table revealed the status of preparation of State Disaster Management Plan, District Disaster Management Plan, Departmental Disaster Management Plans, Sub-Divisional Disaster Management Plans, Block Disaster Management Plans, M.Cs., DMPs, PRI, Panchayats Disaster Management Plans, in the State of Himachal Pradesh. An overwhelming majority of respondents i.e. one hundred eighty four i.e. (60.93%) described the factual position and replied negatively and 92 respondents i.e. 30.47% replied positively and remaining 26 respondents i.e. 8.61% did not say anything.

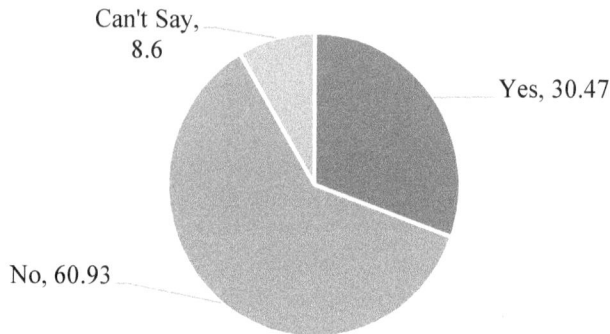

As per website of the H.P. State Disaster Management Authority only State and District level SDMP & DDMPs had been prepared but the line departments like HPPWD, IPH, Industry Department, MCs, PRIs in the State did not bother to prepare their DMPs and get it approve from the State Disaster Management Authority, since there is mandatory provisions contained in the Disaster Management Act, 2005, to get the DMPs be approved from the competent authority.

Table 4: Opinion of the respondents about the mock drills conducted quarterly at the state HQ level and district HQ level in Himachal Pradesh

Sr. No.	Description	Total	Yes		No		Can't say	
			Nos.	%	Nos.	%	Nos.	%
1	Admin. Stakeholders	150	28	18.67	95	63.33	27	18.0
2	Rural Stakeholders	40	03	7.5	27	67.5	10	25.0
3	Urban Stakeholders	40	07	17.5	19	47.5	14	35.0
4	Communities, NGO's, Media & Professionals	72	09	12.5	44	61.11	19	26.39
5	Grand Total	302	47	15.56	185	61.26	70	23.18

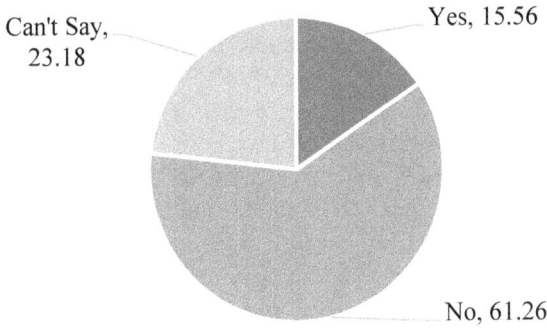

The above table shows the factual position of mock drills conducted at state capital and at the district head quarter level. An over whelming majority of the respondents i.e. 185 opined (61.26 percent) that no mock drill was conducted so far, whereas merely 47 i.e. 15.56 percent opined that in positive and stated that some mock drills were conducted but not in proper interval. The remaining respondents 70 (23.18 percent) did not say anything about the mock drill exercise. As such the overall scenario of disaster prevention and preparedness is not satisfactory and up to the mark in the state of Himachal Pradesh.

13.8. Findings

The main hypothesis of the study has been proved beyond doubt, because in Himachal Pradesh the prevention, preparedness and mitigation activities could not be implemented vigorously in the field and Disaster Risk Reduction measures could not be incorporated in projects and schemes due to lack of coordination, planning, and monitoring mechanism. The line departments like H.P.P.W.D, I.P.H, H.P.S.E.B, H.P.C.C.L, Hydel Dams, Social Justice, Education, Public Relation Department Media NGOs, VOs, Mahila Mandals etc. could not be assigned their role in the Disaster Management. Hence, majority of the line department did not even prepare their Departmental Disaster Management Plans so far. The important findings of the study are as given below:

The Hazard and vulnerability mitigation management initiative could not be launched in the State of Himachal Pradesh.

The prevention and preparedness activities like community

preparedness at the family level also failed as the majority of respondents did not have their family disaster management plan.

The Disaster Risk Reduction could not be implemented in the State so far.

The updation of state disaster management plan, District Disaster Management plan and organizational level DMPs were not updated and upgraded annually. The mandatory mock drills of response forces, task forces could not be conducted regularly at state HQ as well as at district HQ level to check the preparedness level.

The state of Himachal Pradesh also unable to mainstream plans & mitigation strategies into developments plans/projects/schemes at the ground zero level.

13.9. Suggestion and Strategies

- Plan Formulation at every organization level must be prepared as well as existing plans must be updated and upgraded.
- A special campaign should be launched for general awareness among the students and communities through IEC information Education and Communication Network.
- Administrative Preparedness for the worst situation should be readily available.
- An early warning mechanism for natural and man-made disaster should be installed at the critical/vulnerable points.
- Risk management should be assessed in the state and all component of disaster risk be mitigated as follows:

$$\frac{\text{Hazard} \times \text{Vulnerability} \times \text{exposure}}{\text{Capacity (Preventin, Preparedness, Mitigation, Plan, Mockdrills, School Safety, Training and updation of plans and strategies participation of all stakeholders}}$$

- Land use planning should be adopted and stringently enforced through various agencies of the state government.
- The Incident Response System should be notified in the state for efficient and effective management of any incident or disaster.
- Life line structures like H.P. Secretariat, IGMC, Hospital, Schools, District Collectorates etc. must be retrofitted and repaired.
- Mock drills should be conducted regularly at the state headquarter as well as in the district and local level/PRIs/ULB levels.

In conclusion, the results of this study provide some significant results ,which is crucial as Disaster Prevention, Preparedness and Mitigation initiatives in the state of Himachal Pradesh has a dire need to be emphasized for execution and implementation of the National Policy, Disaster Management Act, 2005 as well as State policy on Disaster Management. At the ground level, a huge gaps and shortcomings were found as per the empirical analysis, hence more hard work, appropriate coordination, advance planning, mitigation strategies, involvement of all stakeholders, N.G.O., U.L.B., P.R.Is, Communities, Media experts, Engineers, Architects, Doctors, Para Medical Staff, Contractors and Builders, Sub-Contractors are imperative, therefore, all stakeholders should have to be involved and a participatory mechanism for the prevention, preparedness and mitigation management, so that, a safe and disaster resilient communities could be transformed and culture of prevention, preparedness and mitigation could be inculcated and promoted in the state of Himachal Pradesh.

References

Alexander David (1999), Natural Disaster, Kluwer Academic Publishers, London, pp. 4-5.
Arthur, Bradley T. (2011), "The Disaster Preparedness Handbook: A Guide for Families, Sky Horse Publishing, Inc. New York, pp. 6-7.
Bankoff, Greg Georg Frerks & Dorotheo Hilhorst (2006), "Mapping vulnerability; Disasters, Development and People, Earthscan London (UK), pp. 183-186.
Building PRI Capacities for Disaster Preparedness and Management- A Training Manual, A GOI, U.N.D.P., Disaster Risk Management Programme 2002-2009, UNDP, New Delhi- 11003, India.
Carter, W. Nick (2008), Disaster Management: A Disaster Manager's Handbook, Asian Development Bank, 6 ADB, Avenue, 1550 Metro, Manila, Philippines, pp. 323-330.
Disaster Management Act, 2005. G.O.I, Ministry of Law and Justice, New Delhi.
Disaster Preparedness for Effective Response Guidance and Indicates Package for Implementing Priority Five of the Hyogo Framework, UNO, (2008) New York , A Publication of OCHA & ISDR.

Disaster Response and Management, (2014) LBSNAA, Centre for Disaster Management Mussoorie (Uttarkhand), June 2014, Vol. 2, pp. 1-20. (November 1, ISSN, 2347-2553).

Environment Mater Plan Vulnerability Assessment (Map Volume) Himachal Pradesh, Government of H.P. Department of Environment Science & Technology Shimla-1 (Official Web-Site).

Fernando N.B.J (2001), Disaster Mitigation, in Pardeep Sahni, Alka Dhameja and Uma Medury (Eds.) Disaster Mitigation: Experiences and Reflections, PHI, New Delhi, (pp. 1-5).

First Aid- A Handbook for Community based Disaster Preparedness, Gujarat State Disaster Management Authority and UNDP, Ghandhinagar, Gujarat, (India).

Guidelines for Hazards Assessment and Vulnerability Analysis, ADPC Bankok (ADB) and UNDP.

Gupta, Harsh K. (2003), Disaster Management, Universities Press (India), Pvt. Ltd., Himayatnagar, Hyderabad-500029 (AP), (pp. 100-108)

Himachal Pradesh State Policy on Disaster Management 2011, HPSDMA, Govt. of H.P. Department of Revenue, Shimla - 2.

Himachal Pradesh Vulnerability Atlas (2009), Seeds & SDMA, Department of Revenue DMC Shimla-2

HPSDMA website www.hpsdma.nic.in

Hull William I. (1916), Preparedness, Fleming H. Revell Co. London, pp. 40-45.

India Disaster Report-2013, National Institute of Disaster Management, Ministry of Home Affairs, Govt. of India.

National Disaster Management Plan (NDMP) National Disaster Management Authority, Ministry of Home Affairs, GOI, New Delhi, May, 2016.

Pant, J.C. (2001), The Report of High Powered Committee on Disaster Management, Ministry of Agriculture & National Centre for D.M in IIPA, New Delhi, pp.1-51.

Pelling, Mark (2003), "The Vulnerability of Cities: Natural Disaster and Social Resilience Earthscan Publications Ltd., London UK, pp. 5-7.

Quarantelli E.L., (1998) What is a Disaster,?: Perspectives on the Questions, Rutledge, Park Square Milton Park, Oxon, USA & Canada, pp. 2-3.

Sendai Framework for Disaster Risk Reduction (2015-2030), UNISDR, 9-11, Rue-deVarembe CH-1202, Geneva Switzerland, (www.unisdr.org.) pp. 1-14.

Sinah A and Sharma V.K (1999)," Culture of Prevention", I.I.P.A. New Delhi, p.1-14.

Singh R.B. (2013), Natural Hazards & Disaster Management: Vulnerability and Mitigation, Rawat Publications, Jaipur, (pp. 1-23).

Smith Keith (2013), Environmental Hazards: Assessing Risk and Reducing Disaster, Routledge, 711 Third Avenue, New York, pp.11-14.

Sood R.K. (2012), Hazards and Disaster Vulnerability of the State of Himachal Pradesh Jan-June 2012, Journal of HIPA, Shimla, Administrative Development: A Journal of HIPA, Shimla H.P., Vol. 1, No. 1, pp. 33-57. (ISSN-2319-2976).

State Disaster Management Plan, Himachal Pradesh, Department of Revenue and Disaster Management, Shimla-2.

Thomas, Deborah S.K., Phillips Brenda D. William E. Lovekamp & Alice Fothergill, (2013), "Social Vulnerability to Disaster, C.R.C. Press, Taylor & Francis Group, N.W. Suite 300, Boca Raton, pp. 17-18.

Tidings, NIDM, Newsletter Vol. X, No. 4, Oct-Dec., 2015, National Institute of Disaster Management, Ministry of Home Affairs, GOI, New Delhi.

Wisner, Ben Piers Blaikie, Terry Common and Ian Davis (2003), at Risk: Natural Hazards, people's vulnerability and disaster, Rutledge & UNDP, New York, pp. 49-50.

World Disaster Report (2015), International Federation Of Red Cross And Red Crescent Societies, 17, Chemindes Crets, Po. Box-303 Ch-1211, Geneva 19, Switzerland (Web.Www.Ifrc.Org., UNDP, UNISDRI, OP. CIT., NDMA, NIDM, ADPC.

CHAPTER 14
A COMPARATIVE STUDY ON FINANCIAL INCLUSION OF PUBLIC AND PRIVATE SECTOR BANKS – A CASE STUDY OF NORTH EASTERN REGION

Nitin Gupta

Abstract

India is one of the fastest budding economies of the world. in spite of such a high economic growth our rural population seems to miss the benefits of this growth. Financial inclusion is a new model of economic growth which plays a major role in driving away the poverty. Many countries around the globe have considered financial inclusion as means for better inclusive growth. since nationalization, various efforts were made by banks to expand reach of banking services to the areas not covered under the banking system. however, in 2005 the concept of financial inclusion was formally expressed by the then governor of reserve bank of India. After the formal inception of this worldly known concept, reserve bank of india had taken various measures to include the financially excluded population under the umbrella of banking. both public and private sector banks are regularly encouraged by RBI for strengthening the network of ATMS and bank branches across india. Many initiatives like Business Correspondent (BC) model, opening of no-frill accounts, and expansion of bank branches were taken to expand the reach of banking. Technological developments like automated teller machines (ATM) have been successfully able to transform banking from brick-

and-mortar infrastructure to single delivery point for wide range of banking services. In recent past initiatives like launch of White Label ATMs (WLAs), off-site ATMs and technological developments like national financial switch (NFs) were made by RBI to expand the reach of banking and curb financial exclusion. Looking at the sequence of events launched by RBI, an attempt had been made to conduct a comparative study of public and private sector banks with regard to installation of ATMs in north eastern region of India since 2010 when RBI authorized banks to install offsite ATMs. The study concludes that topographical challenges, safety issues, power failures and connectivity of ATMs were some of the major reasons for lower financial access in these areas.

14.1. Introduction

India is one of the fastest budding economies of the world. In spite of such a high economic growth our rural population seems to miss the benefits of this growth (Pallavi and Bharti, 2013). Financial inclusion is a new model of economic growth which plays a major role in driving away the poverty (Raman, 2012). Its importance arises from the problem of financial exclusion of nearly 3.5 billion people from the formal financial services across the world (Thamotharan and Prabakran, 2013). Rangarajan Committee (2008) defined financial inclusion as the process of ensuring access to financial services and timely and adequate credit where needed by the vulnerable group such as weaker sections and low income groups at an affordable cost. Indian economy though achieved the high growth momentum during 2003-04 to 2007-08, but over 25% of Indians still remain in abject poverty (Dixit and Ghosh, 2013). In 2006, the Government of India constituted a committee on Financial Inclusion which made a wide range of recommendations on the strategies for building an inclusive financial sector and gave a national rural financial inclusion plan (Hameedu, 2014). Reserve Bank of India permitted commercial banks to make use of the services of non-governmental organizations, micro finance institutions and other civil society organizations as intermediaries for providing financial and banking services to unbanked (Aditya, 2014). As of September 2008, approximately 15.8 million bank accounts had already been opened as a step towards achieving 100% financial inclusion (Minakshi, 2009). Many banks these days are planning to tap the prospects in un-organized sector. North eastern region (Assam, Arunachal Pradesh, Meghalaya, Mizoram, Nagaland, Manipur, Tripura and Sikkim) of India still remain as a challenge for financial inclusion. The ratio of current and savings accounts over per 100 adults was found to be 40.9% in Meghalaya and 19.5% in Manipur, which shows that the inequalities in accessibility to banking services is very broad and extensive (Thangasamy, 2014). Since nationalization significant banking development was made in these areas, but starting with low base, development in banking still lags behind in comparison to other states on country. Northeast being recognized as special category region, government of India needs to give special attention for developing roads, air networks, telecom facilities and other communication networks for strengthening the market linkages (Chakma, 2014). Even after the advancement of technology in banking, frequent power failures, security issues, difficult terrains have always restricted in spreading banking facilities in northeast. It is now important for banks to explore alternative sources of energy for ATMs to ensure their continuous connectivity in northeastern region of India.

14.2. Objectives of the Study

1. To analyze and compare the financial inclusiveness of public and private sector banks with respect to number of ATMs installed in northeastern states of India.
2. To study and compare the region wise geographic and demographic penetration of ATMs in India.

14.3. Review of Literature

In previous years many studies of financial inclusion have been conducted to understand the status of inclusiveness in Indian banks. This section of the study provides with a summary of some existing literature on financial inclusion.

Financial inclusion may be defined as the process of ensuring access to financial services and timely and adequate credit where needed by the vulnerable group such as weaker sections and low income groups at an affordable cost (Rangarajan Committee, 2008). The percentage of financial inclusion in the different states of the country varies differently. For instance Kerala, Maharashtra and Karnataka accounts for higher rate of financial inclusion but the states such as Gujarat, Manipur, Assam, Bihar, Uttar Pradesh, and Madhya Pradesh, etc. stand poorly on the grounds of financial inclusion (Dixit and Ghosh, 2013). It was observed that among socio- economic factors, income is positively associated with the level of financial inclusion. Moreover electronic connectivity, information availability, road network, telephone facility, internet usage also play positive role in enhancing financial inclusion (Mandira & Jesim, 2008). In a study conducted on financial in India 59% of adult population in the country have bank account and 41% of the population is unbanked, northeastern region has the highest unbanked population (Bhole and Jitendra, 2009). It was found that geographic peculiarities were the reason for slow progress of banking in northeastern states. The population per branch (i.e. 19465) was found to be higher in comparison to All India level which is 13916 only (Thangasamy, 2014). As Northeastern states lag behind due to communication gap, geographical constraints and it is difficult to build brick and mortar structure of banks in each vicinity. Therefore, it is imperative for government to highly promote the movement of self-help groups (Saha, 2015) and promote the extensive use of ATMs (Automated Teller Machines) instead of brick and mortar branches to explore the untapped rural north east. Other than this it is also important to promote sustainable industrial development, increase agricultural productivity, financial education in the states of north east (chakma, 2014). Hence a coordinated effort of all stakeholders, commercial banks, reserve bank and governments is required for increasing banking penetration and enhance financial inclusion in the region.

The above mentioned studies point out that northeastern region of India have been affected by financial exclusion. In recent past installation of ATMs have been highly promoted by RBI to supplement the traditional method of banking and increase the accessibility of banking. In backdrop, an initiative has been taken to study the current status of work done on financial inclusion in northeastern states by public and private sector banks of India.

14.4. Research Methodology

This study is conducted to analyze the financial inclusiveness in public and private sector banks with regard to ATMs installed in northeastern states of India. The study is purely based on secondary information collected from various RBI publications, namely Basic Statistical Returns and ATM & card statistics and various other bulletins. The scope of the study is limited to the analysis of ATM penetration of public and private sector banks over the period of 2014-2016. Statistical tools like percentage method and ratio analysis were used to analyze the trends of ATMs installed. Findings of the study were then presented in the form of figures and tables to make comparative analysis of both public and private sector banks.

14.5. Results

Since the period of nationalization, India has been making various efforts to promote inclusive growth. However intensive efforts have been made after formal inception of financial inclusion in 2005. The Government of India and RBI had implemented various measures like No-frills accounts, BCs (Business Correspondent Model), SGHs (Self Help Groups) and expansion of bank branches for enhancing financial inclusion in various states of India. Technological developments like ATMs had supplemented the brick and mortar structures and have become a single delivery point for wide range of banking services. The policy initiative of installing offsite ATMs taken in 2010 resulted into remarkable change in the number of ATMs installed by public and private sector banks. By March 2011, public sector banks had minimum one ATM on every ten thousand saving accounts, whereas this figure was 3 in case of private sector banks.

Even after the tremendous growth in ATM installation, northeastern states lagged behind the other states of India in this regard. The region wise percentage distribution of ATMs given in figure 1 below shows that northeastern states have the least number of ATMs in comparison to other regions of India.

Figure 1: Region Wise Percentage Distributions of ATMs (March, 2015)

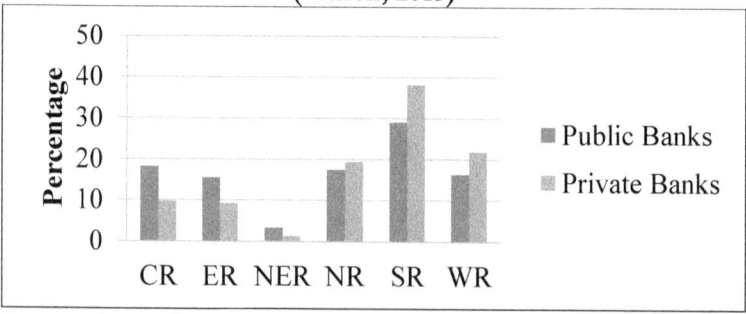

Source: Gupta (2016), A Comparative Study on the Performance of Public and Private Sector Banks, Shoolini University.

Looking at the lowest penetration of ATMs in northeast, an initiative has been taken to conduct the comparative analysis of public and private sector banks on the penetration of ATMs in northeastern states on India. The findings of the same are presented below:

14.5.i. Number of ATMs per ten thousand savings accounts

It has been observed that as the numbers of saving accounts are increasing for enhancing inclusive growth, hence it generates the requirement of installing more number of ATMs. Therefore, it becomes imperative to study the penetration of ATMs over number of saving accounts.

Table 1: Number of ATMs per Ten Thousand Saving Accounts

States	2014		2015		2016	
	Public	Private	Public	Private	Public	Private
Arunachal Pradesh	2.3	9.3	2.2	9.9	2.2	6.3
Assam	2.0	9.0	1.7	7.4	1.7	2.4
Manipur	1.8	10.9	1.9	8.7	1.6	7.3
Meghalaya	2.2	9.1	2.2	6.8	2.2	5.4
Mizoram	2.5	10.2	3.4	9.0	3.1	8.2
Nagaland	3.2	7.7	3.5	6.3	2.7	6.2
Tripura	2.1	9.7	1.9	15.4	2.0	1.3
North Eastern States	**2.0**	**9.1**	**1.9**	**8.0**	**1.8**	**2.7**
Other Regions						
Eastern states	1.3	7.9	1.3	7.2	1.1	4.0
Northern States	2.0	4.8	1.9	4.1	1.7	3.7
Western States	1.6	3.3	1.5	3.3	1.5	3.1
Southern States	1.4	4.4	1.5	4.3	1.6	4.0
Central States	1.2	7.1	1.2	6.4	1.1	5.4

Source: Basic Statistical Returns, ATM & Card Statistics, (Various Issues, RBI)

Table 1exibits that during year 2014, in case of public sector banks all the states except Nagaland had minimum 2 ATMs over ten thousand saving accounts, whereas private sector banks had highest 10.9 ATMs in Manipur and 10.2 ATMs in Mizoram. But further in 2015, penetration of ATMs in case of private sector banks reduced with the increase in number of savings accounts. Further, Table 4.1 shows that from 2015 downward trend was witnessed in both public sector banks and private sector banks. The figures reveal that significant change was witnessed in Tripura, wherein the number of ATMs per ten thousand saving accounts got reduced from 15.4 in 2015 to 1.3 in 2016. The above table 1 concludes that private sector banks had higher penetration in terms of savings accounts as compared to private sector banks. The lesser number of saving accounts of private sector banks was one of the reasons for higher penetration in comparison with public sector banks. The effect of which can be seen in the inter-regional comparison, wherein in 2014 and 2015 both public and private sector banks of northeastern states were ahead of all other regions.

14.5.ii. Geographic penetration of ATMs

Geographic penetration determines the outreach of ATMs within the geographical area of particular state or territory. It can be measured in terms of number of ATMs per thousand square kilometers. Larger number of ATMs in per square km. area indicates closer and smaller distances for accessing banking services. Results of geographic penetration in north eastern states are presented in table 2.

It depicts that in terms of accessibility public sector banks are better performers then private sector banks. The above figures reveal that in year 2014 Assam showed highest penetration with 31.8 ATMs per 1000 sq. km. in public sector banks, and 5.4 in case of private sector banks. The area of concern witnessed was Arunachal Pradesh where the penetration was 2 and 0.2 in public and private sector banks respectively. With the increasing trend till 2015, total number of ATMs in northeastern states was 16.8 and 2.7 in case of public and private sector banks respectively. It also showed that Arunachal Pradesh, Manipur and Mizoram are the states where financial inclusion drive needs to be strengthened for better penetration. By the end of year 2016, penetration of public sector banks was 19 ATMs per 1000 sq. km, whereas not much change was observed in case of private sector banks. Study also revealed that northeastern region lagged behind in ATM penetration in comparison with other regions of India.

Table 2: Geographic Penetration of ATMs (Per 1000 sq.km.)

North Eastern States	2014		2015		2016	
	Public	Private	Public	Private	Public	Private
Arunachal Pradesh	1.7	0.1	2.1	0.2	2.4	0.2
Assam	31.8	5.4	35.5	5.5	40.2	5.7
Manipur	8.3	1.6	11.6	1.7	11.8	1.8
Meghalaya	65.7	14.9	77.2	13.9	86.1	15.4
Mizoram	3.5	0.9	5.7	1.0	6.0	1.1
Nagaland	13.1	2.1	18.2	1.9	15.7	2.3
Tripura	28.9	4.3	33.6	8.8	38.5	4.8
North Eastern States	**14.4**	**2.5**	**16.8**	**2.7**	**18.6**	**2.6**
Other Regions						
Eastern states	38.8	10.6	46.0	11.0	50.3	12.0
Northern States	28.2	13.8	31.3	13.9	34.2	14.8
Western States	25.9	6.3	41.5	22.3	45.4	24.4
Southern States	50.0	28.4	58.8	31.0	66.1	33.2
Central States	36.9	20.9	31.8	6.8	35.4	7.6

Source: Basic Statistical Returns, ATM & Card Statistics, (Various Issues, RBI)

14.5.iii. Demographic penetration of ATMs

Demographic penetration indicates the number of ATMs per one lakh population. Higher penetration represents better accessibility for banking. The results of demographic penetration with regard to number of ATMs have been illustrated below:

Table 3 exhibits that public sector banks are better performers than private sector banks in terms of ATM accessibility. Public sector banks in Arunachal Pradesh had highest number of ATMs in terms of population, overall 8.4 ATMs over per one lakh persons was recorded in northeastern states, whereas only 1.4 ATMs were found installed in case of private sector banks. In 2015, performance of public sector banks improved, whereas in case of private sector banks increase in penetration was witnessed in Manipur and Tripura.

Figures in the table depicts that in 2016 ATM penetration of public sector banks in northeastern states was 10.2 whereas the number reduced to 1.4 in case of private sector banks. Comparative analysis of northeastern states with other regions depicts that in case of public sector banks northeastern states were ahead of eastern and central region states. This shows that public sector banks are moving in the right direction for accomplishing financial inclusion goals.

Table 3: Demographic Penetration of ATMs (Per 100000 Persons)

North Eastern States	2014		2015		2016	
	Public	Private	Public	Private	Public	Private
Arunachal Pradesh	11.7	1.0	13.9	1.2	14.0	1.0
Assam	8.2	1.4	9.1	1.4	8.9	1.3
Manipur	7.6	1.5	10.6	1.5	9.3	1.4
Meghalaya	9.6	2.2	11.3	2.0	10.8	1.9
Mizoram	7.3	1.9	12.1	2.1	10.9	2.0
Nagaland	9.6	1.6	13.4	1.4	10.0	1.5
Tripura	8.4	1.2	9.7	2.5	9.6	1.2
North Eastern States	**8.4**	**1.4**	**9.8**	**1.6**	**10.2**	**1.4**
Other Regions						
Eastern	6.5	1.8	7.7	1.8	7.9	1.9
Northern	12.7	6.2	14.1	6.3	14.2	6.2
Western	10.8	6.1	12.1	6.5	12.4	6.7
Southern	12.9	7.3	15.1	8.0	16.3	8.2
Central	6.2	1.5	7.6	1.6	7.9	1.7

Source: Basic Statistical Returns, ATM & Card Statistics, (Various Issues, RBI)

14.5.iv. Discussion

The state wise analysis of northeastern states was conducted to know as how far these states have been able to contribute towards financial inclusion. Study showed that northeastern region had lowest ATM penetration in comparison to other regions of India. It was found that total number of ATMs installed in northeastern region were just 3% i.e. 4287 of the total number of ATMs established by public sector banks in India, whereas the percentage was 1% in case of private sector banks (Gupta, 2016). The state wise comparative analysis (Table 2) of public and private sector banks revealed that for better accessibility and to promote technology banking, public sector banks need to work more towards installation of offsite and WLA (White label ATMs) in rural and excluded areas. Further table 3 reveals that Arunachal Pradesh, Manipur and Mizoram had the lowest geographic penetration in both public and private sector banks. The RBI recommended that significant level of exclusion persists in northeastern states and it is important to address the situation immediately by stepping up inclusion drive in these states. As topographical challenges, connectivity issues, frequent power failures and security problems were the major reasons (RBI, 2015) for lower financial penetration in northeastern states. Hence to overcome these problems brick and mortar branches should to be supplemented by technology banking like micro ATMs, Business Correspondents and mobile banking facilities. Efficient usage of alternative sources of energy could be another way out to overcome the problem of power failures in these regions. Moreover, as customer retention & satisfaction is one of the major objectives of banks, hence it becomes imperative that both public and private sector banks should provide better ATM accessibility to its customers (Gupta *et.al*, 2015) and avoid frequent power failures and grievances. The demographic penetration (table 4) revealed that the position of public sector banks in comparison to private sector banks had improved by the end of 2016. The relative position of public sector banks in northeastern states was found to be better than the states of eastern and central region of India, whereas private sector banks lagged behind in this regard. The study concludes that public sector banks are innovatively working towards accomplishing financial inclusion goals, whereas it is important for private sector banks for come forward in big way to contribute towards inclusive drive.

Conclusion

The result of the study concludes that private sector banks were better in terms of ATM penetration with regard to savings accounts as they had lesser number of saving account in comparison to public sector banks. By the end of year 2016, private sector banks had 2.7

ATMs on per ten thousand saving accounts, and 1.8 in case of public sector banks. On the other hand, study revealed that public sector banks are geographically highly penetrated in comparison with private sector banks. By the end of 2016, public and private sector banks had 18.6 and 2.6 ATMs respectively within the vicinity of 1000 sq. km. It was found that due to the topographical challenges, power failures and security issues the geographic ATM penetration in northeastern states was far less than other regions of India. Hence it is important for government and RBI to highly focus on providing banking through micro ATMs and mobile banking in the excluded areas of the region. Alternative sources of energy generation should also be tapped to avoid power failures at ATM branches. In terms of demographic penetration, public sector banks were ahead of private sector banks in northeastern states and also comparatively better then eastern and central region states of India. Hence it is the time when RBI also needs to encourage private sector banks to participate equally to promote financial inclusion in excluded regions of India.

References:

Anjum, B. & Rajeshwari. (2012). Role of Private Sector Banks for Financial Inclusion. *International Journal of Multidisciplinary Research, 1,* 270-280.

Bhle, L.M., & Mahakud, J. (2009). Financial Institution and Markets – Structure, Growth and Innovation. *Tata Mc Graw Hill, 5th Edition, New Delhi.*

Chakma, J.B. (2014). Financial Inclusion in India: A Brief Focus on Northeast India. *International Journal of Application or Innovation in Engineering & Management, 11,* 224-229.

Dangi, S., & Kumar, P. (2013). Current Situation of Financial Inclusion in India and its Future Visions. *International Journal of Management and Social Sciences Research (IJMSSR), 8,* 155-167.

Dixit, R., & Ghosh, M. (2013). Financial Inclusion for Inclusive Growth of India – A Study of Indian States. *International Journal of Business Management & Research, 1,* 147-156.

Dixit, R., & Ghosh, M. (2013). Financial Inclusion for Inclusive Growth of India – A Study of Indian States. *International Journal of Business Management & Research, 1,* 147-156.

Gupta, P., & Singh, S. (2013). Role of Literacy in Financial Inclusion in India: Empirical Evidence. *Journal of Economics, Business and*

Management, 3, 272-276.

Gupta, N. (2016). A comparative of the performance of public and private sector banks. Thesis, Shoolini University, Solan.

Gupta, N., Kesari, & Negi, Y.S. (2015). Comparative Study on Customer Satisfaction of Public and Private Sector Banks – A Case Study of Shimla Town in Himachal Pradesh. Global Journal of Multidisciplinary Studies, 11, 60-70.

Hameedu, M.S. (2014). Financial Inclusion – Issues in Measurement and Analysis. *International Journal of Current Research and Academic Review*, 2, 116-124.

Massey, J. (2010). Role of Financial Institutions in Financial Inclusion. *Banking and Finance Journal*, 4.

Massey, J. (2010). Role of Financial Institution in Financial Inclusion. *FICCT's Banking & Finance Journal*.

Prasad, E. (2010). Financial Sector Regulation in Emerging Markets: An Overview. *NBER Working Paper 16428. Cambridge, MA: National Bureau of Economic Research*.

Ramaji, M. (2009). Financial Inclusion in Gulbarga: Finding Usage in Access. Institute for Financial Management and Research. *Working paper series*, 26, 1-5.

Raman, A. (2012). Financial Inclusion and Growth of Indian Banking System. *IOSR Journal of Business and Management*, 1, 25-29.

Raman, A. (2012). Financial Inclusion and Growth of Indian Banking System. *Journal of Business and Management*, 3, 25-29.

Rangarajan Committee (2008). Report of the Committee on Financial Inclusion, Final January.

Rangarajan Committee. (2008). Report of Committee on Financial Inclusion, January, 2008.

RBI, (2013). Annual Report. Credit Delivery and Financial Inclusion. 75-83.

RBI, (2012). Annual Report. *Credit Delivery and Financial Inclusion*, 83-92.

RBI (2015). Report of the committee on Medium-term Path on Financial Inclusion, 6.

Saha, G.K. (2015). Microfinance Sector Towards Rural Development in North East India. *International Journal of Recent Scientific Research*, 6, 4845-4849.

Sarma, M. & Paise, J. (2008). Financial Inclusion and Development: A Cross Country Analysis. *Indian Council for Research on*

International Economic Relations, 1-28.

Shastri, A. (2014). Financial Inclusion in Madhya Pradesh-A Study with Reference to Rural Population. *Journal of Business Management & Social Sciences Research, 12,* 09-13.

Thamotharan, A., & Prabakran, G. (2013). Role of Private Sector Banks in Financial Inclusion-Issues & Challenges. *Asia Pacific Journal of Research, 10,* 127-141.

Thangasamy, E. (2014). Financial Inclusion in North East India: An Analytical Study. *International Journal of Commerce, Business and Management (IJCBM), 1,* 180-188.

V. Ganeshkumar, C. (2013). Overview Of Financial Inclusion In India. *International Journal Of Management And Development Studies.*

CHAPTER 15
EFFECTIVENESS OF PUBLIC DISTRIBUTION SYSTEM IN ENSURING FOOD SECURITY IN HIMACHAL PRADESH

Tilak Raj and Anuradha Negi

Abstract

The main objective of the study is to discuss the effectiveness of Public Distribution System (PDS) in ensuring food security in Himachal Pradesh. An, attempt has also made to study the major drawbacks of the system in the State. The study is based on the secondary data collected from various sources like journals, books, department of food and civil supplies Himachal Pradesh. To analyze the effectiveness of PDS the National Sample Survey Organization (NSSO) data from 61th and 68th rounds of the public distribution system and other sources of household consumption survey conducted in 2004-05 and 2011-12 has been used. The study concludes that the overall PDS contribution has improved over time and has emerged as an effective tool in providing food security. However, the study found wide inters sector variations in the State. The percentage share of PDS rice, wheat, sugar and kerosene consumed to total consumption has increased in urban areas, but in rural areas this share has declined except wheat which has increased almost double during 2004-05 to 2001-12.

15.1. Introduction

The Public Distribution System (PDS) is a large scale food rationing programme through which the Government ensures food security. Over the years, PDS has become an important instrument of the Governments policy in enhancing food security to the poor. In India, the system was invented by British Government in 1939 as a war time rationing measure and it was improved and modified over the time by Indian Government to protect the food security of poor (Mahalingam & Raj 2016). The objectives of PDS are maintaining price stability of essential commodities, providing access to foods at affordable prices to the vulnerable people and to maintain minimum nutrition level to population (Saxena & Gupta 2014).

The Centre and State government both share responsibility for the functioning and operation of PDS. The Government of India, established the Food Corporation of India (FCI) in 1957, which procures, store and transport the food grains and releases every month for distribution through PDS network all over the country. The responsibility for the actual distribution of the material to consumers is that of the Government of the State and Union Territories.

Public Distribution System is a anti poverty programme and contributes towards the social welfare of the people by supplying essential commodities like rice, wheat, sugar and kerosene to the beneficiaries through the network of Fair Price Shops (FPSs). Every year government spends approximately Rs.750 billion which is one of the biggest of its kind in the world. The planning commission (Government of India, 2005) estimated that for every Rs.3.65 spent by the government, only Re.1 reaches BPL households.

Though the PDS is an important component of the food security programme in India, it was widely criticized on the grounds of corruption, leakage, mis-targeting and inefficiencies in the supply chain. Moreover, the role and working of PDS has undergone several changes since its inception. Until 1991, the PDS provided food subsidy to all beneficiaries without targeting. In 1991, government came with the scheme of Revamped Public Distribution System (RPDS) especially for the remote and tribal areas. In the year 1997, the era of Universal Public Distribution System ended and it was replaced with the Targeted Public Distribution System (TPDS) with benefits intended exclusively for the poor people. This scheme is meant to serve families below-poverty-line (BPL) at 50 per cent of the FCI economic cost. The population above-poverty-line (APL) would continue to receive foodgrains as per the Universal PDS at a price equal to 90 per cent of the FCI's economic cost.

However, the PDS being the largest food security scheme in the Country has criticized on the ground of urban biasness, its failure to serve the poor, diversion of food grains and targeting error etc. The huge amount of diversion of grain has been reported in the PDS and targeting error was also reported under the scheme. There is no doubt that PDS performed well in the State as compare to other states, but there is also a need of PDS reforms in the State.

15.2. Review of Literature

PDS has remained an important instrument of the government food policy. A vast literature is available on different aspects of PDS. Some of the relevant studies done in the recent past are following:

Jha and Srinivasan (2001) examined the cost and benefits associated with the operation of the PDS in India. The study found the inefficiencies in the working of PDS due to inadequate and unreliable identification of beneficiaries, unviable operation of FPS, large scale diversion of food grains to open market, corruption and poor administrative arrangements etc. The study suggested that the Government should focus on reducing cost inefficiencies in the procurement, public distribution system and control the diversion of grain from the PDS to the open market. Study also suggested that there should be universal provision of subsidies for poorer States.

Swaminathan and Misra (2001) investigated the changes in errors of targeting due to shift from a universal to a targeted food subsidy programme. They have used primary data from a village in Maharashtra at two subsequent surveys. Their finding shows that error of wrong inclusion decreased while error of wrong exclusion increased due to the shift from universal to targeted coverage. The study found that the cost of administrating a targeted programme was higher than the cost of administrating a universal programme.

Ghumaan and Dhiman (2013) studied the status of Public Distribution System and its relationship with the problem of food security. The study found that PDS plays a relatively more important role in food security of the households rather than poverty reduction. It was highlighted that the o PDS has many leakages and weaknesses which create obstacles in its efficiency. The study found that in 2001-02, 18.2 percent of PDS rice and 67 percent of PDS wheat were diverted to the open market. Finally, they gave some suggestions for better functioning of PDS which includes higher procurement, lager coverage, improved distribution, lower diversion and viability of fair price shops by giving them higher margin.

Singh (2014) analyzed the functioning and effectiveness of PDS on the front of price rise, poverty alleviation and hunger. The study was based on secondary sources and to check the effectiveness of PDS, log linear model was used. The empirical results showed that the PDS performed very well in the later phase (1991 onwards) as compared to early period on the front of controlling inflation and reducing poverty. It was concluded that the role of PDS in reducing poverty was better in the rural India and it also helped people to save themselves from starvation and hunger.

Shanmugam and Thomas (2016) investigated the effectiveness and drawbacks regarding the implementation of the activities of Public Distribution System. They also tried to find out the important socio-economic determinants which influences the purchase from PDS outlets. The study was based on primary data collected through the questionnaire. It was found that majority of sample respondents were benefited from PDS and it helped in raising their standard of living. The study also found that inspite of lot of practical problems, PDS was effective in providing food security to the poor. The study suggested that the role of vigilance committee should be transparent, accountable and electronic weighing machines should be introduced at all the fair price shops.

15.3. An Overview of PDS in Himachal Pradesh

Himachal Pradesh is one of the most dynamic hill States of India. It is being a hilly and difficult State of India is largely scattered. The maximum population of the State is engaged in agriculture and allied activities. Despite that, the production of foodgrains is limited as it depends on timely rainfall and weather conditions. Moreover, due to increasing shift towards horticulture crops the area under food grain crops like rice, wheat, barley, other cereals and pulses has witnessed a declined in the State. Therefore to provide sufficient foodgrains to the people is a challenging job for the Government of Himachal Pradesh. The State depends upon all the essential commodities from neighboring States with the help of the Central Government. Therefore PDS becomes more important for hilly States like

Himachal Pradesh.

The PDS is implemented so far by the Government of Himachal Pradesh, to provide essential commodities to the beneficiaries through the network of FPSs. The TPDS was introduced in the State on 1 June 1997. Households were classified under two categories below the poverty line and above the poverty line. The food and civil supplies department ensures that the PDS in the state functions smoothly. In the State there are total 18,27,900 ration card holders out of the total population of 77,33,519 and there are about 4856 FPSs. Presently, under the PDS, the commodities namely wheat, rice, sugar are being allocated by the Center to the States for distribution.

In addition to these commodities the Government of H.P has launched a specially subsidized State scheme to all ration card holders with effect from 1st April, 2007. Under this scheme the beneficiaries are given 1 kg of dal rajmah and 1 kg of iodized salt per family per month for all ration card holders at the rate of Rs. 35 and 4 per kg, 1 kg of dal black masar per family of three and above members per month at the rate of Rs. 55 per kg, 1kg of dal channa per family of five and above members per month @ Rs. 61 per kg and also 1 litre of edible oil per ration card having 1 and 2 members and 2 and above family members per month @ Rs. 90 per litre (Department of food and civil supplies, 2016).

Moreover, for the implementation of National Food Security Act, 2013, the State Government has launched Rajiv Gandhi Anna Yojna on 20 September 2013. Under it beneficiaries would be categorized as antyodaya anna yojna, priority household and other than NFSA which includes above poverty line and below poverty line beneficiaries. Under the antyodaya anna yojana quota fixed as per Government of India is 35 kg of food grains per family per month. However, the State of H.P has bifurcated 20 kg of wheat and 15 kg of rice per family at the rate of Rs. 2 for wheat and Rs 3 for rice. As per the NFSA, 2013, priority household shall be entitled to receive 5 kg food grains per person per month at subsidized rates. The State has divided 3 kg of wheat and 3 kg of rice per family.

Apart from this, the Government of H.P is providing additional food grains to all the below poverty line families with the scale of 35 kg per family per month at the rate of Rs. 5.25 per kg of wheat and Rs. 8.5 kg of rice. Simultaneously, above poverty line beneficiaries are also getting benefits from PDS. The scale of APL wheat atta and rice is being changed every month depending upon the availability of stocks with the H.P. State Civil Supplies Corporation. These scales are uniformly applicable throughout the State except tribal areas of the State (Kinnaur, Lahaul Spiti, Pangi and Bharmour) where 20 Kg. of wheat atta and 15 Kg. of rice are being distributed monthly to APL card holders.

Table 1: Total allocation, off-take percentage of rice and wheat under PDS in Himachal Pradesh during 2003-04 to 2015-16.

(In thousand tonnes)

Year	2003-2004			2015-16		
	Allocation	Offtake	% of Offtake w.r.t. allocation	Allocation	Offtake	% Offtake w.r.t. allocation
Rice	380.52	149.87	39.38	184.09	184.49	100.21
Wheat	217.32	129.40	59.54	323.90	323.24	99.79

Source: Author's calculations using PDS offtake from ministry's bulletin foodgrains data.

Table-1 presents the total allocation, off-take and off-take percentage of rice and wheat from 2003-04 to 2015-16 in the State.

The total allotment of rice during 2003-04 and 2015-16 under PDS was 380.52 and 184.09 thousand tonnes, against which the total offtake was 149.87 and 184.49 thousand tonnes representing an overall percentage offtake of 39.38 & 100.21 percent. It shows that the percentage off take of rice with respect to allocation has increased significantly from 39.38 % in 2003-04 to 100.21 percent in 2015-16.

The off-take percentage of wheat has also increased from 59.54% in 2003-04 upto 99.79 % in 2015-16. It reveals the clear improvement in the working of PDS in Himachal Pradesh.

There was decline in the amount of rice allocation from 380.52 to 184.09 thousand tonnes for the same period whereas the amount of wheat allotment was increased from 217.32 to 323.90 thousand tonnes.

15.4. Household Reporting Consumption from PDS

One of the major problems of PDS is that, although households possessed ration card but they do not purchase PDS commodities from the fair price shops due to poor quality, lower difference between market price and PDS price and irregularities in supply of commodities etc. Table-2 shows the average and percentage monthly household consumption from PDS rice, wheat, sugar and kerosene during 2004-05 and 2011-2012 in Himachal Pradesh.

Table 2: Average and percentage monthly household consumption from PDS during 2004-05 and 2011-2012 in Himachal Pradesh.

Sector	Item	2004-05				2011-12			
		Quantity consumed (kg)			% share of PDS in qty. consumed	Quantity consumed (kg)			% share of PDS in qty. consumed
		From PDS	From other source	Total		From PDS	From other source	Total	
1	2	3		4	5	6	7	8	9
Rural	Rice	9.516	9.462	18.976	50.14	8.97	10	18.97	47.28
	Wheat	5.836	22.077	27.913	20.90	13.73	14.07	27.80	49.38
	Sugar	3.272	2.337	5.609	58.33	2.71	2.36	5.07	53.45
	Kerosene	0.915	0.23	1.145	79.91	0.53	0.19	0.81	65.43
Urban	Rice	2.050	10.616	12.66	16.19	3.15	8.79	11.93	26.40
	Wheat	1.080	17.66	18.74	5.76	6.17	11.98	18.15	33.99
	Sugar	0.876	2.463	3.339	26.23	1.23	2.17	3.41	36.07
	Kerosene	0.715	1.915	2.63	27.18	1.08	0.74	1.82	59.34

Source: Authors calculations based on NSS 61th and 68 round data: public distribution system and other sources of household consumption.

15.5. Share of PDS in Total Consumption of Rice and Wheat:

It is clear from above table that over the period of time share of PDS consumption to total consumption of rice and wheat has increased in both rural and urban areas. The average monthly rural household total quantity consumption of rice and wheat in 2004-05 is estimated to be 18.97 and 27.80 kg out of which 47.28 and 49.38 percent is sourced from the PDS. The contribution of PDS consumption to total consumption in 2011-12 shows a significant rise compared to 2004-05, particularly for rice and wheat. The percentage share of PDS in rice consumption declined to 47.28 percent in 2011-12 from 50.14 percent in 2004-05 in rural sector of Himachal Pradesh. However, the share of PDS in wheat consumption in 2004-05 was 20.90 percent which almost doubles to 49.38 percent in 2011-12. The contribution of PDS consumption to total consumption was highest in rural sector as compared to urban sectors. Moreover, the share of PDS rice and wheat in urban areas had increased over the period of time. In case of wheat consumption in urban areas, PDS share in 2011-12 (33.99 %) shows considerable rise compared to 2004-05 (5.76 %).

15.6. Share of PDS in Total Consumption of Sugar:

In 2004-05, the percentage share of PDS in sugar consumption was about 58.33 percent in rural areas whereas by 2011-12, this proportion had fallen to 53.45 percent. Despite the increase in the use of PDS food grains, the share of PDS in sugar consumption in urban areas has increased modest, 26.23 percent in 2004-05 to 36.07 percent in 2011-12.

15.7. Share of PDS in Total Consumption of Kerosene:

The share of PDS in total quantity consumption of kerosene in rural sector was highest about 79.91percent in 2004-05 which declined to 65.43 per cent in 2011-12. However in urban areas the percentage share of PDS quantity consumed to total consumption in 2011-12 (59.34%) shows a significant rise compared to 2004-05 (27.18 %).

15.8. Food Security Through PDS

Food insecurity is very challenging problem across the world, nearly 795 million people suffer from chronic hunger and almost one billion people live in extreme poverty globally (FAO, 2015). GHI (Global Hunger Index, 2016) shows that the level of hunger in developing countries as a group has fallen by 29 % since 2000 but India is still rated as country with serious hunger.

Every country is trying to tackle these problems. The Government of India has acted to put in place several safety nets to improve incomes and provide protection from shocks for the poor and vulnerable, one of which is the Public Distribution System. Indian Parliament also appeared very sensitive and enacted National Food security Act on 10 September, 2013. This act provides legal entitlement to the poor households for receiving the adequate quantity of quality food-grains at affordable prices to live a life with dignity (The Gazette of India, 2013).

In India, food security system mainly focuses on supply of food grains and this is distributed through the PDS. In the context of widespread poverty ratio, malnutrition and inflation in food prices, access to basic food at reasonable prices remains an important policy intervention (Swaminathan, 2003).

It has now been well established that availability of foodgrains is not the real problem but it is prevailing poverty amongst a large number of household that comes in the way of achieving household's food security. There may be abundance of food but it is no help to the poor households if it has no access to that. (Gaidhane, 2015)

According to the Indian council of agricultural research, there was the phenomenal increase in foodgrains from 196.81 million tonnes in 2000-01 to an all-time high of 265.04 million tonnes in 2013-14, which led to a surplus of foodgrain compared to domestic requirements and contributed substantially to overall exports. Thus, despite the achievement of self-sufficiency in foodgrains production and the prevalence of subsidized distribution of grains, there are millions of poor who lived the below poverty line and are not being able to consume at least minimum levels of calories (Gaidhane, 2015). In this situation PDS plays an important role in providing food security to the poor. Kochar (2005) highlighted the importance of PDS in improving the food security and the study found a low but positive elasticity of calorie intake with respect to PDS subsidy.

The average quantities of rice and wheat consumed by the households are converted into their nutrient content calories (kcals) using the nutritive value of Indian food item. The chart of nutrient contents remains the same in both the NSSO 61th and 68th rounds. Table- 3 provides the evidence that PDS plays an importance role in improving food security by reporting the share of the PDS in total calorie intake from the consumption of rice and wheat. For the overall period from 2004-05 to 2011-12, the percentage share of PDS in calorie intake from rice and wheat has increased both in rural and urban areas. It shows that the PDS is more effective in improving nutritional security in rural areas of Himachal Pradesh.

Table 3: Percentage share of PDS rice and wheat in calorie intake during 2004-05 and 2011-12 in Himachal Pradesh

Sector	Item	2004-05				2011-12			
		Calorie intake (kcals)			% share of PDS in calorie intake	Calorie intake (kcals)			% share of PDS in calorie intake
		From PDS	From other source	Total		From PDS	From other source	Total	
1	2	3	4	5	6	7	8	9	10
Rural	Rice	32925.36	32738.52	65663.88	50.14	31036.2	34600	65636.2	47.28
	Wheat	19900.76	75282.57	95183.33	20.90	46819.3	47978.7	94798	49.38
Urban	Rice	7093	36710.6	43803.6	16.19	10899	30413.4	41312.4	26.40
	Wheat	3682.8	60220.6	63903.4	5.76	21039.7	40851.8	61891.5	33.99

Source: Authors calculations based on NSS 61th and 68 round data: public distribution system and other sources of household consumption.

Also, it was clear from above table that the contribution of PDS in total calorie intake from rice consumption in rural Himachal declined from 50.14 percent in 2004-05 to 47.28 percent in 2011-12. In contrast to this its contribution increased over the time in urban areas.

In case of wheat, the share of PDS in total calorie intake in 2011-12 shows a considerable rise as compared to 2004-05 in both the rural and urban areas. Finally, the study shows that, over the period of time PDS become more effective in ensuring food security in Himachal Pradesh.

15.9. Major Constraints in the PDS in Himachal Pradesh

One of the major problems in the PDS is the large scale diversion of food grains to the open market. Himachal Pradesh is also facing the problem of leakages. As per Balani (2013) PDS suffers from nearly 61 % error of exclusion and 25 % error of inclusion of beneficiaries and in case of Himachal Pradesh there is very high (more than 30 %) leakages through Ghost cards and 25-50 % over all leakage of food grains.

PDS has been criticized on the ground of large scale targeting error in the identification of beneficiaries. There is a problem of inclusion and exclusion of the households. As per the statement by Food Minister of Himachal Pradesh, Bali (2013), number of actual ration card holders in the state was 17.15 lakh, while this figure was exaggerated to be 36.82 lakh in the previous Government records(Daily News and Analysis, 2013).

Irregularities in supply of commodities are another major problem in working of PDS in the State. It was found that even after over half month, the consumers did not get PDS food items like refine, mustard oil and sugar in Himachal Pradesh (Tribune, 2009).

Conclusion

Himachal Pradesh is a foodgrain deficit state and therefore it has to depend largely on the neighboring States for the supply of rice, wheat and sugar. Under such a situation PDS becomes very important in providing food security to the poor in the State. The study based on NSSO data however shows that the role of PDS in meeting consumption requirement of households has increased over time but there was wide inter sector (rural and urban) variations in the State. It was found that the percentage offtake of rice and wheat with respect to allocation has increased significantly 39.38 to 100.21 percent and 59.54 to 99.79 percent during 2003-04 to 2015-16. The percentage share of PDS in sugar consumption in rural areas has declined. Despite the increase in the use of PDS food grains, the share of PDS in sugar consumption in urban areas has increased from 2003-04 to 2011-12. The households reporting consumption of kerosene from the PDS has declined in the rural area and its consumption increased in urban areas of the State. Apart from a marked improvement in PDS consumption the study also indicates the rising contribution of PDS in terms of nutrient gains across rural and urban areas. The share of PDS wheat consumption was highest in both the areas.

References

Balani, S. (2013). Functioning of the public distribution system. [Online] Available from: http://www.prsindia.org/administrator/uploads/general/1388728622~~TPDS%20Thematic%20Note.pdf

Daily News and Analysis. (2013, Dec 18). Public distribution system issue rocks Himachal Pradesh assembly.

Department of food and civil supplies & consumer affairs Himachal Pradseh. (2016). http://admis.hp.nic.in/ehimapurti/welcome.asp

Gaidhane, A. (2015). Understanding the Llnkage between poverty, hunger and food security in India: role of public distribution system as a development input for poverty alleviation – problems and prospects of PDS. *Journal Of Humanities And Social Science*, 56-65.

Ghumaan, M. G., & Dhiman, D. P. (2013). Role and effectiveness of public distribution system in providing food security in India. *Indian Journal Of Research*, *3*(5), ISSN - 2250-1991.

Global Hunger Index. (2016). Global Hunger Index: Getting to zero hunger. *International Food Policy Research Institute*. http://www.ifpri.org/topic/global-hunger-index

Government of Indai. (2005). Evaluation report on revamped public distribution system. Programme Evaluation Organisation , Planning Commission , New Delhi.

Jha, S., & Srinivasan, P. V. (2001). Taking the PDS to the poor: directions for further reform. *Economic and Political Weekly*,

3779-3786.

Kochar, A. (2005). Can targeted food programs improve nutrition? an empirical analysis of India's public distribution system. *Economic development and cultural change*, *54*(1), 203-235.

Mahalingam, B. & Raj, A. (2016). Major drawbacks of public distribution system in India-A Review. *International Journal for Scientific Research & Development*.

Saxena, A., & Gupta, A. K. (2014). Significance of public distribution system in an Indian State -Uttar Pradesh. *International Journal of Management and Social Sciences Research*.

Shanmugam, P., & Thomas, D. K. (2016). Efectiveness of public distribution system : a case study of marangattuoilly panchayat in Kerala. *International Journal of Humanities, Arts, Medicine and Sciences*, *4*(9), 17-26.

Singh, B. P. (2014). PDS: A review of its functioning and effectiveness, since independence. *Research Journal of Economics and Business Studies*.

Swaminathan, M., & Misra, N. (2001). Errors of targeting: public distribution of food in a Maharashtra village, 1995-2000. *Economic and Political Weekly*, *36*(26), 2447-2454.

The Gazette of India, (2013). Ministry of Law and Justice, Government of India The. National Food Security Act , New Delhi.

CHAPTER 16
PROBLEMS & PROSPERITY OF PUBLIC DISTRIBUTION SYSTEM IN HIMACHAL PRADESH-A CASE STUDY WITH SPECIAL REFERENCES TO KANGRA DISTRICT

Ranju

Abstract

India is a vast country where majority of the people live below the poverty line. India's food problem continues to be the most serious problem, scarcity of food & essential commodities affects adversely the economy along with the life of the people. Without the freedom of the hunger, other freedoms are of little significance. Planning and Economic development sound hollow indeed when the majority of rural masses are not able to get minimum quantity of food and essential commodities at reasonable price. Without proper distribution of food and essential commodities to the poorer and vulnerable rural masses, India's hope for improving human welfare, achieving social justice and securing democracy will be futile efforts. So, a system was established in 1939 such as "Public Distribution System". It is a sum of three words Public+Distribution+System which means a system of distribution of necessary goods & services among people by central govt. & state govt. The need of public distribution system as we know that "Poverty Alleviations & eradication of hunger" are two vital objectives of rural development programmers in India. Apart from that in 2013 National Food Security Act was established to maintain security & safety of food to the beneficiaries. So the study was conducted to determine some of problems & prosperity of PDS in Himachal Pradesh & strategies' they use to minimize these challenges. A case study of Kangra district in H.P was conducted. Pilot survey & Multistage Sampling technique were employed to collect the data. A sample of 160 beneficiaries & 20 F.P.S were selected. Two data collection techniques were used: Structured questionnaire & in depth interview. The gathered information was analyzed using statistical package of social science. Finding of the study showed that some of problems occur in Kangra district of H.P includes, quality of commodities, working hour, transparency, distribution pattern, black marketing. The respondents recommended that govt. & community should create secure conditions & policies for them to cope up the current situations.

16.1. Introduction

PDS is a combination of three words PUBLIC +DISTRIBUTION+SYSTEM. It means a system in which essential commodities is distributed among people by govt. at reasonable prices. It is an Indian food security system established by Government of India, under Ministry of Consumer Affairs, Food & Public Distribution are managed jointly by state govt. in India. This scheme was launched in India on June 1947 but established in 1939 as Public Distribution System. Major target of this scheme was to distributes the subsidized food & non subsidized food items to the weaker section or needy one by maintaining the RATION CARD, issued by the local authority.

The major commodities distributed includes, staple food grains, such as wheat, rice, sugar, pulses, kerosene along with the fertilizer, through a network of Fair Price Shops(F.P.S) also known as ration shops established in several states across the country. Food corporation of India a govt. owned corporation i.e. process & maintains the PDS. The need of public distribution system as we know that " Poverty alleviation and eradication of hunger" are two vital objectives of rural development programmers in India. The major target set by the ministry such as eradication of rural poverty & inequality by providing justice to the poorer one or needy one. According to the (Economic Review, Directorate & Statistic H.P). It was clubbed with the minimum needs programmers (MNP) in the 7TH five year plan with the network of about 4,51,000 fair price shops for the distribution of commodities worth over rs.150 billion to about 180 million households throughout the country, PDS perhaps the largest distribution network not only in India but in the world.

According to (S. Shankaran 1981) The role of the govt. in an economy varies according to the economic system followed by it. In capitalistic economy the role of the govt. in controlling business enterprise is reduced to minimum & vice versa, in socialism system irrespective of such an economic system, the govt. modern days try to control the working of economic system, through economic planning & active participation in the industrial activities. As such in mixed economy the govt. through effective & rational interference in the economic, business, monetary & fiscal sectors, tries to achieve its goals & objectives of welfare.

On the recommendations of some committees & in view of old PDS performance the govt. introduced "Targeted Public Distribution System " from June 1997. The main objective of the scheme was to supply the necessary commodities for the poor section of society. Under this schemes entire population of the country was divided into two categories:

- APL (Above poverty line)
- BPL (Below poverty line)

PDS is a poorer's welfare scheme run by central & state govt. jointly for satisfactory upbringing of rural masses. But it doesn't seems to be a easy task due to different kind loopholes in working. Which causes insignificance contribution towards different welfares schemes run by the govt. for social welfare or rural development. But this system had given a positive living by providing an essential commodities which leads a satisfactory level to their basic needs . It can be said that PDS has given pleasure of living or satisfactory living to the rural masses.

But apart from that it is noticed that PDS is a welfare scheme but huge amount of loop holes are running together in the path of welfare projects or programmers. Problems in the path of welfare projects causes a big obstacle for bettermenship of the society. Such as by passing wrong entries in the ration card without acknowledging the ration card holder, not providing the original slips of subsidized ration receipt, non availability of F.P. Shopkeeper during the working hours, misuse of the material by selling the same in the bigger shops such as black marketing, poor quality of material, these are the loopholes which are major issue in up bring of society as smooth level.

According to (Mahendran & Indrakant) revealed in their study that PDS run by govt. in rural masses plays a positive role such as poor people are very happy & utilized to meet their basic needs by distributing the free rice, color TV, fan, mixer & other basic needs commodities. Lifestyle of rural castle people has improved. Welfare schemes run by govt. in state of Tamil Nadu leads the development of socio economic factors from the grassroots.

According to (Joshipura & Joshipura 2013) pertained in his study " Technical & Financial Feasibility of I.T enabled PDS. By implementing I.T on PDS is not only establishing a cost effective system but also has a greatest possibility to avoid leakage or loopholes & Crotch of commodities from the PDS.

According to (Dreze & Khera) the author suggest that PDS had both + & - perspective in India. Positive perspective lies in clear evidence such as India's PDS now has a effective impact on rural poverty. The impact is particularly large in states with well-functioning of PDS such as important tool of economic security for the rural masses in many states. Negative perspective is that PDS still has very little impact on the rural poverty in U.P & West Bengal where PDS reforms are long overdue. Another author Sharma (Food Security in India - A Comment) 17.2% of world's population have been living in India. So it can be said that most populated counrtry in the world is India. But according to the World 's hunger Index India's condition is pitiful i.e. 25% (30 crore) people of India can't even have two times meal. Due to green revolution India contribute a unique specter of overflowing godowns & decomposing grains on the other hand, while millions of populations go to bed hungry. Wastage of food due to negligence & poor storage should be announced as criminal offence.

According to Hussain (2012) food that there is a lot of misappropriation of supplies in the system. There is Fair Price Shop (FPS) within a two km radius for every ration card holder. Kashmir is a region which has a comparative advantage for cash crop production and is dependent on imports mainly for food. Under the targeted PDS, the centre had identified 24% of the population as being BPL and the allotments to the state had been reduced from the time of the universal PDS. Ration shop owners would get less profit and more incentive to sell their goods in the black market as it is much more profitable.

Government in J & K is not serious about the supplies provided to the general public. The supplies either is of least quality or is not provided at proper time resulting into huge crises in the state in general and Kashmir in particular. The pubic in Kashmir is properly dependent on thee supplies for their survival as there is no production of sugar and other commodities supplied through PDS.

Svedberg (2012) analyzed the case for and against replacing a reformed version of the current PDS with a targeted and differentiated cash transfer scheme. He proposed that such a scheme could benefit more than two-third households and extend the PDS outreach to large poor communities. He expressed a concern that providing unconditional cash to poor households will reduce the labor supply but increase significantly the amount of nutritional intake of the poor. He also added that increase in suggested a targeted and differentiated all India cash transfer scheme based on bio-metric UID Cards to curb use of ghost cards.

Banerjee (2011) empathized in his study entitled "Decentralized procurement and universalized PDS" that decentralization of food procurement could facilitate universalization of the pubic distribution system under the proposed National Food Security Act of the diverse array of foodgrains available across the country only rice, wheat and sugar are provided from the ration shops in most areas. The other crops like millets, coarse cereals, pulses, oilseeds, etc, which are the part of the diet of people across the country are surprisingly not available in ration shops. Most of these "other" crops grew in rain fed conditions-an overwhelming majority (between 60% and 70%) of Indian agriculture is rain fed and an array of crops grows in these regions, yet our procurement and public distribution relies only on three crops. This, we shall demonstrate, is because of a flawed strategy of the green revolution (GR henceforth) paradigm.

Rai (2011) found in their study entitled "Performance Audit of Food Security in Orissa and UP" that among 3250 total surveyed households, more than one third (34.2%) had no ration card whatsoever 22.5% of respondents households identified "full quantity of grain not provided" as a major problem faced by them in availing their food grain entitlements under the PDS. "Irregular availability of grain at the PDS shop" was identified by 13.5% of the respondents as a major problem faced by them. Only one respondent in the total samples said that there was over-pricing by dealer. 22.2% of sample households said that there was corruption in the PDS. 33.5% of the respondents said that poor quality of grain was given to them under the PDS. "Lack of cash when grain was available at the PDS Shop" was a problem faced by 21.2% of the surveyed households.

Khera (2011) finds contrary to a common belief that India's Public Distribution System is irreparably dysfunctional; a nine-state survey of the PDS, the respondents received 84-88% of their full entitlement. The implicit subsidy for households below the poverty line from PDS food grains alone is roughly equivalent, in many states, to a week's NREGA wages every month. The revival of PDS can be traced, in large part, to a renewed political interest which manifests itself in state initiatives such as expanded coverage, reduced prices, computerization of stock management, etc. A large majority of the respondents preferred to receive in-kind food transfers rather than cash transfers, expect in Bihar where the PDS is still in very poor shape. Their testimonies, and the survey findings, point to many good reasons to be wary of a hasty transition to cash transfers.

Pal (2011) critically analyzed the functioning of organizations like Food Corporation of India and Central Warehousing Corporation in ensuring procurement, transportation, storage and distribution of commodities provided by the public distribution system. He argues that the current system is extremely corrupt and fails to address issues around storage of stocks, fake supply entries in ration cards, diversion of commodities for sale to open market, bogus ration cards, irregularity and poor quality of food grains. He advocates technical up gradation and policy reforms to ensure transparency, speed up the process and improve performance to solve the above mentioned problems.

Lathi and Narkhede (2010) examined that the problem of food security seems to be an important parameter for economic stability, and for the human kind. It requires three fold activities: Use of safe Genetically Modified crops and use of better Bio-technological seeds and pesticides. Rehabilitation of barren land into cultivation with the fewer use of water resources, use of those crops which requires less water as a prime source as far as India is concerned due to more pressure of use of water comes from community supply for human beings (even at the cost of production activities).

Use of increasing income policies by strategic planning of deployment of natural resources, availability of finance and by trade-off of information technology through bi-lateral policies with the help of Government

16.2. Problem Statement

To know the "Problems & Prosperity of PDS in H.P - A study with special reference to Kanga District"

16.3. Objectives

1. To study the satisfaction level of consumers & F.P.S regarding quality of goods.
2. To identify the various problems faced by beneficiaries of Kangra District.
3. To examine overall performance of PDS.

16.4. Methodology

In order to an appropriate & relevant understanding of problems & prosperity of PDS in H.P-A Study with special reference to Kangra district was conducted. The statistical data for the study have been collected from the Primary sources along with the pilot survey. The primary data has been collected from the 160 consumers & 20 F.P.S. Multistage sampling technique was used to know the existing performance of PDS. The data thus collected have been analyzed by using to suitable tools & statistical package of social science.

16.5. Sampling Design

Sampling design is a design which called as blueprint by another name Multistage sampling is used for seeking information from the respondents for the research. Such as followings:

Figure 1

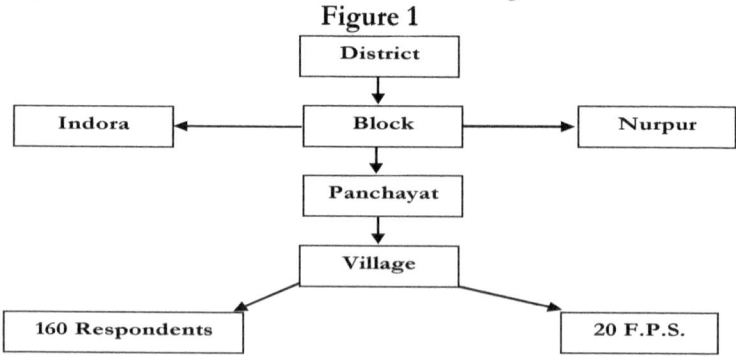

First Stage: This was the multistage sampling design, which includes five stages for following the research pattern. Out of twelve district of h.p Kangra district was selected purposively basis.

Second Stage: In second stage, two blocks from Kangra district were taken on randomly basis. These were: Nurpur & Indora.

Third Stage: The third stage was related to the selection of the local self-government bodies (Panchayats). From each block, two panchayats are taken on randomly basis.

Fourth Stage: In fourth stage from each panchayat two villages were selected on randomly basis.

Fifth Stage: In this stage from each block 90 respondents had been purposively selected spread as 80 households respondents & 10 fair price shops dealer. The respondents were selected on convenience random sample basis.

Table 1: Selection Of Sample

Sr. No.	District	Blocks	No. of Panchayats Selected	Name of Villages	Respondents		Total
					Household respondent	FPS Dealer	
1.	Kangra	Nurpur	Kamnala	Kamnala	20	10	90
				Kathala	20		
			Nurpur	Nurpur	20		
				Jassur	20		
		Indora	Indora	Indora	20	10	90
				Chanour	20		
			Sanour	Sanour	20		
				Maladi	20		
Total	1	2	4	8	160	20	180

16.6. Analysis & Interpretation

16.6.i. Demographic Profile Of The Study Area

The study was conducted in the NURPUR and INDORA block in KANGRA District of Himachal Pradesh. This following section mainly focuses on the demographic characteristics of the study area in terms of gender of the respondents, age, education and family.

Table 2: Profile of Respondents on the basis of Gender

GENDER	No. of Respondents	Percentage
Male	42	26.25
Female	118	73.75
Total	160	100

Source: Field Survey 2015

Note: Figure in parenthesis indicates percentage

For the purpose of this study one hundred sixty participants were purposively surveyed. Response showed that 26.25% of the respondents were male and 73.75% were female. This means that more number of female participants was involved in collecting their monthly quota of gain from the PDS outlet rather than male.

Table 3: Profile of respondents on the basis of age

Age Group	No. of Respondents	Percentage
Upto 25	24	15
25-50	97	60.7
Above 50	39	24.3
Total	160	100

Source: Field Survey 2015

Note: Figure in parenthesis indicates percentage

The distribution of the respondents has been categories on the basis of their age in table 3. From the above table it can be seen that the respondents having age 3up to 25 years, 15% of respondents are in this category, Second category is of respondents having age between 25-50 years and percentage of respondents is 60.7% and third category is of above 50 years, which is 24.3% of respondents are in the category. This shows that PDS entitlements are for all adult age group members who possess a valid ration card.

Table 4: Profile of Respondents on the basis of Education level

Education level	No. Respondents	Percentage
Matric	7	4.3
Plus Two	60	37.5
Graduate	48	30.0
Post Graduate	45	28.2
Total	160	100

Source: Field Survey 2015

Note: Figure in parenthesis indicates percentage

The above table it is found that highest number of participants were educated (37.5%) plus two followed by graduate (30%). Post graduate also formed (8.2%) .only 4.3% respondents were matric holders.The above study shows that maximum no of respondents were educated at some level & were aware of their benefits received from PDS supplies.

Table 5: Profile of Respondents on the basis of Family

Type of Family	No. of Respondents	Percentage
Nuclear Family	129	80.7
Joint Family	31	19.3
Total	160	100

Source: Field Survey 2015

From the above table it is found that out of 160 respondents (80.7%) were living in nuclear family along with that only (19.3%) belongs to joint family. Above study shows that only few respondents were living in joint family & maximum no. of respondents were living in nuclear family or single hold.

Table 6: Profile of Respondents on the basis of Income

Variables	No. of Respondents	Percentage
Below 25000	77	48.2
25000-50000	33	20.6
50000-75000	20	12.5
Above 75000	30	18.7
Total	160	100

Source: Field Survey 2015

As per table it is clear that above table shows the distribution of income of the respondents. This shows that maximum of respondents (48.125%) of respondents having income less than 25000 p.m (20.625%) of the respondents earn an income between 25000-50000 remaining were belongs to other income group. Thus crux of the study represents that majority of the respondents are low income earning individuals irrespective of other opportunities.

Table 7 shows the views regarding the supply of ration among the customers by the govt. The statement shows the negative response regarding the supply of ration. Crux of the table shows that 40 percent of the respondents are dissatisfied with the above mentioned statement. The overall mean has been found 2.05 which is below the average mean at 3 point likertscale. Reason for this is that now days people are more aware about the quality branding of the product so they buy the product at best quality.

Table 7: Opinion of customer regarding supply of Ration

Block	Panchayat	Highly Satisfied	Satisfied	Dis-Satisfied	Total	Mean	S.D	Chi Value	P Value
Nurpur	Kamnala	6 (15)	14 (35)	20 (50)	40	1.75	.630	3.80	.120
Nurpur	Nurpur	16 (40)	16 (40)	8 (20)	40	2.01	.712	.250	.250
Indora	Indora	11 (27.5)	13 (32.5)	16 (40)	40	1.87	.822	.950	.950
Indora	Sanour	7 (17.5)	13 (32.5)	20 (50)	40	1.23	.430	1.96	.275
Total		40 (25)	56 (35)	64 (40)	160	2.05	.858	1.963	.003

Source: Field Survey 2015

Table 8: Opinion of Respondents regarding Existing PDS

Block	Panchayat	Highly Satisfied	Satisfied	Dis-Satisfied	Total	Mean	S.D	Chi Value	P Value
Nurpur	Kamnala	10 (25)	6 (15)	24 (60)	40	2.02	.622	.820	.620
Nurpur	Nurpur	11 (27.5)	13 (32.5)	16 (40)	40	2.30	.803	12.40	.002
Indora	Indora	15 (37.5)	7 (17.5)	18 (45)	40	1.92	.916	4.05	.008
Indora	Sanour	14 (35)	13 (32.5)	13 (32.5)	40	2.03	.741	.060	.96
Total		50 (31.25)	39 (29.39)	71 (43.75)	160	1.65	.739	5.84	.039

Source: Field Survey 2015

The views of respondents regarding existing PDS have been presented above. It shows that majority of respondents 43.75 percent dissatisfied with the statement. With that only 31.25% are only satisfied with statement. Mean value of both block is 2.02& 2.03 which shows almost similar trends. S.D shows the 739 denotes less variation. Chi square value shows significant at 5 percent level. Overall opinion regarding existing PDS has showed difference in opinion of respondents. Crux of the study shows that majority of respondents are not satisfied with existing display which means that there must be need to improve the system.

Table 9: Opinion of Respondent regarding the Distribution of Ration accordingly to member of family

Block	Panchayat	Yes	No	Total	Mean	S.D	Chi Value	P Value
Nurpur	Kamnala	17 (42.5)	23 (57.5)	40	3.01	.762	10.550	.101
	Nurpur	15 (37.5)	25 (62.5)	40	2.01	.862	12.2.	.120
Indora	Indora	22 (55)	18 (45)	40	2.05	.753	8.03	.000
	Sanour	24 (60)	16 (40)	40	2.01	.852	3.06	.203
Total		78 (48.75)	82 (51.25)	160	2.27	.807	8.82	.002

Source: Field Survey 2015

Above table shows the distribution of the ration according to the member of the family. Statement reveals that majority of the respondents are not satisfied with the distribution of ration according to the member of the family. The reason behind this is that every single member demands to get ration on monthly basis not according to the member of family. So crux of the study reveals that majority of the respondents not satisfied with distribution of ration according to the member of the family

Table 10: Opinion of Respondents regarding Quality of Salt

Block	Panchayat	Highly Satisfied	Satisfied	Dis-Satisfied	Total	Mean	S.D	Chi Value	P Value
Nurpur	Kamnala	3	7	30	40	2.30	.640	12.90	.002
	Nurpur	4	9	27	40	1.98	.610	6.10	.032
Indora	Indora	6	12	22	40	1.62	.614	13.04	.040
	Sanour	4	4	32	40	1.78	.831	3.10	.161
Total		17 (10.62)	32 (20)	111 (69.37)	160	1.92	.673	28.40	.189

Source: Field Survey 2015

Above table shows the views of respondents regarding the quality of salt. Salt play vital role in daily need. Without good quality of salt major health issue arise. At present scenario costumers are quality conscious instead of pricing. Above table shows that majority of the respondents are not satisfied with quality of the salt 69.37 percent respondents are not satisfied with quality of salt which means quality of the salt is not good. S.D also show the very less variations in the variables. Crux of the study shows that majority of the responses are not satisfied with the quality of the salt so there is need to be improve the quality of salt.

Table 11: Opinion of Dealers regarding quality of material

Particulars	Highly Satisfied	Satisfied	Dis-Satisfied	Total
Rice	4 (20)	10 (50)	6 (30)	20 (100)
Wheat	5 (25)	9 (45)	6 (30)	20 (100)
Edible oil	4 (20)	9 (45)	7 (35)	20 (100)
Sugar	-	3 (15)	17 (85)	20 (100)
Salt	-	4 (20)	16 (80)	20 (100)
Pulses	-	14 (70)	6 (30)	20 (100)

Source: Field Survey 2015

Above table shows the view of fair price shopkeeper in regard to the quality of material supplied by the govt. to the different patterns of the society. 50 percent of the majority of the dealer is satisfied with the quality of rice. Reason behind this that they said quality is not bad as weaker and other section of the society regular use it. 45 percent of the majority is satisfied with the quality of wheat supplied by the govt. in the society. 45 percent of the majority is satisfied with the edible oil. Reason behind this is that majority of the society use it. Pluses are of good quality. Sugar & Salt is not of good quality because majority of the dealers are not satisfied with this supply reason is of low quality.

Table 12: Opinion of Respondents Regarding quality of commodities

Block	Panchayat	Highly Satisfied	Satisfied	Dissatisfied	Total	Mean	S.D.	Chi Value	P Value
Nurpur	Kamnala	12	14	16	40	1.50	.720	2.40	.206
	Nurpur	11	10	19	40	1.60	.821	4.91	.120
Indora	Indora	13	14	13	40	2.20	.741	.070	.871
	Sanour	14	8	18	40	1.90	.716	.624	.810
Total		50 (31.25)	46 (28.75)	66 (41.25)	160	1.80	.748	5.84	.041

Source: Field Survey 2015

The views of respondents regarding quality of goods supplied by government have been presented in the table. It shows negative response of the respondents for this statement. It is clear from the table that 41.25 percent of respondents dissatisfied with this statement. Overall mean value has been found 1.80 which is below average mean at 3 points of Likert scale. This indicates that most of the respondents dissatisfied or satisfied with quality of goods. It is found that nowadays people are more aware about the quality, branding of the product and they want to buy those goods which are of best quality. This is useful to convey that people are not satisfied with quality of goods as majority of the panchayats has shown their dissatisfaction for this statement.

Table 13: Opinion of Respondents regarding working hour of shop

Block	Panchayat	Highly Satisfied	Satisfied	Dissatisfied	Total	Mean	S.D.	Chi Value	P Value
Nurpur	Kamnala	10	5	25	40	3.06	.670	6.01	.049
	Nurpur	12	9	19	40	1.09	.716	1.84	.390
Indora	Indora	10	12	18	40	1.36	.605	6.64	.012
	Sanour	6	12	22	40	1.24	.570	1.9	.000
Total		38 (23.75)	38 (23.75)	84 (52.5)	160	1.68	.640	4.01	.041

Source: Field Survey 2015

Most of the FPS in the state functions from 9AM to 6PM because majority of the shops are in the hands of co-operatives and

H.P. State Civil Supplies Corporation. In above table consumer attitude towards the working hours of the FPS are being analyzed. It is evident from the table that 52.5 percent respondents dissatisfied with this statement. The overall mean value has been found 1.68 which is below average mean at 3 points of Likert scale. This indicates that the most of the respondents dissatisfied with the statement. As it is found that PDS shops in the villages are not open at time. The calculated value of S.D has been found .640 which shows less variation in the responses of respondents. On applying chi square test of goodness of fit its calculated value has been found insignificant at 5 percent level of significance accepting null hypotheses.

Table 14: Opinion of Respondents regarding overall performance of PDS

Block	Panchayat	Highly Satisfied	Satisfied	Dissatisfied	Total	Mean	S.D.	Chi Value	P Value
Nurpur	Kamnala	14 (35)	12 (30)	14 (35)	40	2.30	.641	3.610	.171
	Nurpur	12 (30)	5 (12.5)	23 (57.5)	40	2.10	.629	12.21	.000
Indora	Indora	14 (35)	10 (25)	16 (40)	40	2.12	.610	5.170	.010
	Sanour	12 (30)	6 (15)	22 (55)	40	2.01	.728	11.32	,001
Total		52 (32.5)	33 (20.6)	75 (46.87)	160	2.13	.652	27.150	.021

Source: Field Survey 2015

The views of respondents regarding overall performance of PDS have been presented in the table. It shows negative response of the respondents for this statement. It is clear from the table that 46.87 percent of respondents dissatisfied with this statement. Overall mean value has been found 2.13 which is below average mean at 3 points of Likert scale. This indicates that most of the respondents dissatisfied or satisfied with overall performance of PDS. It is found that nowadays people are more aware about the quality, branding of the product and they want to buy those goods which are of best quality. This is useful to convey that people are not satisfied with overall performance of the PDS as majority of the panchayats has shown their dissatisfaction for this statement.

Conclusion

At the end it is concluded that PDS is an important tool for eradication of hunger & poverty alliviation. But due to loopholes, working of PDS had been effected badly, such as poor quality of material supplied by the fair price shopkeeper, no proper timing of working hours, majority of the people are not satisfied with contribution of the material according to the member, apart from that majority of the people's view regarding the overall performance is also not good due to huge amount of loopholes. For this necessary steps must be taken for the betterment of the current PDS.

References

Economic Review, Directorate of Economics & statistics H.P, Shimla, 1992, P.P 1-15.

Shankaran, S. (1981) Business Economy (Progressive Corporation, Bombay) p.447.

Mahendran, A. Indrakant, S. (2014). Public Distribution System in Tamil Nadu, India: Rice Supply Scheme of Prosperous, Problems and Policy, International Journal of Academic Research in Public Policy and Governance, Vol. 1, No. 1, (January), pp. 23, www.hrmars.com.

Dreze, Jean, Khera, Reetika. (2013). Rural Poverty and the Public Distribution System, *Centre for Development Economics*, Working Paper No. 235, Department of Economics, Delhi School of Economics, p. 11.

Sharma, A. (2014). Food Security in India: A Comment, *Himalayan Journal of Contemporary Research*, Vol. 3, No. 1 (January-June), pp. 724.

Joshipura, N. M., Joshipura M. H. (2013). Technical and Financial Feasibility of Information Technology Enabled Public Distribution System, *Prabhandhan: Indian Journal of Management*, Vol. 6, No. 1 (January), p. 22.

sHussain, B. (2012). Efficiency of Public Distribution System in Kashmir: A Micro Economic Analysis, *International Research Journal of Social Sciences*, Vol. 1 (4), (December), pp. 24-27.

Svedberg, P. (2012). Reforming or Replacing the Public Distribution System' with Cash Transfers *Economic & Political Weekly*, Vol. 47 (7), (February), pp. 53-62.

Banerjee, K. (2011). Decentralized Procurement and Universalized PDS, *Economic and Political Weekly*, Vol. XLVI, No. 52, (December), p. 19.

Rai, P.(2011). Performance Audit of Food Security Schemes in Orissa and UP, *Centre for Environment and Food Security*, New Delhi, pp. 8-10.

Khera, R. (2011).Revival of Public Distribution System: Evidence and Explanations, *Economic and Political Review*, Vol. XLVI, No. 44-45, (November).

Pal, B. (2011). Organization and Working of Public Distribution System in India: A Critical Analysis, *International Journal of Business Economic & Management Research*, Vol. 1, No. 1, pp. 40-48.

Lathi, B.J., Narkhede, Parag.. (2010). Food Security in India: Concepts, Realities and Innovations, *Global Journal of Business Management*, Vol. 4, No. L(June), p. 80.

CHAPTER 17
GLOBALIZATION AND INDIAN IDENTITY

Jitender K. Bhanwal

17.1. Introduction

Globalization is not a new concept but it has acquired a new significance and dimensions in face of the changed scenario of international balance of forces often the collapse of communism in Soviet Union and other EEC and disintegration of the socialist system. People want to unshackle themselves from the grip of regulating political and economical regime. They are tiring to learn to treat the world as one entity, throwing to the dustbin all sorts of economic barriers, which inhibit free flow of world's financial and technological resources. Capital has now assumed a more pronounced global character. This upsurge and diversification has brought sea changes in economics and politics of both advanced and developed countries. The end of the cold war has necessitated the development of capital, which has been hitherto going into war industries, in advanced capitalistic counties the need to increase the rate of export of capital has assumed greater importance. The word globalization is the key word, which means world as', a single market. It gives us awareness about latest technology and product so that we keep out identity m' this world. A multi-polar new world, which encompasses an enormous movement of goods, will change the whole concept of trading through globalization. It is a concept in it entirely. Globalization does not mean imploring homogenous solutions in a pluralistic world. It means individual identity. It means nourishing local insights, but it also reemploying communicable ideas in new geographies around the world. For nearly two centuries prior to the Independence in 1947, India's Economy was subservient to the economies of the European nations. Actually, it was the mass time disruptions occurred and the trade sanctions imposed during the tenures of World Wars-1 and II that helped to loosen these tight reins and hence, tentative development of indigenous trade, industry and markets could occur. After independence, the policymakers were faced with the challenging task of nation building, which they attempted to accomplish through the implementation of five year, development plans. The national economy was protected from the cyclical as well as episodic disruptions in the world economies through import export restrictions, reservations, and barriers to the entry of foreign capital and a self-imposed frugal life style of the masses. Even after decade and half it has not been possible to pinpoint one single causes, that caused the fiscal fiasco of 1991 and led India to the doorsteps of the World Bank and IMP, seeking a huge loan of USA Seven billion to bail the country out of the balance of payments crises. While agreeing to provide assistance to India the World Bank IMF' combine insisted that the Govt. must put its economy back on rails; in other words integrate it with the emerging global economy (Datt 2001). In his memorandum on economic policies submitted to the IMF, Dr. Man Mohan Singh then Union Minister of Finance, proposed, "The thrust will be to increase the efficiency and international competitiveness of industrial production, to utilize foreign investment and technology to a much greater degree then in past. To improve the growth and rationalize the financial sector, so that it can more efficiently serve the needs of the economy". The major thrust areas of these economic reforms were to be; (i) Fiscal policy reforms (ii) Monetary policy reforms, (iii) Social policy reforms (iv) External policy reforms (v) Foreign and investment policy reforms (vi) Trade policy reforms (vii) Public sector policy reforms (viii) Industrial policy reforms. Globalization was introduced to India, or was rater imposed on it, under the seemingly innocuous name of 'Economic liberalization'.

17.2. Objectives

The following are objective of this project "Globalization and Indian Identity",
A. Global and Indian Social economic impact.
B. Global and Indian Culture
C. Global and Indian Education
D. Global and Indian Agriculture.

17.3. Methodology

Primary and secondary data will be used and different information's are collected from Journals, magazine, newspapers, Internet and books. In the questionnaire only twelve questions were asked and interviews of 30 intellectual persons conducted and views received from these persons analyze and highlighted in this project.

17.4. Limitation

Maximum secondary data and information used and only simple techniques are used due to shortage of time.

17.4.i. Globalization and Socio- Economic Scenario

India is rapidly getting integrated to the global economy, which requires all of us to consider a deeper strategic and geopolitical view of the world. As gradually move into the New Year and plan where we will be relaxing. George W. Bush is repeated for his second term. China is forging ahead to be the prime power of Asia. After Besla, Vladimir Putin is setting the stage for more centerline, political powerful and economically significant,, Russia, Continental Europe is economically floundering with little or no sense of political unity. Amidst unparalleled violence, Iraq attempts and election in 2005. Yasser Arafat is dead with no succession plan in place. Iran and North Korea want to join the nuclear club. There is an alleged Chinese saying, "May you line in interesting time". Today it takes greater meaning. Traditionally, most of Indians are insular in our worldviews. This is partly due to the sheer size of country and its relative lack of integration with world market. It is also cultural and suspected, arises out of a Brahmin cal epistemology, namely, "we are the front of all wisdom, and what and what we don't know, we don't need to know. This position is no longer tenable. India is getting integrated and geopolitical view of the world. In this research work, we shall try just that to present some issues that we as a country should be thinking of as we engage as wider world. In doing so, we shall focus on the US, Europe, Russia and China, Thereafter-we will try to interpret the geopolitical changes in terms of what they may mean for India's political, economic strategy and its identity. Regarding the US Economy the good news is that it is doing for better than Europe and will continue in that view over the next few years. At $ 851 billion, its trade goods and services is about eight times that of India and that will grow at double" digits. And it will be the world's number one market for mobile phones, coal, steel, metals, television, personal computers, while goods, and agricultural and food products. China's GDP, measures urged at market exchange rates will overtake Japan's. The best is yet to come, and one can't even imagine the scale and speed at which it will arrive. There will be no doubt in our mind that China and India will become a major force in global geopolitics the 8.2% GDP growth last year a possible 7% growth tills time around, India is again on a global radar screen. In part, it is because the global investing community has realized that and economy of over a billion people with growth rates above 6% is a space that it cannot, ignore. In part there is an appreciation that the Global market game is China and India instead of China versus India. It also reflects the desire of global majors to adopt sensible geographical de-risking -strategy and India fit into that scheme of things. Therefore the present global economic constellation is quite favorable to us.

17.4.ii. Globalization and Culture

Globalization did not spare the culture of India also. With the unrestricted entry of the western values, costumes and living habits, the Indian culture is shaken to the roots and the social norms have changes beyond recognition. With the ascent of Internet, different culture microcosms are being replaced by a single, world-engulfing telecom. During collection of data out of 30 person 15 responded that globalization will effect Indian culture and 8 responses came that custom cannot be effected by foreign invaders then how it will be effected by the globalization. Seven responses came, that culture couldn't be affected by globalization. As a result, the generations - old laid-back way of life has been supplanted by the fierce competition to succeed at any cost. The element of competition is to succeed at any cost. The element of completion, in turn, has significantly influenced people's personal, familial and social lives.

17.4.iii. Globalization and Education

There will be a lot of education specification benefits as well particularly in developing countries. India has not been able to reach a higher level of enrolment in education like those of advanced or middle-income countries. For instance, our level enrolment in education first about six percent of the relevant age group against over fifty percent reached be attainable by middle income Countries. Entry of new institutions might add to the supply of seats and thereby improve the rate of enrolment. The govt. has been finding it difficult to even sustain, leave alone augment, resource allocation for education. The allocation in India stood at about 3.5 percent against a desirable norm of six percent of the Gross Domestic Product. The education, to higher education has declined substantially; private investment induced by Globalization may thus give a boost -to the resource allocation for education. During survey 24- percent viewed that Globalization will not effected the education by 26% responded that globalization will help to provide better and more percentage of persons to acquire education by raising more seats in more institutions, colleges and universities etc. But 50 percent strongly viewed that globalization will affect the Indian education as well educational costlier and it will become difficult to acquire higher education. The education has strong links with culture. Traditionally, its objectives were: physical and intellectual development of the child inculcation of values, self and social knowledge and vocational training. Globalization attend the objectives like self-learning, linked learning, synthesis of knowledge, team working and adaptability, uncultured and professionalism.

17.4.iv. Globalization and Agriculture

Globalization on the one hand, has affected the prices of various agriculture produces. The major negative impact was felt in some rural pockets which were not able to cope with the quality of the imported products and further handicapped by the government's internal policies that were unresponsive to the changes at the global level. At the same time globalization has offered to the consumers more choices with a wider variety or produce at cheaper prices and to the producers, a competitive and growing market. During survey 67 percent responded these will be no impact of globalization on agriculture but 33% responded that globalization will harm the agriculture lot.

17.5. Impact of Globalization on India Identity

The main impact of globalization on Indian identity is explained also its suggestions are given below; Economic globalization also results in the transfer of disturbances from one part of-the world eco* system to its other parts. It also generates disturbances in rational market as the entry of economic agents from outside, such as MNCs affects the fortunes of local economic actors while the deeper economic integration of world provides an apparent autonomy to the working of the global economic system, with its laws of motion, it at the same time registers an overpowering impact on national economies. National economies are increasingly buffered by world economic forces which are not always amenable to effective national control. For examples financial volatility is a permanent feature of today, globally integrate, financial markets',

The element of competition, in turn has significantly influenced peoples personal familial and social of life has been supplanted by the fierce completion to succeed any cost,

Globalization will affect the prices which will effects Indian farmer Erectly. It will also commodities and self-sufficiency concepts needs to redefined because.

Agri-economies like USA do not grow everything themselves. They only grow that which they grow best. Its impact will be harmful for India because Indians never followed USA's concept of production.

Globalization has now become an irreversible phenomenon. There is no alternative but to keep pace with the global environment in the field of education otherwise most of Indian education institution's future will be dark.

The mass migration has led to conflict. The impact of the conflict is not only being felt in the Third World Countries, We must understand that the conflict is part of the globalized phenomenon itself the cultural conflict.

Globalization work in agriculture, as this is still the main source of subsistence for the majority of the world's women. Besides agriculture and often overlapping, most women's work worldwide is taking place in the informal economy and this creates the instability and insecurity of most jobs in the sphere.

Globalization and migration are affecting almost contemporary societies and the femininization of migration being an important issue.

Globalization, liberalization and dependence on market mechanism in education may provide programmes for only those who can afford to pay the market price and that weaker sections of the society will be at a huge disadvantage. It would mean that the private and foreigners providers would monopolize the best students and most lucrative programmes. In a country like India with a huge segment of socio-economic disadvantaged population, it will amount of discrimination.

Rise of Internet and globalization of knowledge will have the potential of creating severe problems for institutions and .systems in poorer countries, The norms values, language scientific innovations and knowledge provides of MNC's and economically and politically powerful nations will relegate to the periphery ideas and practices in developing countries." It becomes very difficult to regulate to the periphery ideas and practices in developing countries. It becomes very difficult to regulate the trade in academic institution programmes, degrees or product across international borders. Huge expenditure on advertisement and marketing will make even substandard courses offered by even unknown institutions appear highly attractive for students and parents who may not be well informed and some advertisement also effects the culture.

17.6. Suggestions and Conclusion

Not more than 10% Indians is aware about the concept of globalization. We are living in the world where money, securities, services, opinions, future information, and software companies and know how assets and memberships are all reached without national sentiments across national boundaries. We should not fear the loss of identity or exploitations by multi-national corporations, but rather improving economy, culture and environment, skills in laborers and" employees, improving systems of education and making it more competitive, strategic and creates more sources of employment, improving agriculture, technology and gain access to overseas markets. The effects of standardization and country of origin is very important in the context of Globalization because this is the very foundation on which this concept has taken shape and grown. Take for instance any product or service, which has been newly introduced into the country brings along with it, its country image. This has a direct impact, especially on the young impressionable minds, who tend to behave in a manner in which they perceive that "Image" to be, Over years of the progress of Globalization, this "Behavior" soon turned into a lifestyle and this "Lifestyle" has now emerged into what has become known as the new "Globalized Culture". Although some were of the opinion that with globalization, the rich will become richer and the poor will become poorer, one cannot deny -the fact that each one of us shares a common dream to see our land fertile and rich, our villages prosperous and our farmer and laborers' affluent and India a proud member of the world economic community. For this, we need to reassert our belief in a three-way partnership between Indians, the financial corporations and consumers both in India and the world. We need, winning strategies and product, moral and national character and partnership to face the coming challenges of the Globalization to protect the Indian identity.

References

Dreze, Jean and Sen Amarty (1998) India: Eco Development and Social Opportunity, New Delhi; Oxford University Press.

Kalam, APJ Abdul and Rajan, YS (1998) India 2020-A Vision for the New Millenium, Penguin.

Stella Antpony and Gran-Am, A. (2002) Handbook of Total Quality Management, New Delhi; Jaics Publishing House.

Muske, Pradip (2004. Globalization and its Impact on Higher Education, University, News: 17 to 23 May 2004,

Rangarajan C. (2003). Globalization and its impact of Kapila, Uma "India-n Economy Science Independence" New Delhi; Academic Foundation.

Najar Baldev Raj (2001). Globalization and Nationalism, New Delhi: Sage Publications.

Joshi, J.P. (2003), Globalizations: A Need for Change in Educational Management System, in : University News, May 19-25.

Sharma S.K. (1997) Globalizations of India Business Education: To be or not to be that's the Question in University News April, 28.

Bhanwal Jitender K. and Sood; Vibha (1995) Profile of Globalization Indian Economy and Challenges Ahead: with special references to Globalization Indian Agriculture Punjab School of

Economics. Guru Nanak Dev. University Amritsar.

Shiva Vandana, Global Ecology, May 2004, The impact of globalization on India's environment

Athyal, Sakhi, Globalization,, youth and Religion in India

Adarsh Kishore, Towards an Indian Approach to Globalization.

Bhanwal Jitender Kumar and Maneet Kumar (Oct. –Dec. 1995) Profile of India's Trade Relation with Asian Countries Economic Affairs Journal vol. 40.

Kumar, Maneet and and Jitnder K. Bhanwal (1994) India's Trade with UK, Economic. Journal.

CHAPTER 18
TEXTILE EXPORT PERFORMANCE IN POST REFORM REGIME: A STUDY AT DISAGGREGATE LEVEL

Manoj Sharma and Rahul Dhiman

Abstract

Textile industry stands out with an exceptional significance in the world economy. Textile and clothing are amongst the first manufactured products produced by an industrialized economy. Textile industry has been a major driver of Indian economy as it contributes significantly towards GDP, industrial production and Indian export basket. The present paper attempts to study export performance of principal commodities at aggregate and disaggregate level. The commodities taken in to account include HS 50 to HS 63. The data has been taken for 24 years i.e. from 1991 to 2015. CAGR will also be calculated for different time periods to highlight key commodities. The findings of the study draw attention to the fact that although India has not been able to enlarge its share in international clothing trade at a quick pace but there are certain commodities which have shown significant export growth in the international market. The present study highlights performing and non performing textile commodities. The commodities which are growing at swift pace include HS 51; HS 52; HS 53; HS 54; HS 56; HS 57; HS 59 and HS 62. Some commodities like HS 50 and HS 60 have shown negative growth rates during various time intervals. The study also provides suitable recommendations to improve the performance of non performing commodities. Industrial policies must be framed in a manner so that the commodities which have not shown growth in the world market can be identified and appropriate strategies can be formulated to enhance their contribution in total textile exports.

18.1. Introduction

The Indian textile industry is a diverse and heterogeneous industry. The products of textile industry are used by everybody. Indian textile sector was predominantly unorganized before the economic liberalization. The Indian Textile Policy of 1985 completely protected this sector whereas the process of liberalization culminated in the textile policy of 2000. The Multi-Fiber Agreement (MFA) of 1974 exempted the textile and garments trade from General Agreements on Tariff and Trade (GATT) disciplines. This was supposed to protect producers to restructure to compete with cheaper imports. In the world economy textile industry is of high significance as it contributes in the industrial production, employment, Gross Domestic Product (GDP), foreign exchange reserves. Textile and clothing are amongst the first manufactured products produced by an industrialized economy. In developed economies, the growth of these industries has ignited a dynamic phase of development through industrialization and growing cross border trade. For developing countries, particularly the LDCs, the textile industry is an appropriate alternative on the path to industrialization due to its high labour intensity and low capital requirements. It has an important share in the export earnings of these countries and provides employment opportunities to young skilled and unskilled workforce. Textile industry has played a decisive role in the early phase of industrialization countries such as Britain, Japan, North America and East Asian economies, including Taiwan, Hong Kong and the Republic of Korea. These countries have relied a great deal on textile exports from 1950s to the mid-80s.

The Indian textile industry holds an important position in the Indian economy. It offers one of the most essential requirements of man namely clothing. It offers the basic requirement of raw materials to the finished products. The Indian textile industry contributes to 14 percent of the total industrial production, 4 percent of GDP, 13 percent of the total export and 5 per cent in world textile exports. The Indian Textile industry possesses some commodities like textile yarn and thread which have comparative advantage in the international market and also can speed up the growth of exports

(Sharma & Dhiman, 2014). Different industries have different factor requirements. Textile industry is heavily relied on both skilled and unskilled labour. Countries like Vietnam, Sri Lanka, Bangladesh, and Mauritius have shown remarkable growth in this sector (Chakrabarty, 2014). Abundant raw material availability of Indian textile industry is another comparative advantage gained by the nation. India is the largest producer of jute, second largest producer of silk, third largest producer of cotton and the fifth largest producer of man-made fibres and yarn. Ramaswamy, K.V. and Gary Gereffi (2000) study the challenges of India's clothing exports in international market. The findings of the study reveal that India's share in global clothing exports has not risen since 1994. The economic reforms of the 1990s have not drastically influenced the clothing sector due to entry limitations such as licensing for large-scale plants. Verma (2000) confirms that textile and clothing industry is impacted with several restrictions. There is an instant need to change in policies, otherwise the industry will be blown away by the competitive global market forces, both in the international market as well as by imports in the domestic territory.

From the above discussion it gets clear that Textile export of India play a critical role towards the economic development of the nation. Previous studies have emphasised upon the commodities at aggregate level only. But the researcher could not come across any such study where commodities at disaggregate level are considered and their export performance is examined. So, the present study is a footstep in this direction. The export performance of various commodities at disaggregated level need to be studied so that week commodities can be identified and appropriate strategies can be formulated. The present paper attempts to study the export performance of principal commodities at aggregate and disaggregate level.

18.2. Objectives of the Study

i. To study the composition and share of India textile exports in the world trade at aggregate level.
ii. To study the export performance of principal textile commodities at disaggregate level.
iii. To highlight the key performing and non performing textile commodities in the world trade and provide recommendations.

18.3. Research Methodology

The present study uses the secondary sources of data such as UN Comtrade database, Ministry of Commerce, Government of India, Economic Survey of India (various issues) and World Trade Organisation (WTO) database. The study period is from 1991 to 2015. There are total 14 commodities at disaggregate level which are studied i.e. HS 50 to HS 63. Compounded Annual Growth Rate (CAGR) is calculated to examine the growth rates in different time periods. Period-I is 1991-2002; Period-II is 2002-2015 and Period-III is 1991-2015. The compounded growth rates has been calculated using following exponential function,

$$Y_i = a\,(b_i)^t$$
$$Log\,Y_i = log\,a + t\,log\,(b_i)$$

Where,
Y_i = export value/ volume/ unit price of ith item,
t = time variable.
The Annual Growth rate (r) can hence be calculated using the formula,

$$r = [antilog\,(logb_i) - 1] \times 100$$
$$or$$
$$= (b-1) \times 100$$

where, b = Slope of semi-logarithmetic trend

18.4. Textile Commodities at 02 Digit Level

The textile commodities at disaggregate level (02 digit) from HS 50 to HS 63 are studied. Table 1 depicts the commodities at 02 digit level.

Table 1: Principal Commodities of Indian Textile Export at 02 digit level

Product Code	Name
50	Silk
51	Wool, animal hair, horsehair yarn and fabric
52	Cotton
53	Vegetable textile fibresnes, paper yarn, woven fabric
54	Manmade filaments
55	Manmade staple fibres
56	Wadding, felt, nonwovens, yarns, twine, cordage, etc

57	Carpets and other textile floor coverings
58	Special woven or tufted fabric, lace, tapestry etc.
59	Impregnated, coated or laminated textile fabric
60	Knitted or crocheted fabric
61	Articles of Apparel And Clothing Accessories, Knitted or Corcheted.
62	Articles of Apparel And Clothing Accessories, Not Knitted or Crocheted
63	Other Made Up Textile Articles; Sets; Worn Clothing And Worn Textile Articles; Rags

18.5. Growth in Total Textile Exports:

Figure 1 depicts the total textile exports from 1991 to 2015. Total textile exports increased from 4865.3 US$M in 1991 to 9381 US$M in 1997. Slight downfall can be observed in 1998 and export reached 9007 US$M. Thereafter significant increase can be seen from 9981 US$M in 1999 to 22701 US$M in 2008. After this period the textile exports reached to 37162 US$M with some fluctuation during 2009 to 2015.

18.6. India's Share in World Textile Exports

India's percentage share in the world textile exports has not risen as expected. A fluctuating trend in Indian share in world textile exports can be observed (See figure 2). The World textile exports were 226085 US $ Million in 1991 and India's textile exports were 5057 US $ Million with a share of 2.23 per cent in the global trade. In 2015 the world textile exports were 74413 US$ M and India's textile exports were 35543 US$ M with a share of 4.77 per cent in the world trade.

Figure 1: Total Textile Exports

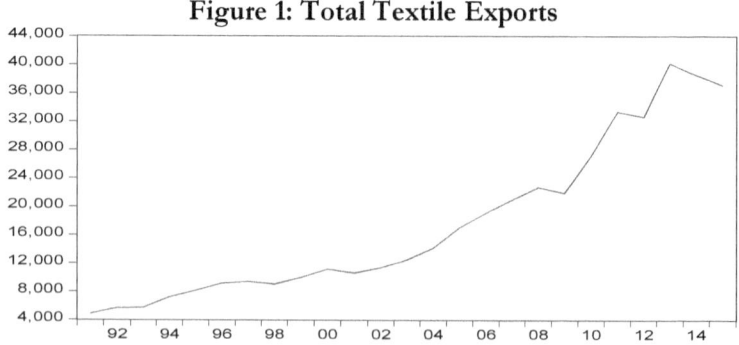

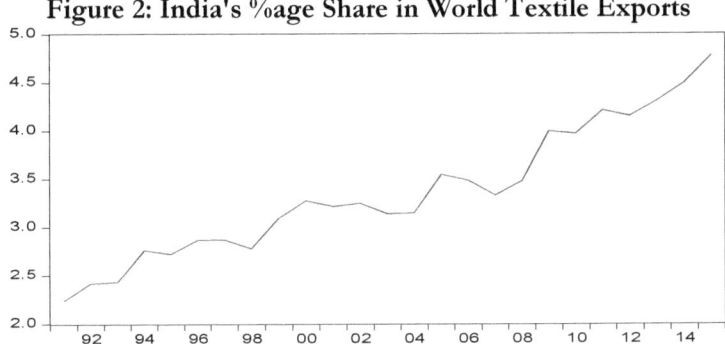

Figure 2: India's %age Share in World Textile Exports

18.7. Export Performance at 02 digit level

i. HS 50: Silk:

In 1991, the export of silk was 128.4 US$M and reached to 403.6 US$M in 2005. After this period huge downfall has been observed and accounted to 111.2 US$M in 2015. Table 3 depicts CAGR for 1991-2002 was 8.54. After this period huge downfall could be seen as CAGR for 2003-15 was -9.2. For the whole period i.e. 1991-2015 CAGR for HS 50 is 2.15.

ii. HS 51: Wool, animal hair, horsehair yarn and fabric

In 1991, the export of the commodity was 25.6 US$M and reached to 110.9 US$M in 1997. After this period huge downfall has been observed and accounted to 53 US$M in 2003. After slight fluctuations the export of the commodity was 180.9 US$M in 2015. CAGR for 1991-2002 was 4.15, 2003-15 was 11.04 and for the whole period i.e. 1991-2015 CAGR for HS 51 is 13.93.

iii. HS 52: Cotton

Cotton remains the key performing commodity in the international market. In 1991, the export of the commodity was 1107 US$M and reached to 2627 US$M in 1997. After slight fluctuations the export of the commodity was 2148 US$M in 2002. Thereafter huge rise can be observed and export was 11294 US$M in 2013. Thereafter downfall can be observed and the export was 7508 US$M in 2015. CAGR for 1991-2002 was 6.42, 2003-15 was 14.03 and for the whole period i.e. 1991-2015 CAGR for HS 51 is 8.69.

iv. HS 53: Vegetable textile fibresnes, paper yarn, woven fabric

In 1991, the export of the commodity was 107.4 US$M, thereafter fluctuations are observed and export was 84.5 USM in 2000. In the year 2008 export was 202.2 US$M and reached to 358.1 US$M in 2015 with fluctuations. CAGR for 1991-2002 was 1.23, 2003-15 was 9.77 and for the whole period i.e. 1991-2015 CAGR is 6.24.

v. HS 54: Manmade filaments

In 1991, the export of the commodity was 218.6 US$M. and reached to 413.8 US$M in 1995. Thereafter fluctuations are observed and export was 306.9 US$M in 1998. After this period huge increase in the export is observed and reached to the maximum level of 2681 US$M in 2013 and with slight fluctuations ended with 2209 US$M in 2015. CAGR for 1991-2002 was 7.94, 2003-15 was 11.08 and for the whole period i.e. 1991-2015 CAGR is 11.87.

vi. HS 55: Manmade staple fibres

In 1991, the export of the commodity was 114.4 US$M. and reached to 38.7 US$M in 1997. After this period huge increase in the export is observed and reached to the maximum level of 2245 US$M in 2011 and with slight fluctuations ended with 2112 US$M in 2015. CAGR for 1991-2002 was 14.95, 2003-15 was 11.2 and for the whole period i.e. 1991-2015 CAGR is 13.42.

vii. HS 56: Wadding, felt, nonwovens, yarns, twine, cordage, etc

In 1991, the export of the commodity was 6.8 US$M. and reached to 55.4 US$M in 1999. After this period slight downfall in the export is observed and reached 49.4 US$M in 2002. After this period huge increase in the export is observed and reached to the maximum level of 428 US$M in 2015. CAGR for 1991-2002 was 18.72, 2003-15 was 20.22 and for the whole period i.e. 1991-2015 CAGR is 16.61.

viii. HS 57: Carpets and other textile floor covering

In 1991, the export of the commodity was 522.7 US$M. and reached to 578.7 US$M in 2001. After this period increase in the export is observed and reached to the maximum level of 1800 US$M in 2014 and ended at 1727 US$M in 2015. CAGR for 1991-2002 was 0.68, 2003-15 was 6.89 and for the whole period i.e. 1991-2015 CAGR is 5.20.

ix. HS 58: Special woven or tufted fabric, lace, tapestry etc.

In 1991, the export of the commodity was 31 US$M. and reached to 41 US$M in 1996. After this period increase in the export is observed and reached at 200 US$M in 2001. After this period downfall can be observed and reached at 98.7 US$M in 2003, thereafter rise in the export can be seen and reached to the maximum level of 407 US$M in 2014 and finally ended at 366 US$M in 2015. CAGR for 1991-2002 was 21.23, 2003-15 was 11.71 and for the whole period i.e. 1991-2015 CAGR is 10.37.

x. HS 59: Impregnated, coated or laminated textile fabric

In 1991, the export of the commodity was 14.8 US$M. and reached to 56 US$M in 1996. After this period downfall in the export is observed and reached at 37.5 US$M in 2000, thereafter rise in the export can be seen and reached to the maximum level of 394 US$M in 2014 and finally ended at 224 US$M in 2015. CAGR for 1991-2002 was 7.59, 2003-15 was 14.9 and for the whole period i.e. 1991-2015 CAGR is 10.95.

xi. HS 60: Knitted or crocheted fabric

In 1991, the export of the commodity was 54.5 US$M. and reached to minimum level of 29 US$M in 1999. After this period rise in the export is observed and reached to 259 US$M in 2014 and finally ended at 238 US$M in 2015. CAGR for 1991-2002 was -7.82, 2003-15 was 19.2 and for the whole period i.e. 1991-2015 CAGR is 7.58.

xii. HS 61: Articles of Apparel And Clothing Accessories, Knitted Or Corcheted

In 1991, the export of the commodity was 541.7 US$M. and reached to maximum level of 7482 US$M in 2014 and finally ended at 7800 US$M in 2015. CAGR for 1991-2002 was 12.38, 2003-15 was 9.8 and for the whole period i.e. 1991-2015 CAGR is 11.77.

xiii. HS 62: Articles of Apparel And Clothing Accessories, Not Knitted Or Crocheted

In 1991, the export of the commodity was 1661 US$M. and reached 3740 US$M in 2000. Thereafter stagnation is observed till 2004 and reached 3755 US$M in 2004. After this period huge increase an be seen and export reached at the maximum level of 9300 US$M in 2015. CAGR for 1991-2002 was 6.84, 2003-15 was 8.3 and for the whole period i.e. 1991-2015 CAGR is 7.11.

xiv. HS 63: Other Made Up Textile Articles; Sets; Worn Clothing And Worn Textile Articles; Rags

In 1991, the export of the commodity was 331.4 US$M. and reached 3740 US$M in 2000. Thereafter increasing trend can be seen and reached to the maximum level of 4712 US$M in 2013.and finally ended at 4600 US$M in 2015. CAGR for 1991-2002 was 12.21, 2003-15 was 9.67 and for the whole period i.e. 1991-2015 CAGR is 11.7.

18.8. Growth Rates at Disaggregate Level

Compounded Annual Growth Rates (CAGR) during different time intervals at disaggregate level (HS 50 to HS 63) can be seen in Table 2. CAGR has been calculated for three different time periods i.e. 1991-2002 as Period-I, 2003-2015 Period-II and 1991-2015 Period-III. Out of fourteen, eight commodities have grown in Period-I and Period-II.

Table 2: CAGR in Different Periods

Product Code	Name	Growth Rate (1991-2002)	Growth Rate (2003-2015)	Growth Rate (1991-2015)
50	Silk	8.54	-9.2	2.15
51	Wool, animal hair, horsehair yarn and fabric	4.15	11.04	13.93
52	Cotton	6.42	14.03	8.69
53	Vegetable textile fibresnes, paper yarn, woven fabric	1.23	9.77	6.24
54	Manmade filaments	7.94	11.08	11.87
55	Manmade staple fibres	14.85	11.2	13.42
56	Wadding, felt, nonwovens, yarns, twine, cordage, etc	18.72	20.22	16.61
57	Carpets and other textile floor coverings	0.68	6.89	5.2
58	Special woven or tufted fabric, lace, tapestry etc.	21.23	11.71	10.37
59	Impregnated, coated or laminated textile fabric	7.59	14.9	10.95
60	Knitted or crocheted fabric	-7.82	19.2	7.58
61	Articles of Apparel And Clothing Accessories, Knitted Or Corcheted.	12.38	9.8	11.77
62	Articles of Apparel And Clothing Accessories, Not Knitted Or Crocheted	6.84	8.3	7.11
63	Other Made Up Textile Articles; Sets; Worn Clothing And Worn Textile Articles; Rags	12.21	9.67	11.7
	Total Textile Exports	7.85	10.22	9.2

The commodities which are growing at swift pace in Period-I and Period II include HS 51; HS 52; HS 53; HS 54; HS 56; HS 57; HS 59 and HS 62. The remaining six commodities have shown fluctuations during Period-I and Period-II. Some commodities like HS 50 and HS 60 have shown negative growth rates during Period-II and Period-I respectively. The study also identified certain commodities which have grown in Period-I then shown decline in growth in subsequent Period-II. Such commodities are HS 55; HS 58; HS 61 and HS 63.

Conclusion

The findings of the study draw attention to the fact that even though India is not competent enough to enlarge its contribution in international trade but still some textile commodities have grown at swift pace. The commodities which are growing at swift pace in Period-I and Period II include HS 51; HS 52; HS 53; HS 54; HS 56; HS 57; HS 59 and HS 62. The remaining six commodities have shown fluctuations during Period-I and Period-II. The study also identified certain commodities which have grown in Period-I then shown decline in growth in subsequent Period-II. Such commodities are HS 55; HS 58; HS 61 and HS 63.The role of the government becomes very vital in this context. An important task in front of the policy makers is to formulate action plan for non performing commodities. Industrial policies must be framed in a manner so that the commodities which have not shown growth in the world market can be identified and appropriate strategies can be formulated to enhance their contribution in total textile exports.

References

Batra, A., & Khan, Z. (2005). *Revealed comparative advantage: An analysis for India and China.* Working Paper No. 168. New Delhi: Indian Council for Research on International Economic Relations.

Chakrabarty. (2014). Textile and Clothing Exports from India – An Analysis of Select Issues. A dissertation presented in part consideration for the degree of Ph.D., IIFT, New Delhi.

Cherunilam, F. (2005). International business - Text and cases. New Delhi: Prentice Hall of India pvt ltd.

Dhiman, R., & Sharma, M. (2016). Textile Exports in South Asia and its determinants: A Literature Review. *Frontiers of New Era for Indian Economy.* (pp 244-251). Bharti Publications: New Delhi.

Dhiman, R., Kumar. R., Gupta, S. & Kumar. M. (2016). Recent Trends in the Bilateral Trade Engagement of India and Canada. *International Journal of Applied Business and Economic Research*, 14 (3): 229-254.

Feder, G. 1983. On Exports and Economic Growth. *Journal of Development Economics*, 12: 59–73.

Griffin, R. W., & Ebert, R. J. (1995). *Business*. New Jersey: Prentice Hall. .

Kathuria, L. (2013). Analyzing competitiveness of clothing export sector of India and Bangladesh: Dynamic revealed comparative advantage approach. *Competitiveness Review: An International Business Journal.* 23(2): 131-157.

Kreinin, M.E. and Plummer, M.G. (1994). Structural change and regional integration in East Asia. *International Economic Journal*, 8(2), 1-12.

Kuldilok, K. S., Dawson, P. J., & Lingard, J. (2013). The export competitiveness of the tuna industry in Thailand. *British Food Journal*, 15(3),328–341.

Mahmood, Z., & Hajji, R. (2009). Revealed comparative advantage of non-petroleum products in Kuwait. *NUST Journal of Business and Economics*, 2(1), 32–41

Nikolić, A., Bajramovic, S., Ognjenovic, D., Lalic, D., &Uzunovic, M. (2011). SEE trade liberalization – new opportunity for agribusiness? *British Food Journal*, 113(1), 78–95.

Ramaswamy, K.V. and Gary Gereffi (2000). India's Apparel Exports: The Challenge of Global Markets. *The Developing Economies*, 38(2), 186-210.

Rudzkis, R., & Kvedaras, V. (2003). Trend *and econometric models of Lithuanian export*. Monetary Studies, 4, 29-51.

Sharma, M. & Dhiman, R. (2014). Study of Post Reform Period of Indian Exports: A Review. *Review of Business & Technology Research*. 11(1), 836-841.

Sharma, M. &Dhiman, R. (2016). Determinants Affecting Indian Textile Exports: A Review. *Biz and Bytes. A Journal of Management & Technology.* 6(2), 193-199.

Wang (2013). *The determinants of textile and apparel export performance in Asian countries.* A dissertation presented in part consideration for the degree of Master of Science, Iowa state University.

Wu, Y. Ch. J., & Lin, Ch. W. (2008). National port competitiveness: implications for India. *Management Decision*, 46 (10), 1482-1507.

CHAPTER 19
WOMEN ENTREPRENEURSHIP AND FINANCIAL PERFORMANCE: MODERATING ROLE OF SPOUSE SUPPORT

Stanzin Mantok

Abstract

This paper aims to investigate the impact of women entrepreneurship on financial performance and the role of spouse support in women entrepreneurship and financial performance link. Data were collected from 169 owner of Small and Medium Enterprises (SMEs) located in an Industrial Hub of North India. Structural Equation Modelling was used to analyse the impact of women entrepreneurship on financial performance. The findings of the study demonstrate that there is a significant weak relationship between women entrepreneurship and financial performance. Thus, the study examine the moderating role of spouse support between them and found that the support from spouse significantly moderate between women entrepreneurship and financial performance The present study is confined to analyses of the women entrepreneurship, financial performance and spouse support of women SMEs operating in India, thus there is a need to conduct research study on large scale women companies operating in India. Beside these, future research can also examine the impact of women entrepreneurship on other constructs viz., life satisfaction of women entrepreneurs and their empowerment.

19.1. Introduction

Since the early age of human civilisation, women have been engaging in one or other forms of entrepreneurial activities. They are known for initiating innovative ways and means to attain sound relationship in family, taking risk to secure family from internal confrontations and possible external threats. Women are naturally blessed with risk-taking ability in life and innovating solutions to the problems at hand in the society. These qualities of risk taking and innovativeness are the core elements for becoming an entrepreneur. Entrepreneurship is widely regarded as the main solution to the growing unemployment problem and ensuring optimum utilisation of physical and human resources resulting in the upliftment of living standard (Sidhu & Kaur, 2006). Women have been striving to contribute to the family's source of financial income either by working at home or by setting up a new business venture outside home (Datta & Gailey, 2012). Creation of a new business unit requires indomitable determination, motivation and ability to optimally utilise available resources to achieve predetermined objective. The likelihood of choosing an entrepreneurship as career is largely determined by the resources people have (Kim, Albrich & Keister, 2006).

Generally, women entrepreneurs across the world find it difficult to procure requisite financial and human resources to start a new venture and get it running smoothly. The main propelling factor for women to become an entrepreneur lies in the fact that they aspire to be financially independent, fulfilling their self-esteem needs, sharing the financial responsibility of the family and above all, testing their entrepreneurial skills in the creation of profitable business ventures. The term "Women Entrepreneurship" has been defined as an act of business ownership and creation that empowers women economically, increases their economic strength as well as position in the society. Women are considered as key players in entrepreneurial activities, making significant contributions to the economic development of the nations across the world (Barringer & Ireland, 2010; Minniti, Arenius & Langowitz, 2005). Despite the significant role played by women in the world economy, there is a paucity of research studies on women entrepreneurship (Ahl, 2006; De Bruin, Brush & Welter, 2006). Because of their peculiar role, women entrepreneurship is gaining attention of academicians and researchers as a novel interest of research in developed as well as developing countries (Brush & Gatewood, 2008; Carter, Shaw, Lam & Wilson, 2007; McClelland, Swail, Bell & Ibbotson, 2005; Verheul, Stel & Thurik, 2006). However, research studies on women entrepreneurship constitute less than 10% of research in the field of entrepreneurship (Brush & Cooper, 2012). During the past decades, academicians and researchers felt strong need to study women entrepreneurship, as women across the world are said to own and control one-third of business ventures in organised sector but majority of business units in unorganised sector are owned by them (Aderemi, Ilori, Siyanbola & Adegbite, 2008). Although men are more inclined to engage in entrepreneurial activity as compared to women in economies across the world (Minniti, Arenius & Langowitz, 2005), but there is higher entrepreneurial tendency among women in developing economies as compared to developed ones (Bosma & Harding, 2007). Hence, it is worthwhile to identify the factors responsible for pushing a woman to become an entrepreneur and to understand expressed or implied ramifications of being a woman entrepreneur.

A firm's potential earning capacity and market capitalisation is reflected by its financial result (Moorman & Rust, 1999). Dess and Robbinson, (1984) put forward an argument that measurement and overviewing of business performance of a firm is the main subject for entrepreneurship academicians. Rumelt and Wensely, (1981) observed that firm's market performance has a positive correlation to better financial performance. The benefit of sound market performance facilitates easy introduction of innovative products, attracts new customers and enables firm to encounter market uncertainties apart from keeping all stakeholders contended. Neely, Gregory and Platts, (1995) conceptualised performance as a process of measuring efficiency and effectiveness of actions. They further classified performance in quantitative and qualitative aspects, where qualitative refers to market share, customer retention aspects while quantitative comprises of return on investment (ROI), return on assets (ROA), profitability. Sharabati, Jawad and Bontis, (2010) measured performance evaluation from three angles, viz., profitability, productivity and market share. Working for demand creation and introducing innovative products aggressively help in boosting firm's performance (Ireland, Hitt & Sirmon, 2003). Women entrepreneurs with higher entrepreneurial orientation tend to attain greater financial performance as compared to less entrepreneurially oriented women. The study contributes to the existing literature in two ways; (i) it analyses the impact of women entrepreneurship on firm's business performance and (ii) examines the moderating role of spouse support between women entrepreneurship and business performance.

19.2. Hypotheses Formulation

Entrepreneurial skills among highly aspiring women entrepreneurs help them to attain satisfaction in terms of personal and business outcomes of their firm. Study conducted by Datta and Gailey (2012) reported that women entrepreneurs in a society like India successfully pursue their career in entrepreneurship to gain certain financial performance. Women entrepreneurs experience positive results of being an entrepreneur in business and individual life (Ufuk & Ozgen, 2001). More specifically, Desai et al. (2011) concluded that women entrepreneurs in India are minimally stressed, live balanced life and most contended with their chosen career. Having achieved initial ambitions, entrepreneurs focus on quantitative performance indicators and long-term quality objectives for future success (Carter & Cannon, 1992). Robb and Watson, (2012) revealed that women entrepreneurs are on par with male in the matters of acquiring skills and resources required for starting-up their ventures and found to have performed almost equally in all performance measurement parameters. Moreover, Logan, (2014) reported that women owned enterprises witness profitable business performance. Thus, on the basis of above statement, the present study framed first hypothesis:

H1: There is a positive association between women entrepreneurship and financial performance.

Spouse cordial support helps entrepreneur to avoid and overcome emotional breakdown. Cramer (2004) acknowledged the valuable effect of spouse support in maintaining relationship satisfaction. Spouse consistent support is a prerequisite for maintaining sound work-family balance for women entrepreneurs and leads to effective financial performance. Parasuraman, Greenhaus and Granrose (1992) found that partner's support helps enhancing work-family balance. Rani (1996) found that women entrepreneurs accord top priority to spouse, children and relationship with them. This tendency helps them maintaining optimum equilibrium between professional demand and family matters. On the basis of above contemplation, we design our second hypothesis:

H2: Spouse Support moderated the relationship between women entrepreneurship and financial performance.

19.3. Research Methods

19.3.i. Sample Design and Data Collection

To test the hypotheses, the data was collected from 169 SMEs women entrepreneurs from Ahmedabad city of Gujarat. The study chooses Ahmedabad because the women population is larger in Ahmedabad district as compared to other districts of Gujarat (Census 2011, Government of India, Gujarat state). A list of 574 women SMEs engaged in manufacturing was acquired from Gujarat Chambers of Commerce and Industry (GCCI women wing), Ahmedabad. The contacted industries were chemical, dyes and intermediates and hosiery and textiles. Based on the five-point Likert scale, a survey instrument was constructed for gathering requisite data pertaining to the research question.

19.3.ii. Generation of Scale-items

The study used three major constructs, viz., women entrepreneurship, spouse support and financial performance. Three dimensions of entrepreneurial orientation, i.e., innovativeness, proactiveness and risk-taking were adopted (Covin & Slevin, 1989), to understand the women entrepreneurship of SMEs in Ahmedabad. The study borrowed five items to measure spouse support of women entrepreneurs. Furthermore, financial performance was measured through four items namely revenue growth (RG), market share growth (MSG), net profit (NP) and return on investment (ROI). A 5-point Likert scale was used for each item ranging from 'strongly disagree' (1) to 'strongly agree' (5).

19.4. Data Analysis

The study used two different techniques to analyse the common method variance (Podsakoff,

MacKenzie, Lee & Podsakoff, 2003). First, confirmatory factor analysis (CFA) single-factor model was used in which all the manifest variables of the latent constructs were loaded onto first-order CFA and in this regard, the study revealed poor model fit (CMIN/df= 8.93; GFI= .54; AGFI= .21; NFI= .14; TLI= .13; CFI=.12; RMSEA=.14). Second, we examined the correlation matrix of the latent constructs and found that 0.575 is the greatest value in the correlation matrix (Table 1), which is less than the threshold limit of 0.90 (Pavlou, Liang & Xue, 2006). Thus, these results confirm that the common method variance is not a problem in the present study.

19.4.i. Descriptive Statistics

Table 1 shows the mean, standard deviation and correlation co-efficient of control variables, viz., firm's age, firm's size, manager's age and qualification, and the main variables, viz., women entrepreneurship, spouse support and financial performance.

Table 1: Mean, Standard Deviation and Correlation Matrix

S. No.	Variable	Mean	S.D	1	2	3	4	5	6	7
1.	Firm Age	13.6	9.31	--						
2.	Firm Size	16.1	14.8	.37*	--					
3.	Manager's Age	52.6	6.62	.16	.31*	--				
4.	Qualification	3.68	1.16	-.27	-.15	.57**	--			
5.	Women Entrepreneurship	4.08	0.57	.01	-.27	.05	.01	--		
6.	Spouse Support	4.91	0.32	.030	.01	.18	.07	.28	--	
7.	Financial Performance	4.30	0.45	-.31	.02	.01	.07	.26	.04	--

S.D= Standard Deviation; $n = 169$; * $p < 0.05$; ** $p < 0.01$; ***$p<0.00$ (2-tailed).

As shown in the table, the average age of the firm is 13.64 years while that of the manager is 52.63 years. In addition, the highest correlation exists between women entrepreneurship and their spouse support whereas the lowest correlation is being observed in case of women entrepreneurship and financial performance. CFA was performed to assess fitness, reliability and validity of latent construct. Fit indices of measurement model reveal that the Chi-square statistics was less than recommended 5.0 level and GFI, AGFI, NFI, TLI and CFI values exceeded the recommended value of .90 (Inman, Lair & Green, 2009; Hoe, 2008).

19.4.ii. Reliability and Validity of the Constructs

Reliability is tested through composite reliability and the value of composite reliability of all the latent constructs is above .90, which indicates internal consistency of the data. The composite reliability, average variance extracted and the Cronbach alpha of all the constructs are shown in Table 2. The table reveals that the threshold criterion for establishing reliability and validity through AVE, composite reliability and Cronbach's alpha stands fulfilled.

In addition, validity of the scale has been established through construct validity, which includes convergent validity (Lim & Ployhart, 2006) and discriminant validity (Fornell & Larcker, 1981). The descriptive statistics of the study are shown in Table 3. Convergent validity has been established through factor loading and average variance extracted and it gets established as majority of factor loadings and average variance extracted are above .50.

Table 2: Reliability and Validity of Latent Constructs

S. No.	Constructs	Average Variance Extracted	Composite Reliability	Cronbach's Alpha
1.	Women Entrepreneurship	0.992	.991	.869
2.	Spouse Support	0.962	.977	.984
3.	Financial Performance	0.617	.987	.708

Table 3: Descriptive Statistics of Measurement Models

Construct	Mean	S.D	SRW	t-Value	AVE	CR	α-Value
1. WOMEN ENTREPRENEURSHIP					0.992	0.991	0.869
(a) Innovativeness							
Focus on tried product	4.15	.61	0.659	3.892			
Launched new product line	3.82	.97	0.856	4.539			
Radical changes in product line	3.72	.95	0.776	-			
(b) Risk-taking							
High risk apatite	4.27	.65	0.830	5.216			
Goal oriented	4.19	.74	0.761	4.901			
Aggressive exploitation of opportunities	4.21	.73	0.839	-			
(c) Proactiveness							
Imitativeness in action	4.17	.76	0.930	2.239			
Initiative oriented	4.17	.76	0.858	2.291			
New product and technology introducer	4.04	.62	0.372	-			
2. SPOUSE SUPPORT					0.962	0.977	0.984
Attention to spouse	4.32	1.62	0.961	--			
Co-operative and supportive spouse	4.04	1.68	0.959	31.06			
Due attention to spouse despite being busy and engaged	4.81	1.52	0.962	31.78			
Proper balance between work and married life	4.83	1.52	0.964	32.08			
Provide strength and support.	4.89	1.46	0.964	32.08			
3. FINANCIAL PERFORMANCE					0.617	0.987	0.708
Revenue growth	3.96	.407	0.418	--			
Market share growth	3.80	.466	0.618	4.310			
Net profit	4.00	.393	0.786	4.437			
Return on investment	4.14	.523	0.622	4.327			

Note: S.D= Standard Deviation; SRW= Standard Regression Weight; AVE= Average Variance Extracted; CR= Composite Reliability.

Discriminant validity analysis is estimated to examine the degree to which a construct is distinct from other constructs (Hair, Black, Babin, Anderson & Tatham, 2009). Table 4 shows that each explained variance estimate on the diagonal is greater than the corresponding inter-factor squared correlation estimates below the diagonal (Malhotra, 2007). Thus, discriminant validity gets established, thereby implying that major constructs are unique.

Table 4: Discriminant Validity of Latent Constructs

S. No.	AVE	Women Entrepreneurship	Spouse Support	Financial Performance
1.	Women Entrepreneurship	**(0.992)**		
2.	Spouse Support	.0125	**(0.962)**	
3.	Financial Performance	.0056	.0077	**(0.617)**

Note: Average Variance Extracted (AVE) on the diagonal and squared multiple correlation between constructs below the diagnol.

19.5. Results And Discussion

The three major constructs (viz., women entrepreneurship, spouse support and financial performance) under the study have been analysed as reflective and multidimensional. On the basis of SEM, we analysed the relationship between women entrepreneurship and financial performance and found positive significant relationship between them, but have weak relationship (β=.156; p=.003). Hence, H1 stands supported (Table 5). SEM results show that there is a weak relationship between women entrepreneurship and their financial performance. Thus, the present study analyse the moderation of spouse support between women entrepreneurship and their financial performance. The hierarchical regression was used to analyse the moderation of spouse support and it was found that spouse support fully moderates the link between women entrepreneurship and their financial performance (β=.166; p=.032), leading to the acceptance of H2 (Table 6).

Overall the study shows that there is a weak relationship between women entrepreneurship and their financial performance. The support from their spouse fully moderates the link between women entrepreneurship and financial performance. Thus, the study depicts that women can run their enterprise successfully only if they have their spouse support. Spouse cordial support helps women entrepreneurs to avoid and overcome emotional breakdown. The results finds support from the study conducted by Parasuraman,

Greenhaus and Granrose, (1992) which found that spouse support helps enhancing work-family balance, which lead women enterprise successfully. Further, the study of Rani, (1996) found that women entrepreneurs accord top priority to spouse, children and relationship with them. This tendency helps them maintaining optimum equilibrium between professional demand and family matters.

Figure 1: Moderation of Spouse Support between Women Entrepreneurship and Financial Performance

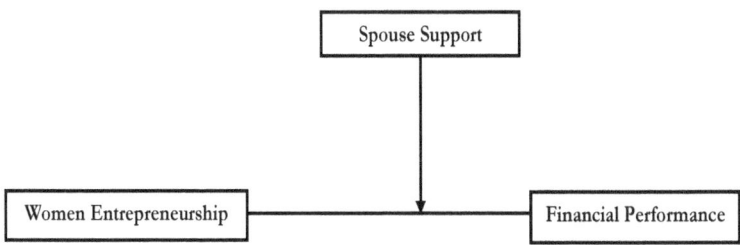

Table 5: Results of the Impact of Women Entrepreneurship on Financial Performance

Relationships	SRW	t-Value	p
Women Entrepreneurship → Financial Performance	.156	2.942	.003

Note: SRW= Standardised Regression Weight

Table 6: Test of Moderation

Control Variables	Model 1	Model 2	Model 3	Model 4
Firm's Age	-.002 (.97)	-.003 (.96)	.012 (.87)	.019 (.80)
Firm's Competitive Intensity	-.064 (.40)	-.665 (.40)	-.052 (.50)	-.045 (.55)
Business Experience	-.023 (.76)	-.022 (.78)	-.049 (.53)	-.043 (.58)
Independent Variable				
Women Entrepreneurship		.009 (.912)	.003 (.917)	.015 (.847)
Moderator				
Spouse Support			.168 (.034)	.153 (.051)
Interaction				
Women Entrepreneurship * Spouse Support				.166 (.032)
R^2	.005	.069	.032	.059
ΔR^2	-	.064	-.037	.027
Adj R^2	.013	.019	.020	.024
F-Value	.26 (.854)	.197 (.940)	2.31 (.03)	3.61 (.000)

19.6. Managerial Implications

The study contributes to the relevant literature in two different ways; First, most of the existing studies on women entrepreneurship primarily focused on identification of problems being faced by women entrepreneurs and finding their solution, but we moved a step further by exploring the latent factors that prompt a woman to become an entrepreneur and resultant outcome of starting a business unit. Secondly, the present study examines how entrepreneurial orientation of a woman enables her to achieve financial performance. The findings of the study shall facilitate government agencies to devise appropriate programmes and policies for encouraging and promoting women entrepreneurship in a country.

The results of the study have certain inferences, which need proper attention of government, academicians, policy makers and society at large. Though women belonging to business family in Gujarat enjoy easy social acknowledgement of being an entrepreneur, yet first generation women entrepreneurs need special care and social acceptance of society to encourage budding young entrepreneurs. Policy-makers are required to introduce appropriate schemes or programmes so as to encourage more and more young women to embark upon becoming a successful entrepreneur. Financial institutions and friends are found to be reluctant in providing financial aid to newly created women owned firms. Hence, it is the need of the hour that various financial institutions accord equal consideration without any gender discrimination while extending financial assistance. Moreover, the concept of interest subvention has to be introduced by government agencies to persuade young women entrepreneurs to avail loan facilities from financial institutions.

Conclusion

The purpose of the study is to examine the moderating role of spouse support between women entrepreneurship and their financial performance in an emerging economy context like India. The study found that the support from their spouse plays an important role in promoting their enterprise financially sound. In any society, becoming an entrepreneur is considered as an uphill task, as it involves accumulation of social support, procurement of sound human resources, raising adequate financial capital and above all, making things happen in most desired way. For married women entrepreneurs their spouse support is very essential because Indian women always want to balance their work and life. Easy availability of all these resources and competency to manage these limited resources in a resource constraint environment facilitate prospective women entrepreneurs to start her venture successfully. We found that conducive social atmosphere in Gujarat helps many women to start their business unit successfully. Independence and flexibility in working hours aid experiencing certain intrinsic feeling of empowerment among women entrepreneurs because they feel psychologically empowered to convert their business ideas into a successful business unit. Moreover, their spouse support towards entrepreneurship enables them to perform excellent in their chosen career, which gets reflected in the performance of their firm.

Limitations And Future Research

The present study suffers from certain limitations. Firstly, we considered only three constructs to analyse the financial performance of women entrepreneurs but there are other factors like social capital, financial capital and psychological factors, which may also serve as strong predictors of women entrepreneurship. Secondly, the data was collected from the Ahmedabad city in Gujarat state, where business- friendly social environment inspires prospective women entrepreneurs to choose entrepreneurship as their career but the generalisation of the results need to be examined in other environmental context. Finally, we examined only spouse support as one of the moderator between women entrepreneurship and financial performance but there may be other constructs, like bricolage, life satisfaction, support from family which may moderates the link between women entrepreneurship and financial performance. Future research can verify the results of this study in other environmental and cultural context.

References

Aderemi, H. O., Ilori, M. O., Siyanbola, W. O., & Adegbite, S. A. (2008). An assessment of the choice and performance of women entrepreneurs in technological and non-technological enterprises in South Western Nigeria. *African Journal of Business Management, 2(10)*, 165-176.

Ahl, H. (2006). Why research on women entrepreneurs needs new directions. *Entrepreneurship Theory and Practice, 30(5)*, 595-621.

Barringer, B. R., & Ireland, R. D. (2010). Entrepreneurship: Successfully launching New Ventures. 3rd. Edition, Upper Saddle River, New Jersey: Pearson.

Bosma, N., & Harding, R. (2006). *Global entrepreneurship monitor.* Wellesley/London: Babson College/London Business School, Global Entrepreneurship Research Consortium.

Brush, C. G., & Cooper, S. Y. (2012). Female entrepreneurship and economic development: An international perspective. *Entrepreneurship & Regional Development, 24(1-2)*, 1-6.

Brush, C. G., & Gatewood, E. J. (2008). Women growing businesses: Clearing the hurdles. *Business Horizons, 51(3)*, 175-179.

Carter, S., & Cannon, T. (1992). *Women as entrepreneurs.* London: Academic Press.

Carter, S., Shaw, E., Lam, W., & Wilson, F. (2007). Gender, entrepreneurship, and bank lending: The criteria and processes used by bank loan officers in assessing applications. *Entrepreneurship Theory and Practice, 31(3)*, 427-444.

Covin, J. G., & Slevin, D. P. (1989). Strategic management of small firms in hostile and benign environments. *Strategic Management Journal, 10(1)*, 75-87.

Cramer, D. (2004). Emotional support, conflict, depression, and relationship satisfaction in a romantic partner. *Journal of Psychology, 138(6)*, 532-542.

Datta, P. B., & Gailey, R. (2012). Empowering women through social entrepreneurship: Case study of a women's cooperative in India. Entrepreneurship Theory and Practice, *36(3)*, 569-587.

De Bruin, A., Brush, C. G., & Welter, F. (2006). Introduction to the special issue: Towards building cumulative knowledge on women's entrepreneurship. *Entrepreneurship Theory and Practice, 30(5)*, 585–593.

Desai, M., Majumdar, B., Chakraborty, T., & Ghosh, K. (2011). The second shift: Working women in India. *Gender in Management: An International Journal, 26(6)*, 432-450.

Dess, G. G., & Robinson, R. B. (1984). Measuring organizational performance in the absence of objective measures: The case of the privately-held firm and conglomerate business unit. *Strategic Management Journal, 5*, 265-273.

Fornell, C., & Larcker, D. F. (1981). Evaluating structural equation models with unobservable variables and measurement error.

Journal of Marketing Research, 18, 39-50

Hoe, S. L. (2008). Issues and procedure in adopting structural equation modelling technique. *Journal of Applied Quantitative Method, 3(1)*, 76-83.

Inman, R. A., Lair S. M., & Green J. K.W. (2009). Analysis of the relationships among TOC use, TOC outcomes, and organizational performance. *International Journal of Operations & Production Management, 29(4)*, 341-356.

Ireland, R. D., Hitt, M. A., & Sermon, D. G. (2003). A model of strategic entrepreneurship. *Journal of Management, 29(6)*, 963-989.

Kim, P. H., Aldrich, H. E., & Keister, L. A. (2006). Access (not) denied: The impact of financial, human, and cultural capital on entrepreneurial entry in the United States. Small Business Economics, 27(1), 5-22.

Lim, B. C., & Ployhart, R. E. (2006). Assessing the convergent and discriminant validity of Goldberg's international personality item pool: A multi-trait multi- method examination. *Organizational Research Methods, 9(1)*, 29-54.

Logan, J. (2014). An exploration of the challenges facing women starting business at fifty. *International Journal of Gender and Entrepreneurship, 6(1)*, 83-96.

McClelland, E., Swail, J., Bell, J., & Ibbotson, P. (2005). Following the pathway of female entrepreneurs: A six-country investigation. *International Journal of Entrepreneurial Behavior & Research, 11(2)*, 84-107.

Minniti, M., Arenius, P., & Langowitz, N. (2005). 2004 Global entrepreneurship monitor special topic report: Women and entrepreneurship. Babson Park, MA: Center for Women's Leadership at Babson College.

Moorman, C., & Rust, R. T. (1999). The role of marketing, *The Journal of Marketing, 63*, 180-197.

Neely, A., Gregory, M., & Platts, K. (1995). Performance measurement system design: A literature review and research agenda. *International Journal of Operations & Production Management, 15(4)*, 80-116.

Parasuraman, S., Greenhaus, J. H., & Granrose, C. S. (1992). Role stressors, social support, and well-being among two-career couples. *Journal of Organizational Behavior, 13(4)*, 339-356.

Pavlou, P. A., Liang, H., & Xue, Y. (2006). Understanding and mitigating uncertainty in online environments: A principal-

agent perspective. *MIS Quarterly, 31(1)*, 105-136.
Podsakoff, P. M., MacKenzie, S. B., Lee, J. Y., & Podsakoff, N. P. (2003). Common method biases in behavioral research: A critical review of the literature and recommended remedies. *Journal of Applied Psychology, 88(5)*, 879-903.
Rani, D. L. (1996). *Women entrepreneurs*. New Delhi: APH Publishing Corporation.
Robb, A. M., & Watson, J. (2012). Gender differences in firm performance: Evidence from new ventures in the United States. *Journal of Business Venturing, 27(5)*, 544-558.
Rumelt, R., & Wensley, R. (1981). Market share and the rate of return: Testing the stochastic hypothesis. Manuscript in Preparation, University of California. Los Angeles.
Sharabati, A. A. A., Naji Jawad, S., & Bontis, N. (2010). Intellectual capital and business performance in the pharmaceutical sector of Jordan. *Management Decision, 48*(1), 105-131.
Sidhu, K., & Kaur, S. (2006). Development of entrepreneurship among rural women. *Journal of Social Sciences, 13(2)*, 147-149.
Ufuk, H., & Ozgen, O. (2001). Interaction between the business and family lives of women entrepreneurs in Turkey. *Journal of Business Ethics, 31(2)*, 95-106.
Verheul, I., Stel, A. V., & Thurik, R. (2006). Explaining female and male entrepreneurship at the country level. *Entrepreneurship and Regional Development, 18(2)*, 151-183.

CHAPTER 20
A FUZZY LOGIC APPROACH TO OPTIMIZE LOW COST CARRIERS PERFORMANCE

Pratima Mishra and Somesh Kumar Sharma

Abstract

To sustain in current volatile and dynamic environment, with growing complexity, aviation industry is facing ever increasing competition in term of improving performance. Due to this, Low Cost Carriers competitiveness has received considerable attention in the recent years. Low cost carriers are the airlines that follow low cost service to provide air travel at lesser price. The growth of Low Cost Carriers (LCCs) had a significant impact on airline competition, airline business models and air travel in general and has provided a chance for many new airlines to emerge, grow and survive in a challenging market. Therefore, this study explored 4 set of measures (Primary activity efficiency, airport flexibility, profitability and growth) and 16 influential measures of successful LCCs to develop the model using fuzzy logics. The fuzzy logic is a process suitable for dealing with uncertainty and subjectivity, which becomes an interesting auxiliary approach to manage performance of Low Cost Carriers. The fuzzy logic model consists of fuzzification of input, rule evaluation, aggregation of rule output and defuzzification. The results obtained from the model were found correct according to the design model. This result can be used to enhance the performance of low cost carriers in air transport industry. MATLAB- simulation is used to accomplish the desired results.

20.1. Introduction

Research on Low Cost Carriers (LCCs) has received considerable attention in the recent years in the aviation industry (Dwyer et al., 2004; Hudson et al., 2004). To sustain in current volatile, complex and dynamic environment, airlines are facing consistent pressure to improve performance in terms of productivity and profitability (Prajogo and McDermott 2005; Fotopoulos and Psomas 2010). The growth of LCCs has created significant impact on the competition and business models of airlines providing opportunities for many new airlines to emerge, grow and survive in the challenging market. The market share of LCCs increased from 25 to 65 percent in the past decades, while full-service carriers (FSCs) like Jet airways saw their market sliced in half from 70 to 35 percent (Centre for Asia Pacific Aviation, aviation advisory and research body 2016). Graham and Shaw (2008) explained the low cost model in terms of the operational characteristics i.e. high-capacity seating, minimum legal crew, cabin service only at additional cost. Therefore, the prime objective of low cost carriers is to lower its unit costs, so as to provide services at the cheapest costs.

The emergence of LCCs was originally seen in the United States' domestic air travel market in 1978. In India, low cost carriers were introduced by Air Deccan with its first flight on 25th August 2003and fares were half of those of the established airlines. However, the emergence and growth of no frills low cost airlines have radically altered the nature within the airline industry, especially on short-haul routes. Before introduction of LCC, air travel was perceived to be elitist activity in India. By year 2020 India is expected to become the third largest aviation market and is expected to be the largest by 2030.

From a recent survey of literature (Mason, 2001; Francis et al., 2006) it has been noted that this field has made progress in identifying research questions than in answering them, one of them being exploring dimensions of successful low cost carriers. This study explores the four low cost carrier measures including primary activity efficiency, airport flexibility, profitability and growth to assess the performance. It also provides a suitable framework to aviation industry to deal with various performance measures of low cost carriers. This will help aviation industry to evaluate their current practices by understanding passenger's behavioral intention towards their services. A software integrated model is developed using fuzzy logics. Hierarchical representation is used to develop a formal model for qualitative low cost carriers performance.

The remainder of the article is structured in five sections. Section 2, present the dimensions of low cost carriers and their measures. The proposed methodology is explained in section 3. Section 4 presents model development for low cost carriers performance, The results are discussed in section 5, Finally section 6 illustrates conclusions, implication and future work.

20.2. Literature review

Low cost carriers are known for selling cheap deep discount tickets over point to point markets (Xiowen et al., 2006). Dimitra et al., (2012) examined the connections between airport efficiency and LCCs and concluded that with its highly seasonal characteristics the LCC traffic positively affect airport efficiency. LCC exploits penetration pricing to achieve deep market penetration by setting the product/service price as low as possible as compared to full service carriers (Narangajavana et al., 2014). In this study, 4 set of measures and 12 influential sub-measures of successful LCCs have been identified from the literature and discussion with experts and academician in the low cost carrier's area keeping aviation sector in focus that can impact the financial performance.

20.2.i. Primary activity efficiency

It is the first factor of the study which consists of different measures such as fixed/semi-fixed cost of activities, variable cost of activities (operational costs, maintenance cost, labour costs, fuel price etc.), cost of travel (price for specific routes, competitive response and differentiation) and customer oriented target group. LCCs maintain schedule flight punctuality and aircraft turnaround efficiency at airports, in order to minimize system operational costs (Wu and Caves, 2000). Flight delays also add directly to operational cost for an airline. Andrew et al., (2009) developed a decision support tool for managing flight delay costs in pre-departure and airborne phase of a flight, dynamic estimation of passenger delay costs, ATC cooperation are key constraints. They further observed short term opportunities for saving fuel and reducing environmental impacts, and hence some reduction in total operating costs. Maintenance costs are a significant percentage of the total operating costs.

20.2.ii. Airport flexibility

Literature governs the flexibility of an airport in terms of number of airlines operating, number of routes served, airport operational time, airport and air traffic control and airport accessibility (Hickman and Blume, 2001; Juan et al., 2013). Airport flexibility refers to LCCs ability to respond to uncertainties and unforeseen operational conditions caused due to airport oriented aspects. Airport operational time associated with scheduled time performance for an aircraft at an airport, which is further linked to turnaround performance. Block delay and airport capacity utilized increase the risk of long taxi-out times (Diana, 2013). Wu and Caves (2002) developed a cost minimization model to optimize the scheduling of aircraft rotation by balancing the use of schedule time, which is designed to control flight punctuality and delay costs. The growth in the demand for low-cost airlines has coincided with the growth in the airport industry. One attempt by airports to attract such carriers has been to construct dedicated terminals called low cost terminals (Hanaoka and Sarawati, 2011). Air traffic control is the airport governing variable that prevents collisions, organize and expedite the flow of traffic and provide information and other support for pilots.

20.2.iii. Profitability

Profitability is an important issue that must be confronted in the context of sustainable investment. It refers to whether an organization is implementing the business process in a proper manner that will impact the bottom line of the company. It consists of different measures such as net profit, revenue passenger miles, return on investment and financial liquidity. Alessandro (2008) concluded profitability is dependent on the relevance of market size and the presence of rivals on the rout and for profitability, LCC mainly focus on short haul routes which are more of a European characteristic and high density long haul routes are evident in American and Asian markets. In response to increasing demand, airlines may increase capacity by increasing the frequency of flights or they may choose to increase aircraft size which yield operating cost economies (Pitfield et. al., 2009).

20.2.iv. Growth

It is a variable that influence the sustainable growth of a LCC. The different measures of growth include sales growth, market share, net income and earnings per share. Pitfield (2008) stated that market share could be measured either in terms of total number of passenger served by the LCC or in terms of revenue generated by LCC. Market share of a LCC reflect its ability to attract passengers. According to the Chang (2012), financial structure and an element of growth rate is a major factor in the successful management of a LCC which influence its long term future development. Nicolau and Maria (2012) found innovations related to advance customer segmentation and new technologies bring similar growth gains, thereby having the same positive effects on airline value. A brief description of the above explored variables and their measures are represented in table 1.

Table 1: Variables and their measures

Variables	Measures	References
Primary Activity Efficiency (PAE)	**Fixed or Semi Fixed Cost** of activities (associated with lease payments, airport fee, flight equipment cost, and maintenance). **Variable Cost** of activities (associated with fuel, labour (staff) wages, insurance, ground handling). **Ability** to provide travelling experience to customers at less price / Cost of travel. **Cost** of marketing the aimed service (Ability to attract & retain the customer oriented target groups).	Wen & Chen, 2011; Dimitra et. al., 2012, Andy Obermeyer et. al. (2013)
Airport Flexibility (AF)	Flexibility of Airports in arranging facilities Flexibility of Airports in serving no. of destinations through LCC Flexibility of Airports in managing air traffic control Flexibility of Airports in meeting schedules	Hanaoka & Sarawati, 2011; Diana, 2013; Juan et al., 2013.
Profitability (PR)	Ability to generate revenues Ability to generate Revenue Passenger Miles Ability to generate 'return on investment' Financial liquidity	Jost & Sascha, 2012
Growth (GR)	Sales growth Ability to generate market shares Net income growth Ability to generate earnings per share	Pitfield, 2008, 2009

20.3. Methodology
20.3.i. Fuzzy logics

Most of the conventional modelling techniques only deals with quantitative data. Meanwhile, fuzzy modeling approach utilizes both quantitative and qualitative data (Erol & Ferrell, 2003). A fuzzy logic is a tool which provides a mathematical concept to deal with uncertainty in human decision making. It was first introduced by Lotfi L. Zadeh in 1965. Fuzzy set theory has a great potential to treat different sources of uncertainty in various engineering applications (Ross, 2004; and Zimmermann, 1996). The basic concept of fuzzy logics is defined briefly as follows.

20.3.ii. Fuzzy concepts

a) Fuzzy sets and membership functions

Classical crisp set theory contains only one of two values 0 or 1. Only two possibilities exists i.e. whether a member exists in the set or not. The concept of fuzzy set relies heavily on element belonging to a fuzzy set with a certain degree of membership (Tsoukalas & Uhrig, 1996). Membership function in a fuzzy set is represented by $\mu_A(x)$.

$$\mu_A(x): X\ [0, 1]$$

Where $\mu_A(x)$ represents the degree of membership of x in fuzzy set A and X represents universe of discourse. The fuzzy set A is represented as-

$A = \{\mu_A(x1) / x1\}, \{\mu_A(x2) / x2\}, \ldots, \{\mu_A(xn) / xn\}$

Where $\{\mu_A(xn) / xn\}$ represents the membership value $\mu_A(xn)$ associated with xn.

Various type of membership functions can be used in fuzzy analysis such as- Triangular, Trapezoidal, Gaussian, Sigmoid, etc. However, because of their simplicity and ease of application, triangular membership functions (TMF) are widely used (Torlak et al., 2011) as shown in Figure 1.

b) Linguistic variables and fuzzy rules

Linguistic variable is a fuzzy variable that allows presenting vague description in natural language with mathematical terms. In fuzzy expert system, these variables are used in making fuzzy rules. A fuzzy rule is the representation of human knowledge in form of rules (Zadeh, 1973). It is defined as a conditional statement in the form-

IF x is A, THEN y is B
Where x & y – Linguistic variables
A & B- Linguistic values

A fuzzy rule contains two distinct parts. The IF part of the rule is called "antecedent", and the THEN part of the rule is called consequent. The antecedent is a clarification that yield a unique number between 0 and 1, however consequent assign the complete fuzzy set B to the output variable y. Degree of truth of both antecedent and consequent expresses proportional relationship among them which means that if the antecedent is true to some degree of membership then consequent is also true to same degree. This statement represents the logical way to blend compound qualitative assessments (Xu et al. 2002).

Figure 1: Triangular membership function (Yazdani et al., 2011).

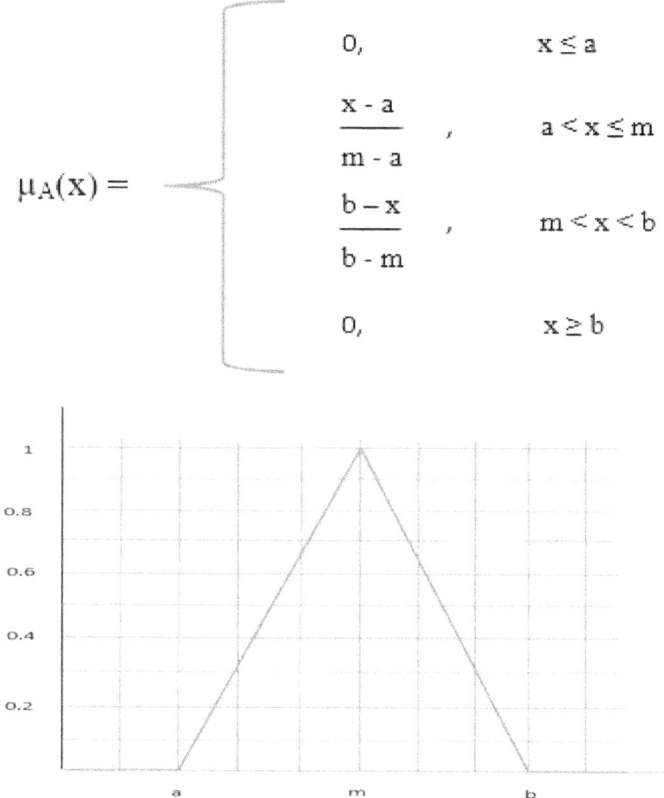

$$\mu_A(x) = \begin{cases} 0, & x \leq a \\ \dfrac{x-a}{m-a}, & a < x \leq m \\ \dfrac{b-x}{b-m}, & m < x < b \\ 0, & x \geq b \end{cases}$$

c) Hierarchical decomposition of variables under fuzzy logics

Developing fuzzy rules in complex domain with a large number of parameters are challenging (Torra, 2002). Let there be n number of variables in system and m number of different fuzzy sets, over the domain of each variable. Then a complete set of m^n different rules will be developed. Dealing with such large number of rules that raises exponentially causes problem, and so named 'curse of dimensionality' (Wang, 1998). Rule hierarchy is a concept to handle the problem of dimensionality. The approach deals with grouping of rules into modules in proportion to their roles in the system (Benitez & Casillas, 2013). Because of hierarchical decomposition, these systems are known as hierarchical fuzzy systems. On the basis of these guidelines, low cost carrier measures were structured into a hierarchy showing the relationship among LCC performance, dimensions of LCC and influencing variables for facilitating the study, as presented in Figure 2.

Figure 2: Hierarchical decomposition of variables under fuzzy logics

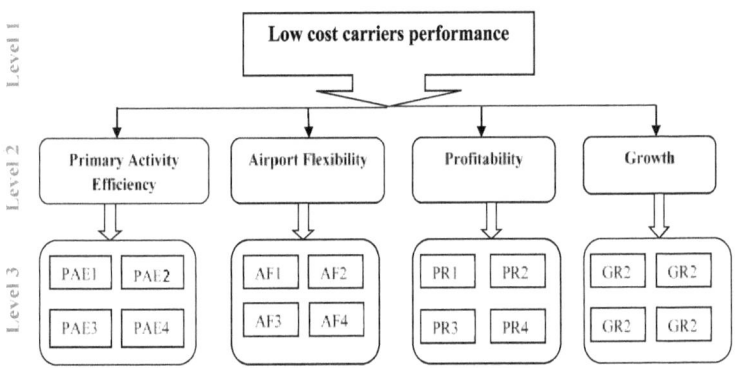

20.4. Model development

In this study, fuzzy logic based model is developed to assess performance of low cost carriers in aviation industry. The primary objective of fuzzy modelling is to construct an input-output mapping that can adequately describe the system behaviour over the complete operational range. Two basic categories of inference systems are used for fuzzy modelling i.e. Mamdani inference system, and Sugeno inference system (Castillo et al., 2007). Among both categories, Mamdani inference system is the most commonly used technique for fuzzy modelling because it allows user to describe the expertise in a more instinctive and more human like manner. In present work, Mamdani inference system is followed that is performed in following four steps described below:

20.4.i. Fuzzification of variables

In the fuzzification process, appropriate fuzzy sets are defined for each linguistic variables by taking suitable crisp values (Cox, 1992). For the crisp inputs (a, b), the membership degree is determined by the intercept of horizontal lines on the vertical axis. Before fuzzification of variables, it is necessary to select the appropriate membership functions for each input and output variables to associate system crisp values with fuzzy membership values. For fuzzification, triangular type of membership function is used in this study. The FIS are built with the help of the explored parameters such as primary activity efficiency, airport flexibility, profitability and growth as shown in figure 3.

Fuzzy values on corresponding universe of discourse such as- low, medium, and high are defined by the subject matter experts. As well as the range of the output variables 0-1 is similarly selected by the experts. The membership functions of input variables are shown in figure 4.

Figure 3: Fuzzy inference system suggested for the model.

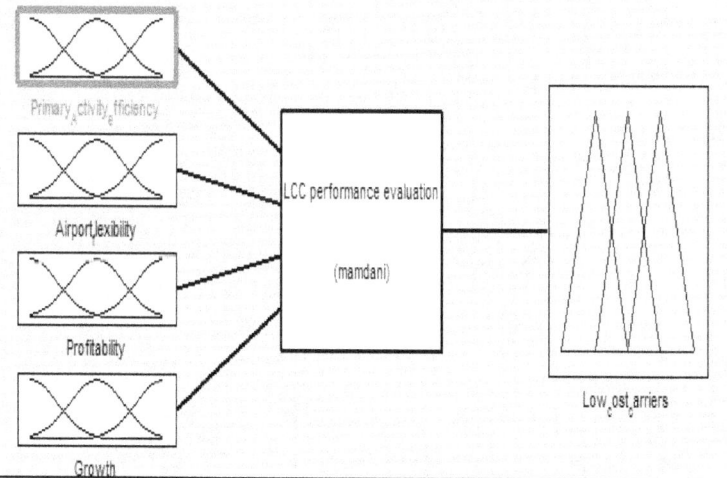

Figure 4: Sample of membership functions for input variables.

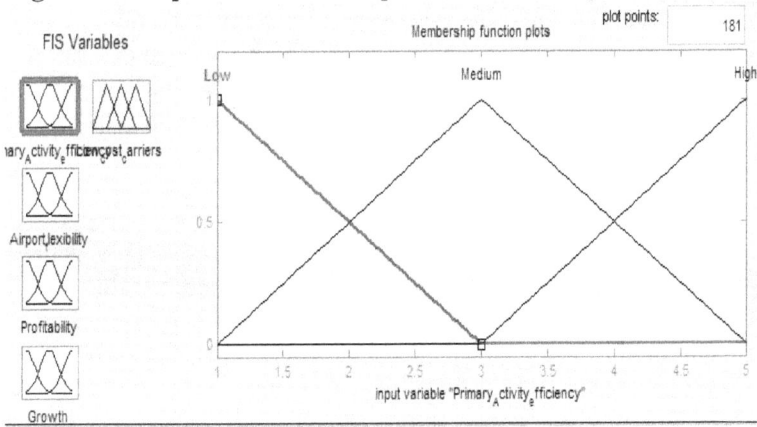

20.4.ii. Rule evaluation

The next step is rule evaluation. A rule is a conditional IF- Then statement, expressed in natural language with applied fuzzified input to the antecedent part and fuzzified output to the consequent part. AND or OR fuzzy operator is used in making rules in case of multiple antecedents. Expert knowledge is required to obtain the rule base (Cox, 1992). Figure 5 illustrates the preparation of fuzzy based rules formed with the help of expert knowledge.

Figure 5: Rule base generated for given input and output variables.

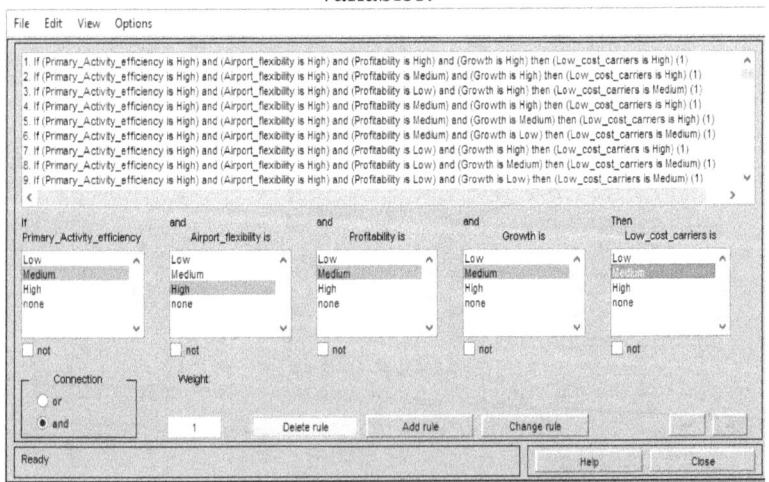

20.4.iii. Aggregation of rule outputs

In this step, output of rules is consolidated into a single output. The clipped or scaled membership functions of all rule consequents are combined into a single fuzzy set. Thus, the list of clipped or scaled consequent membership functions are taken as input in aggregation process, and the output obtained is one fuzzy set for each output variable (Yager and filev, 1994). Figure 6 shows the aggregation of rule outputs into a single fuzzy set.

Figure 6: Rule aggregation for input and output variables.

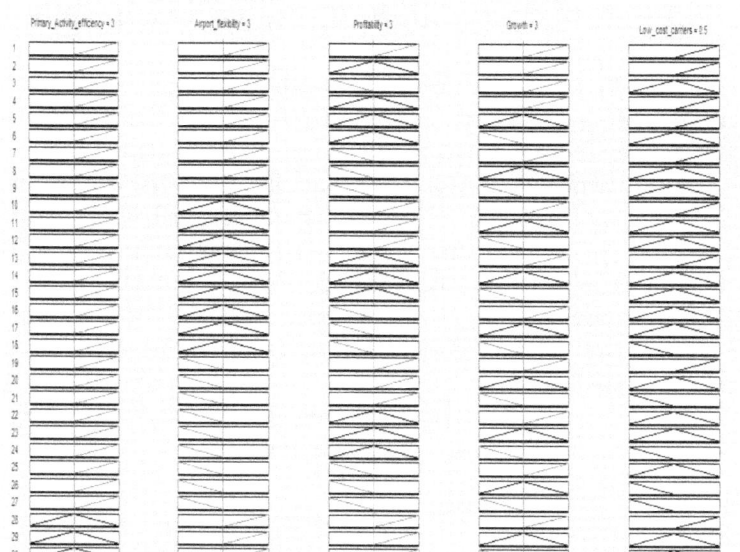

20.4.iv. Defuzzification

The last step, i.e. defuzzification, indicates that output of fuzzy rule is a fuzzy set representing each output or solution variable. But the final output has to be a crisp number. Defuzzification is the mapping of output fuzzy sets into a crisp value, which means that the process creates a value for output variable and produces a quantifiable result in crisp logic (Bajpai et al., 2010). There are several methods or formulas for defuzzification. But "centroid technique" is the most popular one. Mathematically, it is formulated as-

Crisp output = $\dfrac{\int_a^b \mu_A(x)\, x\, dx}{\int_a^b \mu_A(x)\, dx}$

20.5. Results and discussions

Fuzzy Logic toolbox provided by MatLab© software has been used to obtain the optimized values of the input and output variables for LCC performance considered. The results are generated in form of 3-D surface graphs. Total four major performance measures with sixteen process dimensions are taken in this study, as discussed in hierarchical decomposition (Figure 2). Results obtained by the model developed for each performance measures are discussed as follows. The topographic views of results that represent the behavior of input-output variables in response of fuzzy advisory rules are obtained.

Figure 7 represents the behavior of airport flexibility and primary activity efficiency on low cost carriers performance. The horizontal axis defines the input variables i.e. airport flexibility and primary activity efficiency and vertical axis defines the output variable i.e. low cost carriers. This figure shows that if airport flexibility increases from low to medium and primary activity efficiency remains constant from low to medium then performance of LCC remains medium. However, at high value of airport flexibility and medium to high, primary activity efficiency then the performance of LCC increases rapidly.

Figure 7: Surface topography of airport flexibility vs. primary activity efficiency

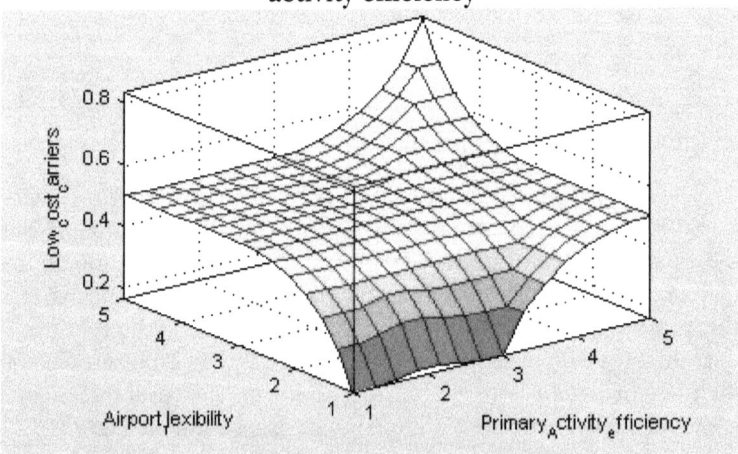

Figure 8 demonstrate the topographic surface view of variables i.e. growth and primary activity efficiency and low cost carriers performance. This shows that if value of growth parameter increases from low to medium and primary activity efficiency increases from low to medium then the performance of LCC remains medium. However with increase in growth and PAE from medium to high, the performance of LCC remains constant at higher value.

Figure 8: Surface topography of growth vs. primary activity efficiency

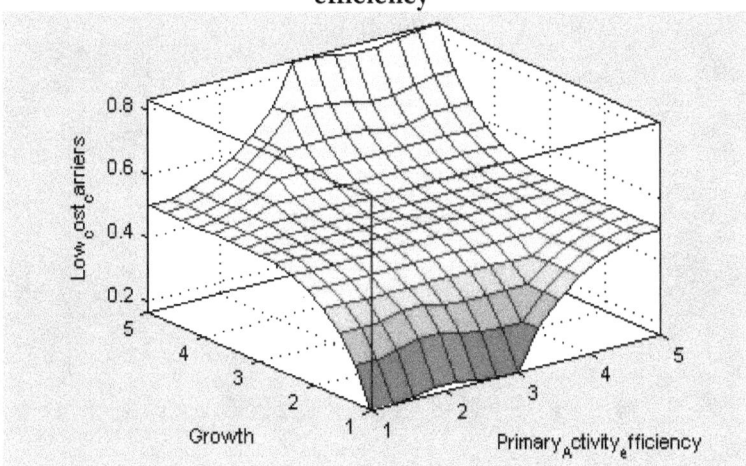

Figure 9 describes the behavior of growth and airport flexibility on low cost carriers performance. IF airport flexibility remains constant while growth increases from medium to high, then the performance of LCC increases rapidly and remains constant at higher value.

Figure 9: Surface topography of growth vs. airport flexibility

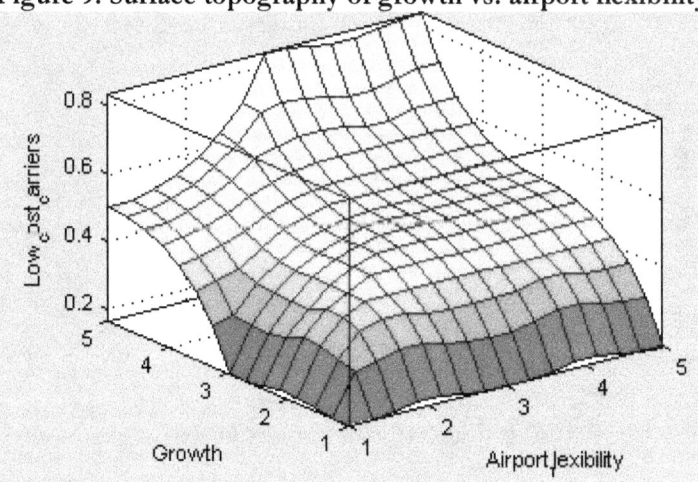

Figure 10 indicates the topographic surface view of profitability and airport flexibility on low cost carriers performance. If the profitability increases from medium to high and airport flexibility also increases from medium to high, the performance of LCC remains constant at maximum value.

Figure 10: Surface topography of profitability vs. airport flexibility

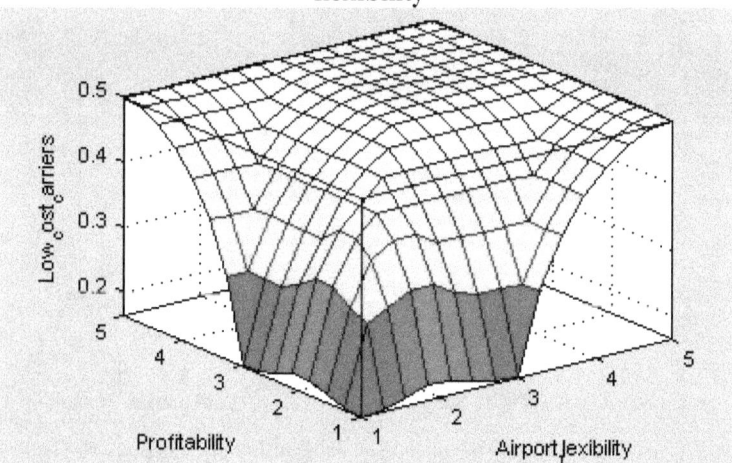

Figure 11 suggest the view of growth and profitability on low cost carriers performance. If the growth increases from medium to high and profitability remains constant at any value then the performance of LCC increases rapidly and remains constant at maximum value.

Figure 11: Surface topography of growth vs. profitability

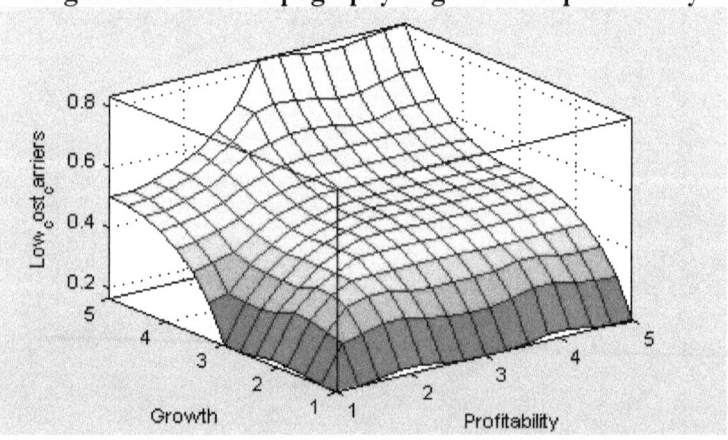

20.6. Conclusions, implication and future work

In this research, the measures of LCC performance are examined. Major four variables and sixteen their influencing variables are explored thorough literature study. Analysis of LCC performance is carried out by developing a model using fuzzy logics. All the results obtained after the implementation of fuzzy logic advisory rule system shows good agreement with the findings of numerous researchers. The result shows that input variables considered for the study are most influencing measures for improving LCC performance.

Findings of present study can provide effective guidelines to the aviation industry to improve LCC performance. The practitioners and aviation industry can use these explored variables to produce a quality product in single attempt.

In the present model, only four variables have been considered for study. Other parameters can also be considered for measuring the LCC performance. Furthermore, instead of fuzzy logic optimization techniques like adaptive neuro-fuzzy, genetic algorithm etc. can be used for the measuring of LCC performance.

References

Alessandro, Oliveira (2008). An empirical model of low-cost carrier entry. *Transportation Research Part A*, 42 (4), 673-695.

Andrew, Cook, Graham Tanner, Victoria Williams and Gerhard Meise (2009). Dynamic Cost *indexing – Managing airline delays costs*. *Journal of Air Transport Management, 15(1)*, 26-35.

Andy Obermeyer, Christos Evangelinos and Ronny Püschel (2013). Price dispersion and competition in European airline markets. *Journal of Air Transport Management*, 26(4), 31-34.

Bajpai, S., Sachdeva, A., & Gupta, J. P. (2010). Security risk assessment: Applying the concepts of fuzzy logic. *Journal of Hazardous Materials*, 173(1), 258-264.

Benitez, A. D., & Casillas, J. (2013). Multi-objective genetic learning of serial hierarchical fuzzy systems for large-scale problems. *Soft Computing*, 17(1), 165-194.

Castillo, O., Melin, P., Kacprzyk, J., & Pedrycz, W. (2007, November). Type-2 fuzzy logic: theory and applications. In Granular Computing, 2007. GRC 2007. *IEEE International Conference on* (pp. 145-145). IEEE.

Chang, Yu - Chun (2012). Strategy formulation implications from using a sustainable growth model. *Journal of Air Transport Management*, 20, 1-3.

Cox, E. (1992). *Fuzzy fundamentals. IEEE spectrum, 29(10), 58-61.*

Diana, Tony (2013). An application of survival and frailty analysis to the study of taxiout time: a case of New York Kennedy Airport. *Journal of air Transport Management*, 26, 40-43.

Dimitra, Pyrialakou, Matthew Karlaftis and Michaelides, Panayotis (2012). Assessing operational efficiency of airports with high levels of low-cost carrier traffic. *Journal of Air Transport Management*, 25 (1), 33-36.

Dwyer, Larry, Robert Mellor, Zelko Livaic, Deborah Edwards, and Chulwon Kim (2004). Attributes of Destination Competitiveness: A Factor Analysis. *Tourism Analysis*, 9 (1-2), 91-101.

Erol, I., & Ferrell, W. G. (2003). A methodology for selection problems with multiple, conflicting objectives and both qualitative and quantitative criteria. *International Journal of Production Economics*, 86(3), 187-199.

Fotopoulos CV, Psomas EL (2010). The structural relationships between total quality management factors and organizational performance. *Total Quality Management Journal*, 22(5), 539–552.

Francis, Graham, Ian Humphreys, Stephen Ison and Aicken, Michelle (2006). Where next for low cost airlines? A spatial and temporal comparative study. *Journal of Transport Geography*, 14, (2), 83-94.

Graham, Brian and Jon Shaw (2008). Low-Cost Airlines In Europe: Reconciling Liberalization And Sustainability. *Geoforum*, 39 (3) 1439-1451.Web.

Hanaoka, Shinya and Saraswati, Batari (2011). Low cost airport terminal locations and configurations. *Journal of Air Transport Management*, 17(5), 314-319.

Hickman, Mark and Blume, Kelly (2001). Modeling cost and passenger level of service for integrated transit service. *Computer-aided scheduling of public transport*, Berlin: Springer.

Hudson, Simon, J. R. Brent Ritchie, and S. Timur (2004). Measuring Destination Competitiveness: An Empirical Study of Canadian Ski Resorts. *Tourism Hospitality Planning and Development*, 1 (1), 79-94.

Jost, Daft and Sascha, Albers (2012). A profitability analysis of low-cost long-haul flight operations. *Journal of Air Transport Management*, 19, 9-54.

Juan, Carlos Martin, Hector Rodriguez-Deniz and Augusto Voites-Dotra (2013). Determinants of airport cost flexibility in a context of economic recession, *Transportation Research part E: Logistic and Transportation Review*.

Mason, Keith (2001). Marketing low-cost airline service to business travelers. *Journal of Air Transport Management, 7 (2), 103-109*.

Nicolau, Juan Luis and Maria, Jesus Santa-Maria (2012). Gauging innovation worth for airlines. *Journal of Air Transport Management*, 20, 9-11.

Narangajavana, Yeamduan, Fernando J. Garrigos Simon, Javier Sanchez Garcia, Santiago Forgas *Coll (2014). Prices, prices and prices: A study of airline sector. Tourism management. 41, 28-42.*

Pitfield, David (2008). The Southwest effect: A time-series analysis on passengers carried by selected routes and a market share comparison. *Journal of Air Transport Management*, 14(3), 113-122.

Pitfield, David (2009). Some speculations and Empirical Evidence on the oligopolistic Behaviour of competing low-cost Airlines. *Journal of Transport Economics and Policy*, 39(3), 379-390.

Prajogo DI, McDermott CM (2005). The relationship between TQM practices and organizational culture. *International Journal of Operations Production Management*, 25(11), 1101–1122.

Ross, T (2004). *Fuzzy logic with engineering applications*, 2ed. Chichester: John Wiley & Sons.

Torra, V. (2002). A review of the construction of hierarchical fuzzy systems. *International journal of intelligent systems*, 17(5), 531-543.

Torlak, G., Sevkli, M., Sanal, M., & Zaim, S. (2011). Analyzing business competition by using fuzzy TOPSIS method: An example of Turkish domestic airline industry. *Expert Systems with Applications*, 38(4), 3396-3406.

Tsoukalas, L. H., & Uhrig, R. E. (1996). *Fuzzy and neural approaches in engineering*. John Wiley & Sons, Inc.

Wang, L. X. (1998). Universal approximation by hierarchical fuzzy systems. *Fuzzy sets and systems*, 93(2), 223-230.

Wen, Chieh-Hua and Chen, Wei-Ying (2011). Using multiple correspondence cluster analysis to map the competitive position of airlines. Journal of Air Transport Management, 17(5), 302-304.

Wu, Cheng-Lung and Caves, Robert (2002). Towards the optimisation of the schedule reliability of aircraft rotations. Journal of Air Transport Management, 8(6), 419-426.

Yager, R. R., & Filev, D. P. (1994). *Essentials of fuzzy modeling and control.* New York.

Xiowen, Fu, Mark Lijesen, and Oum, Tae (2006). An analysis of Airport pricing & regulation in the presence of competition b/w Full Service Airlines & Low Cost Carriers. *Journal of Transport economies & policy*, 40, (3), 425-447.

Xu, K., Tang, L. C., Xie, M., Ho, S. L., & Zhu, M. L. (2002). Fuzzy assessment of FMEA for engine systems. *Reliability Engineering & System Safety*, 75(1), 17-29.

Zadeh, L. A. (1973). Outline of a new approach to the analysis of complex systems and decision processes. *IEEE Transactions on Systems, Man, and Cybernetic*, 3, 28-44.

Zadeh L.A. (1965). Fuzzy sets. *Informations and Control.* 8, 338-353.

Zimmerman, H. (1996). *Fuzzy Set Theory and its Applications,* 3rd ed., Kluwer, London

Contemporary Research in Business & Management

ABOUT THE EDITOR

Dr Manoj Sharma is presently working as Assistant Professor, Department of Management & Humanities, National Institute of Technology Hamirpur, Himachal Pradesh [INDIA]. He attained his PhD, MPhil and PG degrees in Economics from Himachal Pradesh University, Shimla (INDIA). He also earned MBA Degree with dual specialization in Marketing and Human Resource. During twelve years of research and teaching, the author has published more than twenty research papers in National and International Journals. He has also participated, presented and chaired technical sessions in more than twenty-five National and International Conference in India and abroad. His areas of interest are Agriculture Economics, International Business, Environmental Economics, Transportation Economics, Human Resource Planning & Development and Service Marketing. Dr Sharma has also served to various universities and institutes in different capacities. He is also the life time member of Indian Economic Association and Indian Commerce Association.

www.ingramcontent.com/pod-product-compliance
Lightning Source LLC
Chambersburg PA
CBHW050159230526
45470CB00001B/167